D1520771

VLSI SIGNAL PROCESSING:
A Bit-Serial Approach

The VLSI Systems Series

Editors   LYNN CONWAY
             CHARLES SEITZ

VLSI SIGNAL PROCESSING:
A Bit-Serial Approach

PETER DENYER AND DAVID RENSHAW

University of Edinburgh

ADDISON-WESLEY PUBLISHING COMPANY
Reading, Massachusetts · Menlo Park, California · Wokingham, England
Don Mills, Ontario · Amsterdam · Sydney · Singapore · Tokyo
Mexico City · Bogota · Santiago · San Juan

Printed in Great Britain by R.J. Acford.

Library of Congress Cataloging in Publication Data

Denyer, P.B. (Peter B.), 1953–
  VLSI signal processing.

  Includes index.
  1. Integrated circuits—Very large scale integration—Design and construction.
2. Signal processing—Digital techniques. I. Renshaw, David. II. Title.
TK7874.D46 1985   621.3819'5835   84–28344
ISBN 0–201–13306–7 (hbk.)

ABCDEF   898765

To F, K_1, K_2
and
to Ann

Foreword

The subject of VLSI systems spans a broad range of disciplines, including semiconductor devices and processing, integrated electronic circuits, digital logic, design disciplines and tools for creating complex systems. The Addison-Wesley VLSI Systems Series is being organised as a set of textbooks and research references that presents the best current work across this exciting and diverse field, with each book providing for its subject a perspective that ties it to related disciplines.

VLSI Signal Processing: A Bit-Serial Approach by Peter Denyer and David Renshaw provides designers of signal processing systems with a coherent approach to creating high-performance, low-cost VLSI systems in an important area of applications. The book presents an architectural methodology that is based on bit-serial arithmetic, which in its VLSI implementation provides a better relationship between area and speed than traditional parallel arithmetic. Exceptional system performance is then achieved by parallelism at the system level. The system description and compilation tools associated with this methodology allow the designer to work at the conceptual and architectural level while being sheltered from the need to craft details at the device and circuit level. The many design examples in the text can also work in the reverse direction, enabling students of VLSI design to access and explore the world of signal processing. Thus this text is also a significant contribution to the field of digital signal processing.

Taken along with earlier work on the structural VLSI architecture and automatic compilation of microprocessor data paths and their controllers, Denyer and Renshaw's work defines a second point in an important new space of knowledge. Using this work as an example, researchers may discover other classes of digital system applications and algorithms that map efficiently onto constrained forms of structural architectures, where layouts of the architectures can then be automatically generated by appropriate VLSI compilation tools. Thus this text can also serve as a resource and example for researchers in VLSI design methodology and VLSI system design tools.

Lynn Conway
Ann Arbor, Michigan, 1985

Chuck Seitz
Pasadena, California, 1985

Preface

As a result of advances in VLSI fabrication technology, all forms of information processing are dramatically reducing in cost. One area in which this effect is most pronounced is the field of real-time signal processing; the continuous flow of data, together with the complexity of many of the algorithms, impose severe computational demands that often cannot be satisfied by general purpose machines or components.

Sample rates depend upon the application, ranging from around 8 kHz for speech systems, through sonar, telecommunication and image processors to tens and hundreds of MHz for real-time radar processors. It is not uncommon for algorithms to require thousands of computational steps to be performed for each signal datum, leading to computational demands exceeding billions of arithmetic operations per second.

These demands can be met in principle by new system architectures which exploit some of the potential concurrency that exists within many of the algorithms. VLSI technology offers a new potential to implement such architectures. Through this technology we expect to see the implementation of powerful real-time signal processing algorithms that previously have been of only theoretical interest. However, the very advances in device technology that are responsible for this revolution also bring a new challenge to product design. Design complexity has become a dominant cost limit in the development of VLSI systems. Without advances in design methodology and tools, manufacturing capability and algorithm development will far exceed our capacity for design.

This text is about such a design methodology for VLSI signal processing using bit-serial architectures. We firstly introduce bit-serial architectures and systems, emphasising their potential and advantages for VLSI implementation. Throughout the remainder of the text we develop a comprehensive environment of methods, tools and components within which system designers may design and implement complex VLSI signal processing systems.

This is not a foundation text, either in signal processing or in VLSI design. Excellent introductions to these topics can be found elsewhere. However, no existing text seems particularly adequate for those system designers who recognise the potential that VLSI has to offer and wish to exploit it. To build a successful VLSI signal processing system requires expertise in all areas from algorithm, through system and circuit architectures to layout. Engineers with this combination of expertise are certainly rare. It is the purpose of this text to span these disciplines and place the system designer within an environment that supports the rapid conception and implementation of VLSI designs.

Custom VLSI is not the only possible approach to the implementation of real-time signal processors, but it is able to provide arithmetic and memory resources that are precisely tailored to the requirements of each application. The advantages of the custom VLSI solution have in the past been offset by the high costs traditionally associated with long development timescales and multiple design iterations. These overheads have made custom design unattractive for medium and low volume markets, and for products requiring rapid development. More seriously, the *ad hoc* techniques in general use cannot be extended to cope with VLSI complexities without greatly exaggerating these disadvantages. This is a restrictive situation that prohibits the proper exploitation of silicon as a development medium for a host of new VLSI systems and architectures. The methods and tools presented in this text overcome these traditional impediments to the custom VLSI solution within the context of bit-serial architectures for VLSI signal processing. The environment is intended to encourage the development of prototype systems in integrated form from the outset.

The text is divided into two parts. Part 1 develops a methodology for the design of bit-serial systems and supports this through the FIRST silicon compiler. Part 2 presents a range of case studies, some generated through FIRST, and some developed independently.

To preserve the integrity of this text we remain exclusively with nMOS technology. This maintains a link with established teaching practice and widely available foundry services. The architectural concepts and CAD tools, with the exception of the cell library, are technology independent. Thus we expect to see their adoption in other VLSI technologies; redevelopments in CMOS technology are already underway.

Acknowledgements
Throughout the programme of research that has culminated in this text, it was a pleasure to work with many colleagues and visitors. Their enthusiastic contributions were invaluable.

We are firstly grateful to our colleagues in the Department of Computer Science at the University of Edinburgh, who collaborated in the development of FIRST; Neil Bergmann (who wrote the first FIRST with us), John Gray and Irene Buchanan (both also with Lattice Logic Ltd, Edinburgh); and to our associates in the Department of Electrical Engineering, Stewart Smith and Jim Nash. A stream of students contributed to the development of the primitive cell library. These included, as masters' students, David Myers, Graham Stewart, Neil Henderson, Martin Jones and Geoff Hunt; and as undergraduates David Talbot, Hugh Wallace, Mark Clinch, Mike Sunners,

Alan Warrington, Douglas Chisholm and Michael Keightley. Early system studies were performed by guest workers Malcolm Rutter, Lawrence Turner and Greg Allen. We are also grateful for the advice and support given at various times by Gordon Hughes, David Rees, Alan Murray and Jim Reid.

We are pleased to acknowledge the financial support of the UK Science and Engineering Research Council, and to thank the University of Edinburgh for providing a conducive and stimulating environment for this activity. Thanks in particular to Jeff Collins and John Mavor, successive Heads of the Department of Electrical Engineering, and to Sidney Michaelson and Peter Schofield of the Department of Computer Science for supporting and encouraging our work. We are grateful to Bill Turner of SERC and the staff of the Edinburgh Microfabrication Facility for device fabrication.

Our text has benefited enormously from contributions by Alan Murray, Stewart Smith, Malcolm Rutter, Dick Lyon, John Wawrzynek and Carver Mead. We would like to thank them all for their sensitive approach to the anticipated readership. Thanks also to series editors Lynn Conway and Chuck Seitz (USA) and Gerry Musgrave (UK).

We are most grateful for assistance in the preparation of this text given by Pam Armstrong, who set the type using facilities provided by David Stewart-Robinson and the Edinburgh Regional Computing Centre. Diagrams were prepared using Jim Nash's SKETCH programme.

The Publishers wish to thank the following for permission to reproduce material in this book: Schlumberger Palo Alto Research for Plate 6 and Figure 12.3; the University of Edinburgh for Plates 1–4; and the California Institute of Technology for Plate 7. Plate 5 is reprinted by permission of the Xerox Corporation.

Peter Denyer   *David Renshaw*
University of Edinburgh, 1985   University of Edinburgh, 1985

Readers interested in obtaining copies of the FIRST silicon compiler for use as a tutorial aid with this text are invited to contact the authors at the address below.

Peter Denyer
David Renshaw

Department of Electrical Engineering
University of Edinburgh
The King's Buildings
Edinburgh
EH9 3JL
Scotland

Contents

Part 1
Methods and Tools

1

Bit-Serial Architectures

1.1 Introduction

Applications of signal processing abound in the modern world of electronics. In the consumer marketplace telephones, disc and tape players, radios and televisions are the most common examples. Commercial applications in telecommunications and control create a widespread demand for higher quality and lower cost signal processing components. In the emerging field of intelligent machines, the man–machine interface is dominated by intensive signal processing tasks in both speech and vision. Military radar and sonar requirements are similarly demanding. Digital Signal Processing techniques offer a flexible choice between quality and price, and the overall cost of this tradeoff continues to decrease with advances in fabrication technology.

The growing significance of DSP applications and the increasing attraction of VLSI implementation are the motivation for this text. The span of expertise required to satisfy these interests ranges from algorithm, through architecture, system and circuit design to circuit layout and simulation. The purpose of this text is to bridge these fields with a unifying methodology that ultimately couples algorithm with silicon. Supporting this methodology with advanced computer design aids opens the use of silicon as a development and production medium for the individual system designer.

1.1.1 Bit-serial approach

Bit-serial architectures are distinguished by their communication strategy. Digital signals are transmitted bit sequentially on single wires, as opposed to the simultaneous transmission of words on parallel buses (Figure 1.1). This distinction is the key to many inherent advantages for bit-serial as a VLSI strategy. Most significantly, bit-serial transmission leads to efficient communication within and between VLSI chips. This is an outstanding advantage where communication issues dominate, as in many signal processing applications.

We shall see that it is also often efficient for the computation processes themselves to adopt a bit-serial format, often leading to tightly pipelined structures at the bit-level. This is not always the case however; parallel

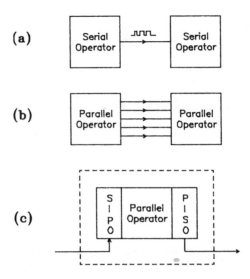

Fig. 1.1   VLSI communication strategies:
  (a)   bit-serial
  (b)   bit-parallel
  (c)   serialised communication with bit-parallel operators.

computation schemes are occasionally convenient. In these cases parallel elements may be used with serialised communications interfaces, as in Figure 1.1(c).

1.1.2 Synchronous systems

Though other variants are possible, we shall deal exclusively with synchronous bit-serial systems. In a synchronous system all communication and computation are ordered in lock-step by a global clock at the system bit-rate. This clock is relatively fast for any given technology; typically tens of megahertz for 3-micron technologies. Asynchronous bit-serial architectures are certainly feasible, and could be a promising solution to the problems of fast synchronous operation beyond Very Large Scale Integration. Although we will not deal explicitly with this form, much of the following material is general with respect to either approach.

The timing of synchronous bit-serial systems is described in units of clock cycles or bit-times, often abbreviated simply as bits without prejudice to the usual connotation of information content. For example, we might refer to a delay of '4 bits'.

1.1.3 The generic operator

We show in Figure 1.2 a generic bit-serial processing element or *operator*. This may perform any signal processing operation on one or more input words and deliver one or more output words after an appropriate delay for the

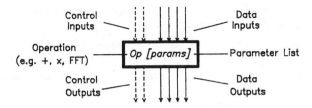

Fig. 1.2 A generic bit-serial operator.

computation process. This delay is called the *latency* of the operator, and it is measured as an integer number of bits, or words and bits. In this text we describe and build an operator-based design environment. An important tenet of that environment is that all operators should have a fixed, known latency. This convention (and others soon to be defined) is always respected even though it is not always trivial to achieve.

Each operator may have an optional set of control inputs, also on single wires. These indicate the arrival of a new word, or group of words, and are generally used to initiate (or terminate) the operation for each set of data. Some operators also have control outputs. These are versions of the control inputs, delayed by the appropriate latency to act as synchronous control inputs for the next (downstream) operator. For the present we shall be concerned with the primary signal functions of these operators. We deal separately with control in a later section.

In principle a third class of operator input signal is possible: the parameter. For example, the gain input to a programmable gain block might be classed as a parameter. In practice this facility is not frequently required in the systems that we shall study, and we class all data to be of two types: signal or control. Where necessary we treat any parameter as type signal.

The adder shown in Figure 1.3 is an example of a serial operator. Assuming an LSB-first data format, this combines successive pairs of input bits through

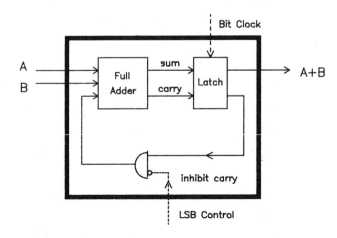

Fig. 1.3 A bit-serial adder.

a full adder stage, latches the sum as an output and feeds back the carry for combination with the next (more significant) pair of input bits. The control requirement in this case is a pulse, synchronous with the arrival of the least significant bits of the two input words; this is used to inhibit any carry resulting from the preceding addition. This operator then has two data input streams, one data output stream, one control input and a latency of one bit.

We shall build systems as networks of such operators, which all perform some signal processing task on words of bit-serial data. Example operators are ADD, MULTIPLY, DELAY, FFT, FILTER, etc. Notice that these are all relatively high level signal processing functions: we shall see that it is possible and desirable to design systems entirely at this level, with no requirement to work at the gate or transistor level. These networks of operators are synonymous with a 'flow-graph' representation of the system. They also correspond directly to the physical realisation; each drawn operator will have a corresponding physical instantiation, and each node a corresponding physical wire. This leads to a very direct route of design and synthesis which we shall explore shortly.

1.1.4   Primitive operators

It is possible to identify a base set of operators, from which a great variety of systems may ultimately be constructed. We call this the set of primitive operators or *primitives*. The set of primitives may be physically supported in the form of blocks of VLSI circuitry (or artwork) which are predesigned for subsequent use at the system level. We present a library of bit-serial primitives in Chapter 4. Some candidates for this primitive library are ADD, MULTIPLY and DELAY, but not FFT or FILTER since these operators can be constructed from the lower level primitives.

In other terms the primitives are a set of standard- or macro-cells, with the special property that they uniformly obey the common generic code set out above. The principal advantage of designing with macrocells is that, once built, their users are spared the task of reimplementing unnecessary detail. However, the principle of common generic type greatly extends this advantage. By carefully defining conventions for data communication throughout the system, and building these into the generic code, we can ensure that the set of primitives, and anything composed of them, can be connected together to produce arbitrarily complex functions without further concern for any electrical, numerical or timing details at their interfaces. This is a very powerful concept which leads to a central technique of system synthesis that we call *functional design*.

1.1.5   Functional design

Functional design hinges simply on the concept that systems are to be built entirely of functional operators of a common generic type. In this way 'machine design [can be] developed and implemented directly at the functional level of conception (Powell, 1981).

An example

By way of illustration, we consider the implementation of a simple function
in silicon. This function is required to produce the magnitude, M, of a complex
number, I+jQ. We use an approximation, due to Filip (1976), known as the
four region approximation:

$$M = \text{Max} \begin{Bmatrix} |I| \\ 7/8|I| + 1/2|Q| \\ 1/2|I| + 7/8|Q| \\ |Q| \end{Bmatrix} \qquad 1.1$$

The principle of functional design is to find an algorithm that will reduce the
function we require to a structured interconnection of lower level functional
cells, ultimately to instances only of the set of primitive functional cells. In this
sense the above approximation is already a possible algorithm, but for the sake
of a more structured implementation we choose to rewrite this algorithm as:

$$M = \text{Max} \begin{Bmatrix} G \\ 7/8G + 1/2L \end{Bmatrix} \qquad 1.2a$$

where

$$G,L = \text{Greater,Lesser } \{|I|,|Q|\}. \qquad 1.2b$$

Figure 1.4(a) is a functional design of this algorithm using a hypothetical set

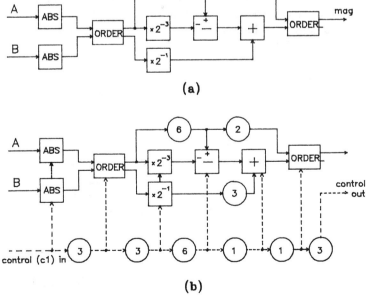

Fig. 1.4 Signal flow-graphs of the complex-to-magnitude approximation:
    (a) flow-graph of the algorithm
    (b) flow-graph of bit-serial implementation, including delay equalisation in signal
        paths and a control network.

of primitive operators. We also refer to Figure 1.4 as a signal flow-graph. To transform this flow-graph into a feasible bit-serial architecture, we need to equalise latency in the signal network, and make provision for the control function. It is essential to equalise the latency on merging signal paths since each operator expects incoming data to be synchronised so that the LSB times match (a further convention). We achieve this by counting the cumulative latency in each signal path, and equalise by inserting compensating delays using a delay primitive (shown here by a circle containing the number of bits of delay). Figure 1.4(b) is such an implementation, including a simple control network. We have not yet discussed control, but it is sufficient for this exercise to note that c1 marks the LSB-time of each new data word, and that the control network shown generates delayed copies of c1 to drive successive operators in the signal chain. Given the existence of a sufficient primitive set it is evident from this example that functional design from algorithm can be a straightforward task.

1.1.6 Hierarchical design

If all operators are of the same generic type (as defined in Figure 1.2), then systems can be hierarchically designed and specified. By this we mean that higher operators may be defined as networks of existing operators, and be used subsequently in the same abstract sense. For example, we might construct a Fourier transform machine from a collection of operators, including complex multipliers, and the complex-to-magnitude converter. These operators are of the common generic type, but are themselves composed of collections of lower

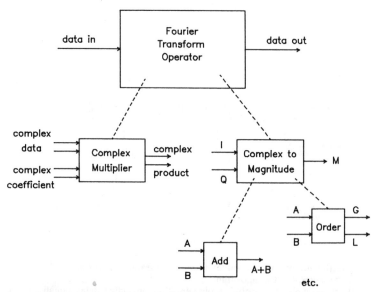

Fig. 1.5   Use of hierarchy in specifying a complex operator.

level operators. The complete Fourier transform machine, however large it may be, is also just another operator obeying the generic code; it has some serial signal inputs, some serial outputs and performs a dedicated function with a fixed known latency (Figure 1.5).

Note that levels in this hierarchy can be mixed. It is perfectly valid to build a system network from any previously defined operators, regardless of their level. Thus we might follow our Fourier transform operator with a simple Adder if required, as in Figure 1.6, despite the existence of Add operators many levels down in the definition of the Fourier transform operator.

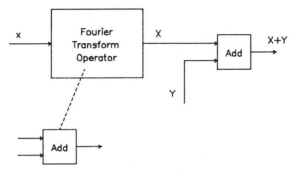

Fig. 1.6   Use of mixed levels in the hierarchy.

1.1.7   A VLSI design environment

Figure 1.4 essentially defines a complete implementation of the complex-to-magnitude algorithm. Consider now a VLSI design environment capable of taking this functional flow-graph as input, of instantiating the required set of bit-serial primitives, of assembling these primitives and routing the network of flow-graph connections between them, and finally wiring input/output pads, and power and clock services to complete a custom chip design. In effect this environment acts as a compiler, delivering low-level code (in this case VLSI mask artwork) from an initial high level program (the flow-graph). We examine this environment and its realisation in the form of a silicon compiler in Chapter 2.

The corresponding implementation in silicon of the complex-to-magnitude algorithm is shown in the photomicrograph of Plate 1, and as an annotated floorplan in Figure 1.7. As a VLSI device this is not particularly impressive: it contains only a few thousand transistors, and might have been implemented on one of the standard parts mentioned earlier. However, as a demonstration of VLSI design technique it is; for we have circumvented all of the traditional hurdles normally identified with this approach. Our design cycle was very fast and required no intimate knowledge of integrated circuit design.

1.1.8   Thesis

The thesis presented in this book is that we may extend these techniques to implement complex signal processing systems as custom VLSI parts, or sets of

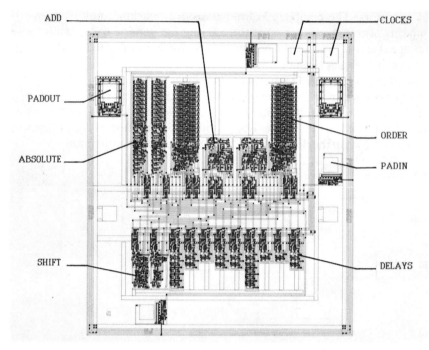

Fig. 1.7 Compiled complex-to-magnitude chip corresponding to the flow-graph of Figure 1.4. See Plate 1 for a photomicrograph of this device after manufacture.

parts. We argue that the dominant complexity problem can be resolved by the technique of functional design, and that working within an appropriate CAD environment, complex systems can be handled on realistic timescales by individual system designers.

1.2   Signals

Having introduced the bit-serial technique, we now need to consider some technical aspects of signal format and timing. Different practitioners may use different formats, as in any scheme of data representation. We will shortly define rigorous conventions on the format used throughout this text, but it is important first to consider the issues involved.

1.2.1   LSB- or MSB-first?

Certain operations, division and sorting for example, are more easily performed on bit-serial data MSB-first. However, the majority of applications of interest to us are dominated by multiply and add operations that are naturally performed LSB-first. For this reason we adopt an LSB-first format. Whenever appropriate we may convert data to parallel format, or even reverse it to MSB-first, as an internal process in any primitive. The LSB-first convention applies strictly and solely as a system communication protocol, it does not restrict the internal format used within any primitive operator.

1.2.2 Timing

We need to ensure correct signal timing by defining the part of the basic bit-cycle during which transmitted data may change, and the part during which it should be stable for sampling by the downstream operator. This convention depends upon the clocking scheme that is to be used. For the purpose of this text we shall deal with systems realised in nMOS technology using the circuit, logic and timing conventions set out in Mead and Conway (1980). Here the basic bit-cycle is defined by a non-overlapping two phase clock, of the type shown in Figure 1.8. The correct operation of this clock scheme requires that successive clocked stages should alternate, and thus that complementary clocks must be used for the input and output processes. We shall decide later the formal issue of which phase to use for which purpose.

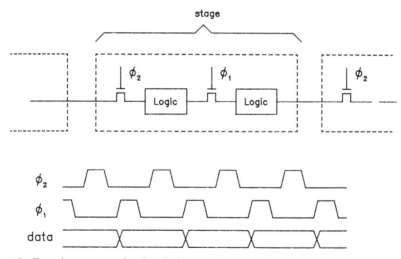

Fig. 1.8 Two-phase non-overlapping clock convention.

1.2.3 Number format

Here we are concerned with the choice between fixed and floating point representations. In general, fixed point operators are simpler and smaller than their floating point equivalents. However, floating point representations are more generally useful in handling large or unpredictable variations in range. Since most of our applications concern dedicated processes whose signal ranges are known or can be predicted at design time, we shall generally adopt the fixed point format.

We also need to choose a consistent arithmetic format: examples include sign-magnitude, one's and two's complement, etc. Again the importance of the multiply and add functions is an influence. Here the arithmetic consistency of the two's complement representation is attractive.

1.2.4   A system wordlength

The length of the fixed point word governs the dynamic range in any system and this may be different in each application. However, it is most convenient if the wordlength is fixed in each specific system. We refer to this as the system wordlength (swl) in any given application. Typically we use values for swl between 12 and 32 bits, but larger values are feasible and not particularly awesome in bit-serial systems (see the case study by Wawrzynek and Mead in Part 2).

1.2.5   Multiple precision

On occasions it is imperative to handle a large dynamic range at strategic points in the system, but it is inefficient to increase the system wordlength for the whole system. Here we may resort to a multiple precision format in which long data words are split into two or more subwords, each equal to the system wordlength. It follows that the number of wires needed for communication is the same as the multiplicity of the representation; normally two and three word formats are adequate.

As an example of the use of the multiple-precision technique, in the matched filter case study given in Chapter 9 we are able to maintain a 14-bit system wordlength but at the same time allow 42-bit (triple precision) working at internal accumulators. The technique seems most often to be useful in processes of accumulation, where data which is very small in significance is coherently amplified to produce a large signal after many iterations.

A useful multiple precision format is shown in Figure 1.9. Here the words on wires of increasing significance are successively staggered, in increments of one word time. This time-skewed representation helps addition and

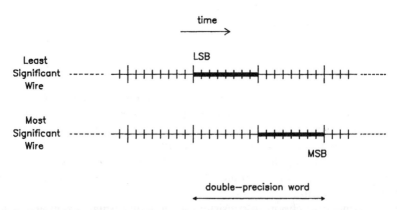

Fig. 1.9   Formatting multiple-precision words by time staggering. Here a double-precision word is represented on two wires.

subtraction processes on multi-wire data, since we can simply assign one such operator to each wire and chain the carry signals. In this way the most significant carry from one addition is passed to the next most significant adder at the correct time to combine with the addend and augend bits of appropriate significance. Figure 1.10 shows this arrangement for a double-precision add operator.

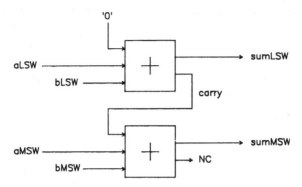

Fig. 1.10   Example of a double-precision operator following the convention of Figure 1.9.

1.3   Operators

We have already indicated that operators are required to conform to the bit-serial convention only at their interfaces. Internally they may adopt whatever signal representation best suits their operation. Thus there may be some internal conversion to bit-parallel, or even bit-reversed serial format, prior to (and following) the desired operation. Figure 1.7 includes several differing internal structures for the set of primitives used on the complex-to-magnitude example.

1.3.1   Latency

We have also indicated the requirement for operators to exhibit a fixed latency. This is an important aid to design. An operator with variable latency would generate problems for delay equalisation in parallel paths, and significantly exaggerate the complexity of controlling such a system.

1.3.2   Time alignment

Design is further simplified if each operator may expect all of its inputs to be synchronous, that is that the LSBs of all inputs will arrive simultaneously. This is somewhat controversial in that it might sometimes be more efficient within an operator to assume that certain inputs become available at different times. This is a good example of the tradeoff between design simplicity and hardware efficiency that is made through such conventions. In practice we adhere faithfully to this convention for the primitive set, but the system designer may disregard it at higher levels if he feels sufficiently confident about keeping track of time in his system. Later, in discussing synthesis practice we advocate the use of time alignment for the initial design, followed by refinement to optimise redundant delays in signal paths.

A common frustration is for two signals to be misaligned by one bit. This situation can be improved if primitives offer an optional one-bit input predelay that can be invoked as part of the primitive structure, to avoid additional routing of the intermediate signal. The use of this facility should be entirely optional, with all primitive inputs conventionally time aligned by default. Figure 1.11 illustrates the beneficial exercise of this predelay option. Wherever the predelay option is used we indicate its presence by a diamond symbol on the relevant input terminal.

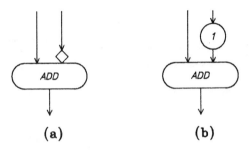

(a)   (b)

Fig. 1.11   Example of the use of predelay:
(a)   in place on one input
(b)   equivalent circuit.

1.4   Control

We have already indicated our intention to construct systems using a functional design style; that is by building networks of fixed function elements. The problem of control here is not primarily one of controlling function, which is the fundamental issue in machines with a central programmable Arithmetic and Logic Unit. Instead we are concerned with controlling the timing or flow of events through a network. At the lowest level this involves the fundamental synchronous bit-clock that controls the flow of all data in the system at the bit-level. Like power supplies, this is globally distributed and its presence is implicit at all of the elements in any functional network. We label this level of control, cycle 0 (or simply c0).

Various other cyclic control signals are needed above c0, as shown in Figure 1.12. The most common of these is the cycle (c1) needed to define the start of new data words on all (or most) of the nodes in a system. An obvious form of this signal is a pulse coincident with the presence of the first, or least significant bit (LSB). Now whereas c0 is globally synchronous, this is usually not the case with c1. Unless we constrain all operators (from primitives up) to have latencies equal to integer numbers of system wordlengths, then the LSB-times of different nodes in the system will differ.

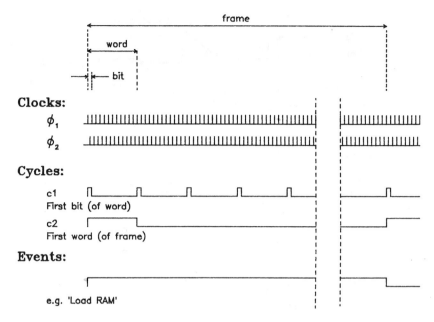

Fig. 1.12   Format of control cycles for bit-serial machines.

The implication is that in addition to specifying the signal network, we need to define a separate control network to deliver control cycles with appropriate timing to each operator in the signal path. We treat this as an independent task and conventionally design the entire signal network before addressing the provision of an appropriate control network. We shall consider this task further as part of a general synthesis methodology in Chapter 6. It is appropriate at this stage, however, to review two alternative approaches.

Our first strategy comes from the realisation that the control network should be identical to the signal network in terms of latency, but not function. One way to realise such a strategy is to provide this control delay as part of the function of each primitive. Here control and data flow through the network together, and whenever a signal enters a new primitive or operator, so does its associated $c1$ control (or one of the control lines is selected if there is more than one). Figure 1.13(a) illustrates the principle of this strategy. However, the provision of the control delay circuitry within each primitive can be wasteful of layout area, especially since many of the resultant control signals are not used.

The second strategy is to realise an independent control network using special control delay primitives, as in the complex-to-magnitude example. Since only a single control path is realised, the duplication associated with the within-primitive scheme is obviated. Figure 1.13(b) illustrates this strategy. A further saving can sometimes be achieved through the realisation that $c1$ is cyclic, and that any version of it delayed beyond the cycle length is identical to a previous version counted modulo the cycle length. This places an upper

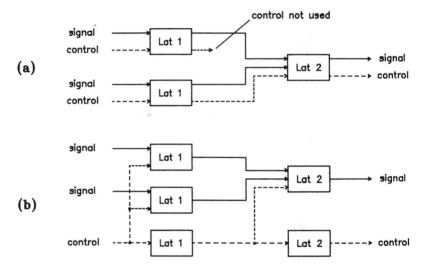

Fig. 1.13 Two approaches to implementing the c1 control network:
  (a)   control delayed within operators
  (b)   orthogonal control network.

limit on the number of different versions of c1 that need to be generated in any network.

Above cycle 1 we may require further cycles. Cycle 2 (c2) is used to indicate the first word of a 'frame' of words, c3 to indicate the first frame of a 'group' of frames, etc. These higher control cycles are commonly used to control multiplexing operations.

The intended operation of our functional networks is a steady-state repetition of fixed cycles of recursions. Occasionally we require discrete *events* to occur. Events are like cycles (in that they last for an integer number of cycles of the next lowest control level), but they do not repeat. Figure 1.12 shows one such event which is used to control the loading of a coefficient store in response to an external 'load' request.

The longest cycle (or event) in any system defines the 'system cycle'. Often this matches the input and output data sample cycle.

As a source of all such control signals we use a special primitive operator, CONTROLGENERATOR. This is realised as a set of synchronous counters, one counting bits to generate the LSB-time pulse, c1, another counting c1 to generate c2, etc. CONTROLGENERATOR is the single source of each control signal in the system; only these signals or delayed versions of them may be used.

The general strategy for control generation is shown in Figure 1.14. This includes an (on-chip) CONTROLGENERATOR, and an (off-chip) crystal-controlled clock source. The clock normally runs at a set bit-rate (typically several MHz). Figure 1.14 also defines a simple asynchronous interface between the serial system and its external environment. The serial clock source is started from an external trigger, and stopped after a complete system cycle

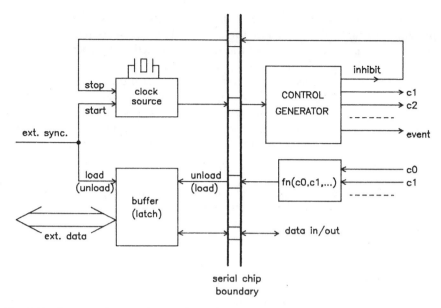

Fig. 1.14   A strategy for control generation and external synchronisation.

by the 'inhibit' line. Data is input through buffer latches which load under control of the external trigger, and unload (into the serial system) under control of the serial clock and related control cycles. This interface maintains timing integrity within the serial system. Uncertainty in the start-up time of the serial clock source causes jitter in the timing of the serial system relative to the external environment. However, it is important only that the system should capture input data, complete its computation cycle, and deliver output data within the cycle time of the external clock.

1.5   Concurrency

One of the attractions of applications in signal processing is that many of the algorithms are predisposed towards parallel or concurrent implementations. (We use 'parallel' here in an architectural sense.) For example, the scalar product of two N-element vectors is obtained as the sum of N products; in principle each of these could be computed simultaneously. The availability of VLSI technology and the amenability of signal processing algorithms to concurrent formulation make this an active field of research.

One example of parallel system architecture is the systolic array (Kung and Leiserson, 1980). The techniques that we shall present are perfectly suitable for the implementation of these arrays, which may be mapped into large concurrent flow-graphs reflecting the array topologies. Indeed an example of a systolic DFT array is given later as a case study.

A consequence of choosing a fully-concurrent solution, however, is that the architecture will dictate the application bandwidth, which is to say that the machine will run as fast as the technology will allow. This could be fine in a high-bandwidth application, but for another application requiring a lower sample rate, the fully-parallel solution, though functionally correct, may be distinctly inefficient in terms of the silicon area employed.

We intend to give consideration to the needs of real-time operation over a range of sample rates, and to consider more generally appropriate architectures for their efficient solution. We will still be interested in concurrency; most of the systems we shall study have multiple processors. However, we are only concerned to provide enough computational power to satisfy the demands of each application, not to produce the fastest possible machine.

We generally achieve this balance by building special purpose bit-serial arithmetic engines to implement the computational requirement, and then 'multiplex' or share these engines among the many repeated processes implicit in the algorithm. We elaborate this process in Chapter 5.

1.6   Conventions

We wish to construct arbitrary functional networks of the type shown in Figure 1.5, possibly incorporating mixed hierarchies. The key to the successful operation of such networks, without any further regard for detail at their interfaces, is to set system wide protocols or conventions on all data transmission.

The purpose of fixing these conventions is thus to conceal unnecessary detail from the user. Once cast into the design of a primitive set, the conventions are automatically inherited by any higher level operators that may be constructed from them. The user of this environment (the system designer) is then free to assemble arbitrary networks as hierarchies of operators and primitives without regard for the underlying protocols that ensure successful communication throughout the system. This frees the designer from an unnecessary task, raises the level of confidence in the design of complex systems, and considerably speeds the design cycle.

As a matter of common sense, we would not suggest that designers should use such an environment without at least some education in the underlying processes, but this does not detract from the principle of the argument given above.

Since we intend to elaborate one particular design environment in this text, we need to define such a set of conventions; indeed we have already introduced many of them. We adopt here the set of conventions proposed by Lyon (1981), with some minor exceptions:

Convention 1:   communication is bit-serial.
Convention 2:   LSB-first.
Convention 3:   signal high = logical 1
                    signal low = logical 0
Convention 4a: on-chip data is stable (between operators) during phi-2
                    (refer to Figure 1.8).

Actually this convention is respected strictly in the silicon parts of the system. As we discuss later (in Chapter 2), it is useful for inter-chip data to be timed one half clock cycle out of phase with on-chip data. Thus the role of the two phases will be transposed in the off-chip parts of any system:

Convention 4b: off-chip data is stable during phi-1.
Convention 5:   numerical format is fixed point, two's complement.
Convention 6:   data wordlength is fixed and constant in each system.
Convention 7:   multiple precision signals are as defined in Figure 1.9.
Convention 8:   operators have a fixed latency.
Convention 9:   inputs to operators are time aligned.
Convention 10:   control cycles have the format defined in Figure 1.12.
Convention 11:   each system has one CONTROLGENERATOR.

1.7   Appraisal of bit-serial architectures

Given this preliminary groundwork we are ready to present an appraisal of the role and advantages that bit-serial systems might have for future VLSI implementation. In this section we consider the relative advantages and tradeoffs with respect to alternative bit-parallel schemes, and in the following section we give a historical perspective.

1.7.1 Communication

Two of the key advantages of bit-serial architecture are evident from the device design shown in Figure 1.7. Firstly, bit-serial networks are easily routed on-chip without the problems of bit-parallel busing. All of the network wiring for our example algorithm is present in the routing channel visible across the centre of the chip. Secondly, all signals entering and leaving the chip do so via single pins. There is rarely a pinout problem in bit-serial parts.

These issues are intuitively related to the realisation that all of the wires in these systems are used at a 100% duty cycle, transmitting data at the fastest serial bit-rate that the technology will support. Buses within bit-parallel systems do not consistently make such efficient use of the available information bandwidth.

A commensurate disadvantage for the serial system is the fixed system wordlength. Except in some of the delay and storage primitives there is no convenient way to exploit the data redundancy that is present in those parts of the system that do not use the full dynamic range offered by the fixed wordlength.

1.7.2 Computational efficiency

In many cases the bit-serial primitives offer efficient implementations of the arithmetic functions in a space–time–energy measure. Here we are primarily concerned with 'operations per second per unit silicon area'. A high score in this measure assures efficient use of silicon area given a fixed requirement on computational throughput. It is well known that pipelining can be used to improve hardware throughput. The bit-serial multiplier is naturally pipelined down to the bit-level, so that its individual components (basically the add function) are continuously used at the best throughput rate that the technology can afford. Parallel multipliers can also be pipelined, but their latency then becomes equivalent to many word-times, making them more difficult to use in a general context.

On a broad comparison between bit-serial and bit-parallel operators assuming a common clock rate, we expect the serial part to process one word every N clock ticks compared with one clock tick in the parallel part, but to contain only 1/Nth of the hardware (one full adder cell opposed to N in the case of an adder). Given a common clock rate and technology base for both implementations we would expect them to be broadly equivalent in terms of an area–time measure AT. (See Ullman, 1984, for an introduction to these measures.) The condition of common clock rate may not hold however, since the tight bit-level pipelining of the serial system should permit a shorter clock period than for the (non-pipelined) parallel system, whose clock period must reflect an allowance for carry propagation in the multiply and add elements. This would be reflected in a reduction of the chip area devoted to the arithmetic processes in the bit-serial part.

Pope and Brodersen (1983) present an alternative programmable signal processing architecture based on a serial-parallel arithmetic unit (bit-serial communication with parallel arithmetic). A comparison with this architecture is interesting because it uses the same order of hardware and time as the bit-serial architecture for multiplication. However, their system has the advantage of supporting multiplication by coefficients represented in a canonic signed digit code. The strength of this scheme is that the number of cycles required to perform a multiplication is reduced from the total system wordlength to the number of significant one's in the recoded coefficient. This can improve the number of cycles by a factor of two or three typically, though the cycle time must be derated to allow for a ripple carry effect. This technique is not readily useful for the types of functional architecture that are of primary interest here because the multiply latency is no longer fixed.

1.7.3 Computational catholicity

We have made a focus of the predominance of multiply and add operations, and of the efficiency of bit-serial implementations of these operations. However, other operations are occasionally required that are not so well suited to bit-serial implementation as these. Division is one such operation. However, as we stated at the beginning, it is important in this methodology only to obey the serial conventions on the communication paths between operators. It is possible to include operators with a naturally parallel orientation provided that their interfaces are serialised, and that they exhibit a fixed latency. Though this may not be optimally efficient, it does represent a practical solution.

1.7.4   System architecture

Though the absolute computational throughput of a bit-serial element may not match that of its bit-parallel counterpart, total system performance is obtained by reducing the problem to several concurrent processes. By using a bit-serial implementation of each of these processes, we may obtain an impressive total system performance, sometimes in excess of the bit-parallel alternative. This concept is illustrated in Figure 1.15.

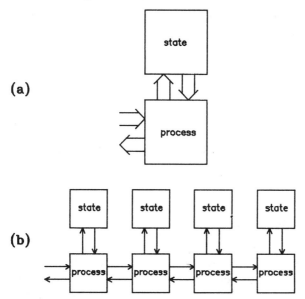

Fig. 1.15   Bit-serial v. bit-parallel architecture:
(a)   bit-parallel formulation
(b)   bit-serial formulation using multiple, smaller, slower processes.

Where the initial algorithm can support the type of concurrent formulation implicit in Figure 1.15(b) there appear to be several inherent advantages to the serial system architecture. These stem from the stronger locality of communication in the serial architecture as compared to the parallel case. In the bit-serial system information is circulated in small loops close to each of the processes. In the larger bit-parallel system, information required at the arithmetic unit from memory may have to travel a long distance to get there. The response time of the memory may slow the system clock rate in this circumstance, as may the time of transmission of the data across a large distance. Both of these issues become progressively more important as advances in technology speed the expected clock rate and permit faster computational units to support more state memory in a given real-time application.

1.7.5   Partitioning

Whenever a system exceeds the bounds of a single-chip implementation it is generally much easier to partition the system with bit-serial architecture. This is partly because the serial system is composed of many finer-grained components, so that it is normally possible to partition at their boundaries, as demonstrated in many of the case studies given later. Even when it is necessary to partition inside a process boundary the partition edges only cross single-wire signal paths, not multiple-bit busses.

Taken together the points covered above suggest several fundamental advantages for bit-serial as a VLSI architecture. Most significantly these advantages seem to be uniformly strengthened with expected improvements in technology. These factors give good cause for optimism about an increasing future role for bit-serial VLSI architectures.

1.8   Heritage

Despite the attractions identified above, bit-serial systems have not enjoyed the general popularity of their bit-parallel counterparts. There is thus a requirement for a more general enlightenment than might be necessary in other fields. Towards this end, and in recognition of earlier work, we present a short history of bit-serial architectures, chips and systems.

1.8.1   Early origins

We are principally concerned with developments of serial architectures for LSI implementation stemming from pioneering work in the 1960s. However, the advantageous tradeoff between hardware cost and performance that is characteristic of serial architecture has proved attractive since the earliest days of digital computing. Examples of specific bit-serial machines may be found in Bell and Newell's catalogue of computing structures (Bell and Newell, 1971). They include the Turing-influenced Pilot ACE (Wilkinson, 1953) and the Pegasus (Elliot *et al.*, 1956).

A second generation serial computer (the Sabrac) is reported by Lehman *et al.* (1963). The initiative behind this development was the projected need for a small, general purpose 'cost limited' computer, for which the authors identified a serial architecture as the best choice.

More recently we find the adoption of bit-serial techniques in several general-purpose array processors. These are generally two-dimensional configurations of simple serial processors (usually a serial adder or Boolean processor) with nearest-neighbour connections. See Fountain (1983) for an excellent summary and bibliography of these architectures. Systolic serial arrays (McWhirter *et al.*, 1985) have also found recent interest. The theme of this text follows the alternative tack of building more complex custom serial processors and systems.

Serial multipliers

The structures of most interest here are characterised by custom serial arithmetic hardware (multipliers and adders) to satisfy the exceptional demand for these functions in digital signal processing applications. Obvious origins lie in early developments in multiplier and adder structure, and there is a path of development from parallel, through serial-parallel to fully serial multiplier operation. The serial-parallel case in particular is closely related; several of the works referenced below are indeed based on this architecture. An early treatment of the parallel, serial-parallel argument may be found in Richards (1955), and the serial-parallel architecture is further developed in Chu (1962).

The first fully pipelined serial multiplier architecture was reported by Atrubin (1965) and was subsequently included in Knuth's seminumerical algorithms (Knuth, 1969). The first multiplier of this type to be specifically optimised for the need of signal processing (generating rounded single word products instead of full integer results) is described in Jackson *et al.* (1968).

Following this, Lyon (1976b) is a classic reference on the architecture of bit-serial pipelined multipliers. His architecture combines common serial formats and two's complement representation for both multiplier and multiplicand.

1.8.2 Methodology

The theme of this text is based on a particular architectural methodology for serial systems that we trace from the following contributions.

Jackson, Kaiser and McDonald (1968)

The foundation work on bit-serial architecture for signal processing was reported by Jackson *et al.* (1968). Their paper presents 'an approach to the implementation of digital filters' that advocates parallel system architecture using serial two's complement arithmetic. They perceptively identify four key features that remain as relevant to VLSI today as they did to potential LSI at that time:

- Filters can be constructed from a small set of relatively simple digital circuits.
- The circuit configurations (our primitives) are highly modular and thus well suited to LSI (VLSI) construction.
- The system configurations are highly flexible in terms of realising a wide range of filter forms.
- Arithmetic units (the computational kernels of the filters) can be easily multiplexed, providing for efficient hardware utilisation.

Powell and Irwin (1975, 1978, 1981)

In a series of successful early hardware developments (see below), Powell and Irwin strongly advocate the concept of 'functional parallelism', or the use of many slow elements to achieve enormous total computational power. They demonstrate this through a series of system constructions employing large arrays of bit-serial computational elements. They further demonstrate pioneering concepts in multiplexing to achieve high throughput rates in excess of the serial system word, and even bit-rates.

Lyon (1981)
In 1981 Lyon published a seminal paper on an architectural methodology for VLSI bit-serial systems. This work sets out the principles of establishing a library of primitive bit-serial elements, and the importance of setting global conventions to simplify the construction of complex networks of these elements.

Denyer, Renshaw and Bergmann (1982)
The authors extended Lyon's methodology and combined it with new methods in VLSI design to implement a silicon compiler for bit-serial VLSI systems (Denyer *et al.*, 1982; Bergmann, 1983). The methodology and tools are the focus of this text.

1.8.3   Hardware

Early chips
In the mid 1970s a series of LSI realisations were reported that substantiated JKM's vision. These ranged from discrete serial multipliers to an early complete second order section on a chip. Mostly these devices were realised in p- and n-channel MOS technologies supporting bit rates up to 2 or 3 MHz.

The first of these devices appeared at the 1975 IEEE International Solid State Circuits Conference. Edwards *et al.* (1975) presented a pMOS chip that implemented a dual second order filter section around a single serial multiplier. In the same session at that conference Powell and Irwin (1975) showed a 'computational element' chip which contained two serial multipliers to compute the general function ab $\pm$ cd. The CE was useful in implementing a family of FFT processors (see below).

Hampel *et al.* (1975) reported an advanced 24-bit serial-parallel multiplier implemented in CMOS/SOS technology that ran at 18 MHz.

The following year saw the publication by Cheng and Mead (1976) of a further double multiplier chip. The architecture of this device was based on a pre-publication version of Lyon's multiplier. This device differed from Powell and Irwin's CE in that it used modified Booth recoding to halve the number of add cells required, and also used a shared data channel which the authors showed was useful in building both second order sections and complex arithmetic functions such as the FFT.

The earliest merchant supplied device (the Am25LS14, an expandable 8-bit serial-parallel multiplier) was announced in 1976. The utility of this device was unfortunately restricted by a lack of related serial support components. Also in that year Kane (1976) reported a high speed 4-bit multiplier featuring fully serial, two's complement operation at 20 MHz.

Later devices
Later devices (both LSI and VLSI) followed these early themes quite faithfully. Technological improvements permitted steadily increasing packing

densities and speeds, but the filter and FFT applications remained predominant at least into the early 1980s.

Baldwin *et al.* (1978) reported a further 4-bit fast serial-parallel multiplier in bipolar technology, operating up to 44 MHz.

Adding to their CE chip, Powell and Irwin (1978) reported three new devices; a first order filter section, a cursive character generator and a matrix operator in an impressive development of applications around a common set of functional elements in one technology.

Ohwada *et al.* (1979), realising the benefit of a library of general functional elements, developed a set of chips featuring serial multipliers, long variable shift registers and general linear arithmetic elements. These devices were implemented in CMOS technology running at bit rates greater than 23 MHz.

Caldwell (1980) described a programmable serial processor (and controller) including two serial multipliers, for a range of speech synthesis applications in industrial, consumer and research environments. These devices are particularly suited to the implementation of lattice filters for LPC speech synthesis.

JKM's vision of a general integrated filter bank using the multiplexed second order section was realised by Adams *et al.* (1981) in their FAD (Filter And Detect) chip, and by Lyon (1981) in his Filters chip (see the case study in Part 2 of this book). Lyon's arithmetic kernel computes a second order section in 2 microseconds and includes sufficient state memory for a multiplex factor of 32. This theme has been continued by Myers and Ivey (1984) in the development of their STAR chip.

An alternative approach to the filtering problem is presented by Van Ginderdeuren *et al.* (1983). Their interest is in minimising the silicon area per pole in a dedicated (non-alterable) filter implementation. Using a tight serial pipeline and carefully compacted layout, they succeeded in matching the area per pole of alternative analogue implementations.

Further work by Wawrzynek and Mead on a new multiply/interpolate structure (for use in a music synthesis system), and by Lyon on a new programmable bit-serial architecture (with application in speech recognition) are included as case studies in Part 2 of this book.

Recent work by Linderman *et al.* (1984) includes a bit-serial radix-4 computational element and control circuitry on a single chip for fast FFT applications.

Systems

Freeny *et al.* (1971) reported an impressive pre-LSI system using a serial architecture for 'modularity of design, flexibility, and resulting economies'. The system implemented an FDM/TDM translator (also called a transmultiplexer) for 24 voice channels using several hundred ECL chips.

A good example of the use of the Am25LS14 part is given by Miranker (1978). This clever microprogrammed architecture made use of the unusual features of the device in a signal processing application of the sort for which it was not well suited.

Perhaps the most impressive work on integrated hardware is that performed by Powell and Irwin who constructed several large machines from bit-serial LSI operators. Powell and Irwin (1975, 1978, 1981) report the construction of a series of FFT machines ranging up to a 1024 point unit (the VFFT-10) that processed 10 MHz complex data in real time. This is achieved using arrays of relatively modest CE chips running at 2 to 3 MHz bit-rates. The low pin count of the serial CE (18 pins) encourages its assembly in compact physical arrays.

The authors further describe the Matrix Functional Processor (MFP), a flexible machine for the solution of recursive matrix equations encountered in boundary value problems, image filtering, adaptive beamforming and non-linear optimisation problems. They show an 8×8 MFP board designed to invert complex matrices of dimension 256×256 to an accuracy of 16 bits in 28 iterations. The architecture of the MFP is strongly systolic and is exemplary of the use of bit-serial techniques in such applications.

References

Adams, P.F., Harbridge, J.R. and MacMillan, R.H., 'An MOS Integrated Circuit for Digital Filtering and Level Detection', *IEEE J. Solid-State Circuits*, vol. SC-16, no. 3, pp 183–190, 1981.

Atrubin, A.J., 'A One-Dimensional Real-Time Iterative Multiplier', *IEEE Trans. on Electronic Computers*, pp 394–399, 1965.

Baldwin, G.L., Morris, B.L., Fraser, D.B. and Tretola A.R., 'A Modular High-Speed Serial Pipeline Multiplier for Digital Signal Processing', *IEEE J. Solid-State Circuits*, vol. SC-13, no. 3, pp 400–408, 1978.

Bell, C.G. and Newell, A., *Computer Structures: Readings and Examples*, McGraw-Hill, New York, 1971.

Bergmann, N.W., 'A Case Study of the FIRST Silicon Compiler', pp. 413–430 in *3rd Caltech Conference on VLSI*, ed. R. Bryant, Computer Science Press, 1983.

Buric, M.R. and Mead, C., 'Bit-Serial Inner Product Processors in VLSI', *Second Caltech Conference on VLSI*, pp. 155–164, 1981.

Caldwell, J.L., 'Programmable LSI Devices Implement Diverse Speech Synthesis Algorithms', *IEEE Computer Society Int. Conf.*, pp 207–209, 1980.

Cheng, E.K. and Mead, C.A., 'A Two's Complement Pipeline Multiplier', *IEEE Int. Conf. on Acoustics, Speech and Signal Processing*, pp 647–650, 1976.

Chu, Y., *Digital Computer Design Fundamentals*, McGraw-Hill, 1962.

Denyer, P.B., 'Introduction to Bit-Serial Architectures for VLSI Signal Processing', in *VLSI Architecture*, ed. Randell and Treleaven, Prentice-Hall International, 1983.

Denyer, P.B., Renshaw, D., Bergmann, N., 'A Silicon Compiler for VLSI Signal Processors', *Proc. ESSCIRC 82*, pp 215–218, Brussels, 1982.

Edwards, G.P., Jennings, P.J. and Preston, T., 'A MOS LSI Double Second Order Digital Filter Circuit', *IEEE Int. Solid-State Circuits Conf.*, pp 20–21, 1975.

Elliot, W.S., Owen, C.E., Devonald, C.H. and Maudsley, B.G., 'The Design Philosophy of Pegasus, a Quantity-production Computer', *Proc IEE*, Pt B, vol. 103, Suppl. 2, pp 188–196, 1956.

Filip, A.E., 'A Baker's Dozen Magnitude Approximation and Their Detection Statistics', *IEEE Trans. Aerospace and Electronic Systems*, vol. AES-12, pp 87–89, 1976.

Fountain, T.J., 'A Survey of Bit-Serial Array Processor Circuits', in *Computing Structures for Image Processing*, ed. Duff, Academic Press, 1983.

Freeny, S.L., 'Special-Purpose Hardware for Digital Filtering', *Proc. IEEE*, pp 633–648, 1975.

Freeny, S.L., Kieburtz, R.B., Mina, K.V. and Tewksbury, S.K., 'Design of Digital Filters for an all Digital Multiplex-Time Division Multiplex Translator', *IEEE Trans. on Circuit Theory*, vol. CT-18, no. 6, pp 702–711, 1971.

Hampel, D.H., McGuire, K.E. and Prost, K.J., 'CMOS/SOS Serial-Parallel Multiplier', *IEEE Solid-State Circuits*, vol. SC-10, no. 5, pp 307–313, 1975.

Heightley, J.D., 'Partitioning of Digital Filters for Integrated Circuit realisation', *IEEE Trans. on Communication Theory*, vol. COM 19, no. 6, pp 1059–1063, 1971.

Jackson, L.B., Kaiser, J.F. and McDonald, H.S., 'An Approach to the Implementation of Digital Filters', *IEEE Trans. on Audio and Electronacoustics*, vol. AU-16, no. 3, pp 413–421, 1968.

Kane, J., 'A Low-Power, Bipolar, Two's Complement Serial Pipeline Multiplier Chip', *IEEE J. Solid-State Circuits*, vol. SC-11, pp 669–678, 1976.

Knuth, D.E., *The Art of Computer Programming*, vol. 2: Seminumerical Algorithms, Addison-Wesley, 1969.

Kopec, G. and Miranker, G.S., 'Programming a Microcoded Processor for Speech Waveform Generation', IEEE Comp Soc. 11th Workshop on Microprogramming, 1978.

Kung, H.T. and Leiserson, C.E., 'Algorithms for VLSI Processor Arrays', in *Introduction to VLSI Systems*, Mead and Conway, Addison-Wesley, 1980.

Lehman, M., Eshed, R. and Netter, Z., 'Sabrac – A New Generation Serial Computer', *IEEE Trans. on Electronic Computers*, pp 618–625 1963.

Linderman, R.W., Reusens, P.P., Chan, P.M. and Ku, W.H., 'Digital Signal Processing Capabilities of CUSP, A High Performance Bit-Serial VLSI Processor', *IEEE Int. Conf. on Acoustics, Speech and Signal Processing*, pp 1611–1614, 1984.

Lyon, R.F., 'Two's Complement Pipeline Multiplier', U.S. Patent 3,956,622, 1976 (a).

Lyon, R.F., 'Two's Complement Pipeline Multipliers', *IEEE Trans. on Communications*, pp 418–424, 1976 (b).

Lyon, R.F., 'A Bit-Serial VLSI Architectural Methodology for Signal Processing', in *VLSI 81*, ed. Gray, Academic Press, 1981.

McLaughlin, P.T., 'A Single Chip Speech Synthesis System', *IEEE Int. Solid-State Circuits Conf.*, pp 32–33, 1981.

McWhirter, J.G., Wood, D., Wood, K., Evans, R.A., McCanny, J.V. and McCabe, A.P.H., 'Multi-bit Convolution using a Bit-Level Systolic Array', *IEEE Trans. Circuits and Systems*, pp 95–99, 1985.

Mead, C. and Conway, L., *Introduction to VLSI Systems*, Addison-Wesley, 1980.

Miranker, G.S., 'A Digital Signal Processor for Real Time Generation of Speech Waveforms', *Proc. 5th Annual Symposium on Computer Architecture*, New York, 1978.

Myers, D.J., Ivey, P.A., 'STAR – A VLSI Architecture for Signal Processing', *Proc. Conference on Advanced Research in VLSI*, pp 179–183, 1984.

Ohwada, N., Kimura, T. and Doken, M., 'LSI's for Digital Signal Processing', *IEEE Trans. on Electron Devices*, vol. ED-26, no. 4, pp 292–298, 1979.

Pope, S.P. and Brodersen, R.W., 'Macrocell Design for Concurrent Signal Processing', in *Third Caltech Conference on Very Large Scale Integration*, ed. Bryant, pp 395–412, Computer Science Press, 1983.

Powell, N.R., 'Functional Parallelism in VLSI Systems and Computations', in *VLSI Systems and Computations*, ed. Kung, Sproull and Steele, Springer-Verlag, 1981.

Powell, N.R. and Irwin, J.M., 'A MOS Monolithic Chip for High-Speed Flexible FFT Microprocessors', *IEEE Int. Solid-State Circuits Conf.*, pp 18–19, 1975.

Powell, N.R. and Irwin, J.M., 'Signal Processing with Bit-Serial Word-Parallel Architectures', *SPIE*, vol. 154, pp 98–104, 1978.

Richards, R.K., *Arithmetic Operations in Digital Computers*, Van Nostrand, 1955.

Rubinfield, L.P., 'A Proof of the Modified Booth's Algorithm for Multiplication', *IEEE Trans. on Computers*, pp 1014–1015, 1975.

Ullman J.D., *Computational Aspects of VLSI*, Computer Science Press, 1984.

Van Ginderdeuren, J.K.J., De Man, H.J., Goncalves, N.F. and Van Noije, W.A.M., 'Compact NMOS Building Blocks and a Methodology for Dedicated Digital Filter Applications', *IEEE J. Solid-State Circuits*, vol. SC-18, no. 3, pp 306–315, 1983.

Wilkinson, J.H., 'The Pilot ACE', in *Automatic Digital Computation*, National Physical Laboratory, Teddington, pp 5–14, 1953.

Zollo, S., 'Digital Filter Handles 24-bit Data', *Electronics Week*, 22 Oct, 1984.

2

A Silicon Compiler

Here and in the following two chapters we consider the implementation of bit-serial processors as custom VLSI circuits. This may seem to be a tall order; as any practitioner may confirm, casting a system into silicon can be a daunting task. In the previous chapter we identified many of the attractions of the medium, but these appear to fade rapidly in the face of multi man-year investments for each algorithm or system that we might like to implement. In one form or another, this problem has deterred the use of silicon, other than as a volume production medium for the last decade. However, our aim lies in the opposite direction; that is to encourage the use of silicon as a development medium from the outset. In this chapter we develop some methods and tools that simplify and accelerate the custom design of complex VLSI signal processing systems.

2.1 An issue of complexity

There are two reasons why VLSI circuit design is a complex task: the span of representations is large, and the degrees of freedom are many. It is our purpose to constrain both of these factors in order to bring competent VLSI design within the grasp of the systems designer. This is not to imply that the systems designer cannot acquire the necessary skills for custom VLSI design, rather it stems from a simple belief that he is most productive at designing systems, not laying out circuits.

We firstly consider the span of representations, which can be large even in the most structured of designs, stretching from algorithmic considerations at the highest level, down to the final detail on a piece of polysilicon at the lowest. One strategy is to abstract a simplified set of design idioms, to reduce the mental 'baggage' that needs to to be carried around by the designer. This approach is advocated by Mead and Conway (1980). We have found this technique to be successful only to a limited extent, because it does nothing to reduce the span of representations. The 'tall thin men' are rare that can manage such a span with sufficient competence. Certainly we would not expect every systems designer to possess these abilities, or even to be interested in acquiring them. We propose therefore to truncate this span. This is possible within a restricted application area (such as signal processing), or within a restricted architectural style, by building systems from a limited set of predesigned functional modules. The system designer need no longer be concerned with the task of generating correct circuits and layout, rather his task is to assemble these modules in order to realise some desired system function. This is not unlike TTL system design, in which the designer is freed from any concern of circuit detail within the package, but here the concept is more powerful. Our set of modules will be specifically tailored to signal processing, and will be consistent within that domain at a level that has never been realised in TTL. Furthermore, our modular functions will not be rigidly fixed. Instead they may feature some parameterisation; for example we may call multipliers of various resolutions, or delay elements of arbitrary length, as single modules.

With the introduction of this module/system interface we have structured the problem into two separate tasks. The system designer needs no information below this boundary (he will simply call and use modules in the confidence that they are correct), while the module designer needs no information above it. This interface is a pivot in our methodology. It has a bearing on many other issues, including the attainment of performance and the partitioning of floorplans. We suggest that it would be productive to look for such pivots in other domains.

We mentioned two key reasons for the complexity of the implementation process. The second of these is an excess of freedom. Throughout the design process there are myriad possible alternatives in translating a system function into two dimensions of blank silicon. This can be seen even at the most elementary level by asking a group of students to lay out some simple circuit function; the results are as varied as the students themselves! Much of the process of custom VLSI design is a cascade of such alternatives through which designers loop, searching for ever more optimal solutions. Depending on a mixture of deadlines, artistic skill and previous experience, this can be an extensive process which is not necessarily warranted if we are more concerned with functional implementation than optimal packing density. To constrain this process we have imposed a precise design style by eliminating alternatives at each step. What results is a controlled style of system synthesis and chip composition which yields results that are close to optimal, but which is nevertheless painless and rapid to execute.

This chapter is devoted to the development of such a constrained VLSI design style, and to its automation in the form of a powerful design tool, the silicon compiler.

2.2   The silicon compiler ...

The term 'silicon compiler' was first coined to describe original work by Johannsen (1978,1981). Since that time it has been the cause of much controversy and interest. Classical compilers take as input some high-level description of the function to be executed and produce as output a list of low-level (normally machine-level) code which will run on a machine to execute the function. Compilers were developed to avoid the tedium and errors consequent in producing long lists of such low-level code, when the tasks themselves could be described much more concisely at a higher level. Few, if any, would now question the advantage of this approach to software engineering, for the complexity of the tasks to be performed at machine code level lies well beyond normal human capability. In one respect this situation bears a strong similarity to the VLSI design problem.

In similar vein, the silicon compiler is a tool which takes a high-level functional description as input but produces, instead of machine code, a detailed chip mask geometry. The advent of such tools for VLSI system design is leading to a minor revolution in design. Suddenly, years of manual design and layout are replaced by a program which can do the same task orders of magnitude more quickly. Before considering the development of such a capability for the class of bit-serial processors, we note some important changes in technical approach and attitude that have already become apparent to us.

First and foremost, the silicon compiler greatly reduces the obstacle of complexity. With this, silicon becomes a much more flexible and rapid hardware development medium. There follows a commensurate advantage in the marketplace when a product in integrated form can be designed more quickly.

Secondly, the silicon compiler offers a single high-level interface to the user. This dramatically extends the community of potential users, to include many system designers who need no knowledge of specialised chip design and layout, save some elementary guidelines on sensible chip sizing and partitioning. The silicon compiler permits the system designer to concentrate on what he is good at – designing systems.

Thirdly, because the implementation process is automated (and assuming that this process has been verified) it becomes error-free, or 'correct by construction', so that the user is assured of a correct implementation at the first attempt. Considering the cost and time factors involved in the fabrication process, this becomes an essential feature, for in general it is not possible to debug and modify the integrated part. We believe that the combination of first-time correctness, along with a rapid design cycle and high-level user interface will make the silicon compiler a prime system development tool of the future.

Fourthly, from the viewpoint of software tool development, the silicon compiler provides a framework for integrating software for VLSI. Finally, in this capacity it also provides a technique for organising and storing previously engineered layout knowledge into a system which allows rapid access and use of the complex information it contains.

2.3 ... in perspective

It would be wrong to view the silicon compiler as an end in itself; it is one of several parts in the process of producing an integrated system. We show a simplified view of the total process in Figure 2.1.

Our aim is to get from some informal system specification through to a good working system. We also entertain the further aims that this route should be rapid, and successful at the first attempt. These conditions are essential for custom VLSI to become a truly attractive and competitive development medium.

A major part of the process is maskmaking and silicon fabrication, which we lump together under the heading 'silicon foundry'. Designers have no part in this; they are primarily concerned with translating the system specification into a set of mask descriptions which, after fabrication, will yield the working function. We identify this as a second pivotal point, since the foundry interface may also be well defined in terms of design rules, tape formats, etc.

The silicon compiler is also a major link in the process, translating a formal description of the system into a set of mask geometries in a single step. It therefore becomes a crucial tool in speeding the development cycle, and in helping to guarantee a correct implementation.

The remaining obstacles to our goal now lie at the start and end of this chain. At the beginning, it is the task of a designer to formulate the system description to the compiler. Whilst a high-level language helps this process, it is well known that writing programs is error prone – not because of the compiler but because of the programmer! This is clearly a weak link in the chain, threatening the chance of producing a system correctly at the first attempt. The solution is to provide, in parallel with the compiler, a system simulator that is driven from the same system description entered to the compiler. Using this simulator, the designer is able to verify that the system he is describing will perform the function he intends. In practice the designer spends much of his time in this loop, which provides an encouraging environment for experimentation. The designer is free to explore at the higher architectural levels, where his creative talents are arguably most effective, with access to the compiler for rapid feedback on chip sizes. This is in marked contrast to the traditional approach, where architectural decisions must be fixed early on, and any later changes at this level can be very costly in terms of circuit design investment. With the silicon compiler, no significant commitment is made to any device until the moment of submission to the foundry.

At the end of the implementation path the remaining task is to test the manufactured wafers and packaged parts. As we suggest in Figure 2.1, this

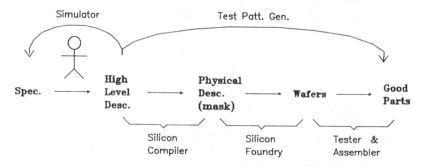

Fig. 2.1 Steps in the progress of producing an integrated system.

process is quite as significant as the compilation and foundry services. It is also traditionally tackled on an *ad hoc* basis, though there is now a general realisation that this must change. At the worst, without sufficient forethought, the design may prove to be untestable. We therefore need a comprehensive and speedy design-for-test methodology, and this is presented in Chapter 7. The subject is included here because we also wish to automate the testing process, remove the 'ad-hocery', and make this an invisible and rapid step. In particular, we intend to generate test patterns automatically from the single formal system description.

Taken together, the silicon compiler, system simulator and automatic test pattern generator offer a complete environment in which complex VLSI systems can be rapidly and correctly synthesised at the first attempt. Reductions in the overall system development timescale will be dramatic, but the absolute figure depends critically on foundry turnaround time. A target of around four man weeks for system synthesis and compilation does not seem unreasonable from our development studies.

2.4   A FIRST compiler

Much of the following discussion relates to a particular silicon compiler that was developed in Edinburgh to demonstrate our methods (Denyer *et al.*, 1982, 1983; Bergmann, 1983) The compiler is called FIRST, for Fast Implementation of Real-time Signal Transforms, and also because it was our first attempt.

It was our intention from the outset to demonstrate some real systems, so FIRST was targeted at the technology then available to us, 5 micron nMOS. We stress that the reader should not measure the merit of the approach by the level of system integration associated with this technology. The ideas and methods presented here are intended as a general approach to VLSI signal processing. It is our ambition that they will be applied across many future technologies.

FIRST then is simply an interpretation at one technology level of the general methodology set out in this book. The overall structure is shown in Figure 2.2. It can be seen to support the major components that we identified above as a complete environment for system implementation. Each of the elements is described below. We begin with a short description of the language compiler, but leave discussion of the system description language itself to Chapter 3. We examine the physical design subsystem, which plays the central role of VLSI implementation, and follow with descriptions of the simulator and automatic test pattern generation (ATPG) facilities.

2.4.1   The language compiler

The input language compiler has to satisfy two requirements. At the input it should support a high-level system description language, which we will develop in Chapter 3. Notably this will include representations of structure and parameterisation to support concise system definitions. At the output it must

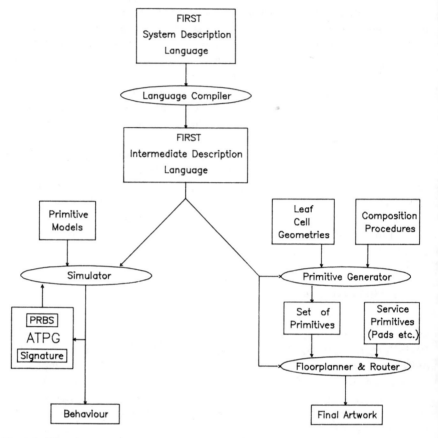

Fig. 2.2   The primary structure of FIRST.

deliver a flattened and evaluated list of primitive modules and their interconnections, for assembly or simulation. As any other compiler it should include checks and warnings on syntax, but in this case it might also check for open (undriven) nodes and other prerequisites of network integrity.

2.4.2   The physical design subsystem

A general composition strategy
The central system/module interface that was developed in Section 2.1 suggests a general composition strategy, in which modules are maintained as tight physical clumps of layout, to be wired together according to the system design. This obvious approach is nevertheless a powerful one, and its advantages are worthy of examination. Most importantly, the high functional level of the modules secures a low connection-to-layout ratio. All of the internal connections between gates and transistors are compact, and externally invisible. This is not the case for example with gate-array and standard-cell techniques, where modules are at the gate level only. In that case all functions

must be reduced to the gate level, where inflexible positioning results in an inefficient wiring scheme. By permitting custom module layout we take advantage of any implied regularity and structure in, say, a multiplier or delay element. Also we allow a degree of local optimisation to be applied in designing such elements. This leaves only the relatively sparse interconnection of operands and results between modules. Here the bit-serial architecture works to advantage, for these signals are generally single wires only. We are never faced with attempting to get a multi-bit bus across a chip, or worse still several such buses.

A constrained floorplan

As a first constraint we secure a target floorplan architecture. The datapath (Mead and Conway, 1980; Sherburne *et al.*, 1981; Batali *et al.*, 1981; Shrobe, 1981) is an excellent example of a target floorplan for bit-parallel architectures. A successful alternative architecture, again with bit-parallel organisation, was proposed by Siskind *et al.* (1981) where the need for constrained architectures is also recognised. A wider variety of styles is feasible for bit-serial systems. For the present we restrict our discussion to a simple floorplan aimed at 4 to 6 micron nMOS technologies.

We have labelled this floorplan style, shown in Figure 2.3, 'Manhattan Skyline' for the similarity it bears to a cluster of skyscrapers and their reflection in the water. It comprises a central communication channel, flanked by two rows of bit-serial primitive modules. Signal routing is implemented through the central channel only; there is no intimate connection between neighbour modules. Thus modules communicate by receiving and transmitting data via the channel across the 'waterfront'. Chip input and output signals are routed to peripheral pads via the ends of the channel. To gain some familiarity with this architecture the reader is invited to study some of the detailed design

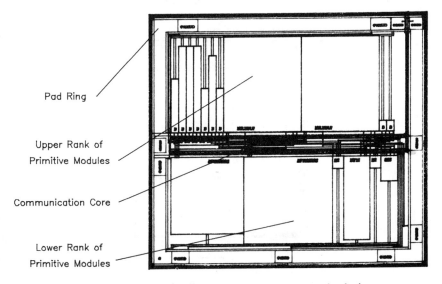

Pad Ring

Upper Rank of
Primitive Modules

Communication Core

Lower Rank of
Primitive Modules

Fig. 2.3 A simple floorplan schema for FIRST, suitable for 5 micron technologies.

examples given later in this book. Note that, as expected for bit-serial architectures, the communication core rarely dominates the chip area.

The simplicity of this floorplan style belies some important advantages. Signals in the communication channel are for the most part routed in metal, beginning and ending in short stubs of diffusion (or polysilicon). This is a useful feature where the technology offers only one low-impedance, low-capacitance interconnection medium (in this case a single level of metal). We shall also see that the single channel is easy to route, and that module ordering to minimise chip area is a realistic task.

Supplying services

Having chosen a particular floorplan style we now consider the provision of common services (global power and clock buses) throughout the chip. The relatively simple floorplan structure means that this need not be a complex task. In fact we are faced with two well defined sub-tasks; servicing the modules, and servicing the pad ring. Our proposal is to provide service ducts along the waterfront for the modules, and a service ring around the pad channel, as shown in Figure 2.4. This principle is easily extended to arbitrary floorplan conventions if the module service duct is allowed to become a flexible 'umbilical cord', routed around arbitrary module placements.

One problem with this arrangement is the need to maintain low impedance power and clock buses as far as possible. Normally this means maintaining these buses in metal for the most part. There is no problem when more than one metal layer is available, for then power and clock lines can be crossed without resorting to a relatively high impedance diffusion or polysilicon crossunder. However, when only one metal layer is available it becomes impossible to supply power from the duct to an adjacent module without using at least one crossunder. The solution is to split one of the power rails (VSS say)

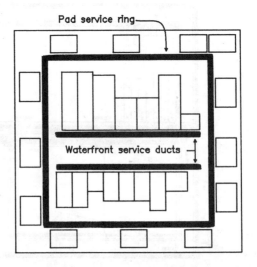

Fig. 2.4   Preliminary supply services for primitive modules and pads.

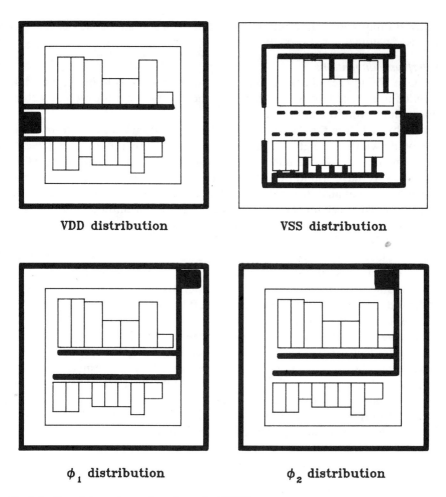

VDD distribution   **VSS distribution**

ϕ_1 **distribution** ϕ_2 **distribution**

Fig. 2.5 Complete service routing scheme for FIRST.

away from the duct and route it separately on the opposite side of the modules. As shown in Figure 2.5 it then becomes possible to route power to all modules, and cells within modules, without crossunders. A similar solution exists for the pad channel, supplying VSS and VDD from opposite sides of the ring.

Figure 2.5 shows the complete service routing schema for FIRST based on these principles. It includes fixed positions for each of the supply pads (at opposite ends of the communication core), and for the clock pads, phi1 and phi2. Without altering this scheme it is possible to replace the clock pad pair by an on-chip clock generator if this is preferred.

In addition to its role as a power bus, VSS is also sometimes used as a source for signals of 'zero' value (000...00). Thus a secondary VSS bus is also routed within the waterfront duct for this purpose. It has a higher impedance than the main power buses (because of crossunders) and so may not generally be used as a power source. A convenient exception to this rule is the use of this bus to power input and output buffers to modules which span this service duct, as discussed below.

Waterfront conventions

We have already set electrical and signalling conventions to be respected at module interfaces. Now we can complete the interface specification by setting geometric conventions at the waterfront.

It is obvious from the later chip plots that there are no absolute restrictions on module width or height. In this respect we give only the recommendation that the module designer attempt to minimise the waterfront dimension, within reason, as we have found this to be an expensive resource. The first formal convention is that all data input and output is restricted to take place along the waterfront. To aid channel routing we also quantise the allowable positions of i/o ports to be at even integer multiples of the wire pitch of the vertical wiring medium. (This will allow vertical wires from opposing rows of modules to interdigitate.) In this case we adopt a standard wire width of 4 lambda,[†] with a space of 3 lambda, giving a total wire pitch of 7 lambda in the diffusion layer. Thus module i/o ports are positioned on a permissible grid of twice this pitch (14 lambda), commencing from coordinate 0 lambda on the extreme left. All of this is illustrated in Figure 2.6.

We have found it convenient to permit the module layout to spread under the service duct for the special cases of input and output buffers, so saving layout area. The use of these buffers, which take a standard form, is illustrated in Figure 2.7 and Plate 2a. The output buffer is the final drive stage attached to every module output. Its design and function are described in Section 2.5. The input buffer is optional on any module signal input port. Its function is simply to delay the input signal by one whole clock cycle (bit-time). This is an

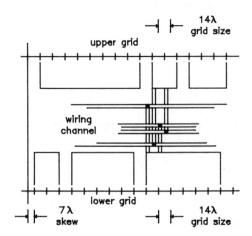

Fig. 2.6 Forcing clean interdigitation by quantising the vertical wire pitch.

---

† Lambda is a unit of linear dimension (Mead and Conway, 1980). Its absolute value depends upon the final choice of technology for implementation

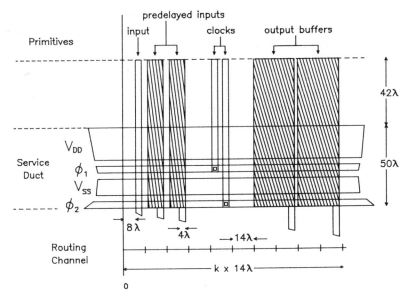

Fig. 2.7 Template for including (optional) input and output buffers under the waterfront service ducts.

expedient facility for handling inputs to modules that have become misaligned by one bit in time. The incorporation of a predelay cell at a module input comes for free (in terms of layout area) in this way, instead of using and wiring an extra module for the sake of a single bit of delay. The incorporation of predelay appears as an option on signal input ports for all primitive modules.

Placement and routing
The tasks of module placement and channel routing are simplified by our previous constraints on the floorplan and waterfront geometries.

Once assembled, modules are placed along the waterfronts and then arranged to meet a criterion of minimum chip area. Some experiments in this process quickly reveal that the overall size of the chip depends on four main factors:

the height of the tallest block on the top row
the height of the tallest block on the bottom row
the length of the longer row
the thickness of the wiring channel

The first three factors depend only on which modules are placed on the top and bottom rows respectively, so the placement algorithm first decides on this subdivision. The modules are ranked in order of height and this string is then divided into two subclasses – tall and short – at whatever point gives the minimum bounding area after placement. Trial perturbations are then made to reduce the area further by making the rows more equal in width. It is occasionally advantageous for example to move a tall block to the bottom row. Throughout these calculations the size of the wiring channel is neglected.

Given this final top/bottom classification, the arrangement of modules within the two rows is next decided. This will have a direct bearing on the width of the wiring channel, and hence on the total chip area. Through experience we have found it unnecessary to use any clever algorithmic approach to determine an optimal arrangement. A good arrangement usually results if the modules are placed in relative groupings that reflect their invocation in the input system description file. Designers tend to write this description in a manner that follows the general flow of information in the system. Such a strategy then leads to closely coupled modules being close together on the chip, with a resultant minimisation of the total wiring net. Since the wiring channel area is in any case only a relatively small proportion of the overall chip area we did not consider the calculation of any more optimal arrangement, though this could be done.

The two rows of modules are now placed in opposition, to either side of the designated wiring channel, and one row is shifted by a single wire pitch (7 lambda). This allows i/o ports from the two rows to interdigitate across the entire width of the channel without concern for coincidences. A simple channel router is used, with metal wires running horizontally and diffusion connections running vertically. Clearly this scheme would be well suited to any two layer process, for example double-layer metal. The top and bottom row offset ensures that connections can be made between any two ports with a single horizontal wire and two vertical wires, that is without doglegs. Figure 2.8 shows a typical wiring channel section.

Once the wiring channel is routed it remains only to place and route the pads (other than the power supply and clock pads which have already been instantiated). These are all either signal or control input or output pads, to be routed from the ends of the central wiring channel. Having fixed the positions

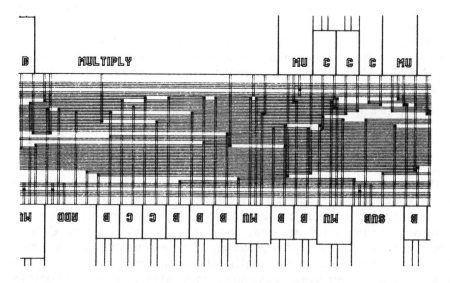

Fig. 2.8   A section from the central communication channel.

of the supply and clock pads, there remain three segments within the pad channel. To allow some control over the eventual device pinout, the user is given the opportunity to assign groups of pads to each segment, and to specify further their order within these segments. The relevant pad primitives (input or output) are then assembled and placed with approximately even spacing within each segment. The pad routing is then implemented by a simple bus arrangement, from the lower and right-hand pad channels to one end of the communication core, and from the opposing edges to the other end of the core. The junction box shown in Figure 2.9 completes the connections between the communication core and the pad bus. Note that it is necessary for the central channel router to have brought any input and output signals to the appropriate end of the channel. More detailed ordering of these signals is not necessary because a good interchange facility is available through the junction box. Once again, this seems a simple if not optimal solution.

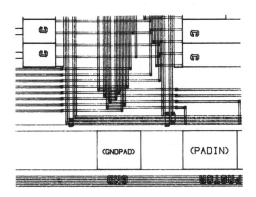

Fig. 2.9   A junction box connecting wires at the end of the communication channel with the pad routing buses.

2.4.3   Module generation

So far we have considered the primitive modules as black boxes, which become available on request. There is no intrinsic requirement for the 'module generator' to be bound in as part of the silicon compiler. This is really an isolated task of silicon assembly. We require modules to be assembled and passed back to the main compiler, in response to specific requests for instantiation.

The purpose fulfilled by module generation is that of producing a block of layout described in some low-level geometric code, for example CIF (Mead and Conway, 1980) or similar. However, we cannot adequately represent each module as a single fixed block of layout. This would permit no variation within the module, as required when calling a delay primitive of so many bits, or a multiplier with such-and-such a coefficient wordlength. It is not expedient to hold a different block of layout to suit each possible variant – e.g. a range of multipliers covering 2, 4, 6, 8, etc. coefficient bits. A more practical approach is to compose each module from a limited set of leaf cells, according to a defined assembly procedure. Such a procedure can take advantage of parameter passing, conditionals and loops to build classes of similar layout macrocells. Thus we represent each primitive as a composition routine in some general programming language which is capable of generating the required low level graphical objects: boxes, wires, polygons, symbols, etc. This approach rests on the development of an 'embedded language' (Johannsen, 1981; Locanthi, 1978; Ayers, 1978) which allows graphical objects to be defined and instanced hierarchically within a conventional high-level programming language.

As an example consider the assembly of a bit-serial multiplier primitive. This

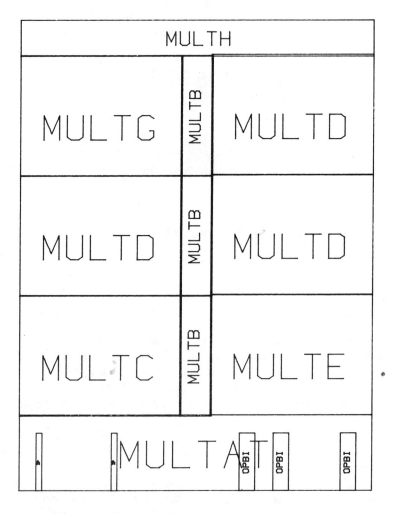

Fig. 2.10 Multiplier composition:
(a) the assembly plan for a multiplier with an odd number of main cells

particular multiplier consists of a cascade of cells, each of which handles the product associated with a pair of bits from the coefficient word. These cells are held as leaf cells of layout in CIF code. The beginning and end cells in the string are special; the intermediate cells are of one type which is repeated as necessary to build a multiplier of the required coefficient wordlength. In order to communicate legally with the central wiring channel, the otherwise linear cascade of cells is doubled over at (or close to) the half-way point, and an additional interconnect cell is used as a link at the folding point. An assembly plan is shown in Figure 2.10(a) for the case of a multiplier with an odd number of main cells.

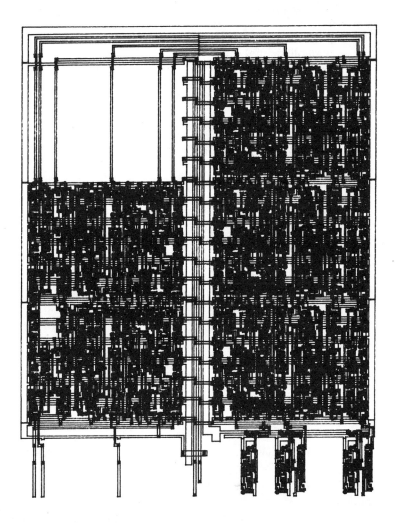

(b) Fully instantiated layout

Given that the sizes of the leaf cells are known (from layout), the following outline for the composition routine, when expanded, may be used to assemble the multiplier as a function of one parameter – the coefficient wordlength:

```
multiply()
{
        declarations
        retrieve parameter values for this instance
        calculate internal constants
        check parameter values
        compose symbol identifier (name)

        if(!symbol__exists(name)) {
                symbol(ttname)
                draw("MULTAT")
                draw I/O buffers
                draw("MULTB")
                draw("MULTC")
                draw("MULTE")
                        for(k = 1;k <= limitb;++k)
                        draw("MULTB")
                        for(k = 1;k <= limitdt;++k)
                        draw("MULTD")
                        if( coeffbits%4 != 0)
                        draw("MULTG")
                        else if(coeffbits > 4)
                        draw("MULTD")
                        draw("MULTH")
                        for(k = limitdb;k >= 1;--k)
                        draw("MULTD")
                        endsymbol()
        }
        evaluate and return height and width
        evaluate and return I/O port relative positions

}
```

Where *draw()* is a function which outputs the CIF shapes of the symbol named as its argument in the correct position and orientation. Note that suitable values for position and orientation must be passed to the *draw()* function and must subsequently be updated for the next call. At this level the details are suppressed for clarity. The function *symbol()* is a routine to generate a CIF definition start and *endsymbol()* to generate a CIF definition end. The function *symbolexists()* is a function which interrogates the data structure generated so far to see whether the symbol has already been defined or not; it returns TRUE or FALSE. The pseudo code given above can be expanded directly into an appropriate high-level language function or routine to define the multiply primitive. An example of full layout generated by such a routine for a 10-bit multiplier is shown in Figure 2.10(b), whilst Plate 2a shows detail of an 8-bit multiplier from a FIRST-compiled system.

This block of layout, representing the full primitive module, is returned to the Physical Design Subsystem of the silicon compiler for placement and routing. There is of course no restriction on the use of a single parameter, several of the primitive examples given later have two or three parameters.

The design of the leaf cells and the related assembly routines is the task of the module designer. As well as meeting the functional and performance specifications set for the module, he must ensure that the geometric conventions are respected at the waterfront. He must pick up the VDD supply along with clocks phi1 and phi2 from the waterfront, and provide a VSS cap along the top of the module. Otherwise his domain is not affected by further external conditions. It need be of no concern to him where, how or why the module is ultimately used.

2.4.4   The behavioural simulator

We have identified above a requirement for a simulator to enable the designer to be sure that the system he describes to the silicon compiler does implement the intended behaviour. Here we are concerned to avoid errors in the high-level system description.

It is also crucial to any guarantee of success that we should be sure to simulate precisely what will be compiled. In practice this is assured only by using the same system description file to drive both the simulator and the compiler and additionally by having some guarantee of isomorphism between the simulation behaviour and the processed layout behaviour. This also has the advantage that the user is presented with only one interface to the software, and that as far as he is concerned only one representation of his system exists.

Some consideration of the role of the simulator (Figure 2.11) and a little experience suggest two major requirements. In terms of overall capability, the simulator must support the concept of a complete system that may be composed of many chips. It is the function of this complete system that is the concern of the designer, not just one chip within it. Secondly, in terms of detailed fidelity, the simulator must preserve accuracy down to the bit-level, which is the finest functional resolution of these systems. The combination of these two requirements is quite forbidding: accurate simulation at bit-level of systems containing perhaps millions of transistors. However, this is the only way to provide a confident verification of the system that is to be fabricated.

One approach to building such a simulator is to work entirely at the bit-level. Primitives are modelled by the Boolean processes they perform, and the state of the entire system network is computed from these at every clock cycle. In practice primitive models at this level are undesirably complex. Also the slavish simulation of the detailed processes within every primitive leads to excessive simulation times. These internal processes are of no relevance to the system designer, who is only concerned with activity at the network level.

In particular, the system designer is concerned with word-level activity within the system network. Words correspond to signal samples and this is the finest level of resolution of interest. This does not imply that we should not maintain bit-level accuracy, but it does offer the possibility of a higher level of abstraction for primitive modelling. Thus the simulator model of a primitive can be based on its word-level function (addition, multiplication, etc.), plus appropriate adjustments to maintain bit-level fidelity. This type of model is illustrated in the following behavioural description of the MULTIPLY primitive:

```
multiply()
{
        declarations
        retrieve control node number for this instance
        if(time of event on control node == time) {

                retrieve signal node numbers for this instance
                retrieve parameters for this instance
                check parameter values, warn if illegal
                compute latency and any other constants required
                if(time of event on any data node != present time){
                        timing warning and diagnostics
                }

                retrieve input signal values
                check formats, warn if out of range
                multiply input values to required degree of precision
                format bytes of product for output
                enter output values, event times and nodes on queue
        }
        else
                timing warning and diagnostics

}
```

There is now no requirement to update every element at every clock cycle. The values on network nodes, which in reality consist of serial bit streams, are modelled as discrete words of data occurring at discrete time intervals. For convenience we deem each word to 'occur' at its LSB time. The simulator now becomes event driven. A word occurrence on any node invokes models of all primitives having that node as an input. New values are then computed for each of the output nodes to 'occur' at the appropriate time (namely the time of the

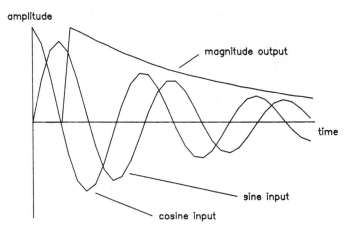

amplitude

magnitude output

time

sine input

cosine input

Fig. 2.11 An example of output from the system simulator (after graphical interpretation). The system is a complex-to-magnitude converter with decaying sine and cosine waves as inputs, producing the illustrated decay envelope as output.

input occurrence plus the primitive latency). The scheduling of occurrences is handled by storing all pending occurrences in a queue. All occurrences due at a given time are removed from the queue, and the new output words are then computed and inserted into the queue at appropriate times.

Input data is entered as a file of occurrences (time and datum), and output data is stored in a similar fashion. It is not hard to interface with this format to produce a user-friendly system. For example, input data may be generated from a set of software 'signal generators' that produce commonly-used waveforms with user controlled parameters. Equally, output data may be interpreted in a graphic form, producing oscilloscope-like traces of signal activity on nodes. In this way it is possible to construct a productive work-bench environment for the systems designer.

Figure 2.11 shows a simulation of this type on the complex-to-magnitude example we studied in Chapter 1. The inputs are two orthogonal sinusoids of equal but decaying amplitude, which should produce a decay envelope at the output. The simulator verifies this behaviour for a run of 32 data samples over several cycles of the sinusoids. Note some initially invalid activity at the output as the pipeline is cleared. Its duration is equivalent to the latency of the operator.

2.4.5 The automatic test pattern generator

The process of automatically generating sets of stimulus and response data for compiled systems is quite straightforward. In Chapter 7 we discuss strategies for testing bit-serial networks. Our conclusion is that with proper clock and control signals applied, reliable tests can be performed by pseudo random binary sequences applied at all signal inputs. An orthogonal set of such sequences, one for each input, is readily generated from a small software module. We may then run the behavioural simulator, with these sequences as input, to generate the expected output sequences, remembering that the simulator preserves bit-level fidelity. The set of all control and signal sequences then forms a complete functional test data set for the device in question.

2.5   Attaining performance

One of the strongest criticisms of silicon compilers has been that of addressing a performance specification in terms of chip operating speed. We have argued the ability of the compiler to produce correct function, but speed is altogether a more analogue, circuit engineering task.

We do not dispute the importance of this factor. Indeed we strongly support such a concern, for it is crucial in the development of real-time signal processing systems. In other areas, novel computing structures for example, it may be a shame if a new processor does not sustain its forecast instruction cycle time, but this does not wholly prevent its use. In real-time applications however, devices and systems are constrained to meet exactingly specified sampling rates, or else fail, though they may function correctly in a logical sense.

Attaining performance specifications is generally a difficult, iterative and time-consuming task. Of course this is precisely the type of situation we wish to avoid, yet it is clear from the above discussion that it is important to find some way of guaranteeing performance as well as function. In this section we describe a method which may be used to guarantee a minimum clock rate for any system composed by the silicon compiler. For perspective, in the case of the 5 micron nMOS version this is specified at 8 MHz, whilst a conservative target for a 2.5 micron CMOS process is 20 MHz. Using the synthesis techniques that are outlined in Chapters 5 and 6, system designers may use this knowledge to construct systems that satisfy arbitrary sample rates, and know that they will be attained.

Different techniques are required at three levels in the hierarchy: maintaining performance within modules, maintaining performance within chips composed of modules, and maintaining performance within systems composed of chips.

2.5.1   Maintaining performance within modules

Conceptually this is the easiest problem to solve, for the domain of the module is never violated by the system designer, nor by the compiler. The module designer has available an arbitrary area of silicon in which to realise the modular function. This domain is unaffected by the ultimate placement and use of the module within a system, so long as the designer meets the full range of interface conventions. It is therefore a well-defined task for the expert module designer to ensure that his circuit and cell designs will maintain the system clock rate under worst-case conditions. This task is eased by the pipelined nature of many bit-serial operators. For the most part these are built from cascaded cells which communicate locally under clock control: loading on internal nodes is seldom dependent on the length of this cell chain. Wherever this is not the case, it is generally feasible to design for worst-case (usually corresponding to a maximum permitted wordlength) without significant sacrifices in overall system area or power dissipation.

2.5.2 Maintaining performance within chips

We now consider how to maintain the system clock rate for arbitrary compositions of modules within chips. In TTL systems speed is guaranteed (for specified fanout conditions) by including sufficiently powerful drivers at the gate outputs. This is the scheme we propose to follow at all module outputs.

Thus to guarantee a system clock rate for arbitrarily connected modules, we require at every module output port a common powerful buffer circuit capable of driving the expected worst-case load within the system clock period. In the case of FIRST, we allowed for a maximum wire length of 10 mm and a fanout of 5 typical modules, for a total load of 10 pF. Note that the buffer consumes one clock phase (half a bit-time) which must be accounted within the overall latency of the primitive. The design of this particular buffer is shown in Figure 2.12. Instances of the buffer can be seen along the waterfront in the full chip plots given later.

In order to maintain the benefit of a high system clock rate afforded by the bit-serial architecture, the module output buffer consumes significant power (3 mW) and silicon area (0.02 mm^2). It would seem sensible to restrict its use on too many occasions within one chip. This is precisely the condition afforded by high-level modules with sparse serial connections.

2.5.3 Maintaining performance within systems

We expect to build systems that are composed of several connected chips. Since the chips themselves contain only connected modules it is not unreasonable to view the system in the same way as a chip. Indeed we will later encourage system design in terms of connected modules without initial regard to chip boundaries and partitioning. However, in an electrical sense we cannot expect the module output buffer of Figure 2.12 to drive an inter-chip load for

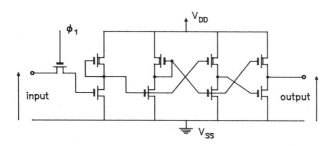

Fig. 2.12   A non-inverting superbuffer.

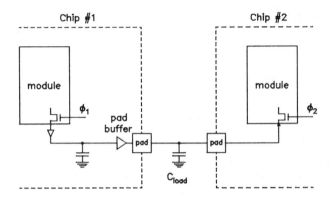

Fig. 2.13 Maintaining high-speed synchronous transmission between chips may not be achieved simply by adding a pad driver. The external load capacitance may be as great as 30 pF.

which it was not intended. This load will include input and output pad capacitance, lead-to-lead capacitance within the device packages, and wire-to-wire capacitance on the printed circuit board. Including the on-chip wiring load we previously estimated, the total load between two modules on separate chips could easily lie in the range 20–30 pF.

A common solution to this problem is to include a further buffer at the pad itself, as shown in Figure 2.13. This is also a dubious solution, however, if we wish to maintain a high system clock rate. The problem lies not in attaining sufficiently fast rise and fall times, but rather in the inevitable propagation delay through the buffer itself. For a system running close to the maximum possible clock rate in a given technology, the cumulative delays through the module output and pad buffers simply may not permit sufficiently fast synchronous data transfer. We propose to maintain a high clock rate therefore by pipelining this transfer. That is to say, by splitting the total delay into clocked segments, none of which contains a delay greater than the system clock period. This process of segmentation can be carried to any extreme, even to the extent of internally segmenting the pad buffer.

We have found it sufficient to add a single pipeline segment apportioned as shown in Figure 2.14 around the pad output buffer (phi 2) and a smaller pad input buffer (phi 1), which is actually a copy of the module output buffer. Note that this maintains proper phasing between the modules where a half stage of delay (say phi 2 only) would have been illegal according to the signalling conventions set in Chapter 1. Naturally we must account for this extra bit of latency across chip boundaries within the overall system timing strategy. There is no other consequence to partitioning.

Through this combination of techniques we are able to maintain the system clock rate throughout systems that are composed of arbitrary connections of chips, in turn composed of arbitrary connections of modules, which is what we set out to do.

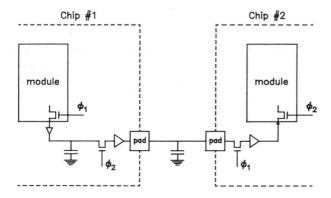

Fig. 2.14   Pipelining the chip-to-chip transfer.

2.6   Technology independence

In the same way that the system designer using a silicon compiler is not concerned with the underlying details of circuit design, he need not be concerned with the fabrication technology.

In the case of FIRST, technology binding occurs in the primitive module library, and also in layout rules for track widths and spaces in the channel router. None of this detail is represented in the FIRST system description language. System definitions therefore become technology independent. This prospect is an exciting one, because it permits the possibility of multiple fabrication vendors, and recommitment in more advanced technologies as they become available. Only in this way can complex systems be specified in a manner that transcends short-term changes in technology.

The prerequisite for commitment of a system in any technology is the existence of a version of the primitive library. We would not underestimate the effort required to implement the library, but the attraction is undeniable if a range of chips are to be developed on any process. In fact we believe that the investment is not greater than for an average custom IC development. This makes the establishment of a verified primitive library an attractive proposition even for a single VLSI system development on a new process. In this context the silicon compiler becomes a means for storing, organising and rapidly accessing cells that have been designed – a kind of limited 'knowledge base' for such cells.

2.7   Correctness and verification

Our stated aim is to produce a functionally correct system at the first attempt. It is unacceptable that time and money should be spent on fabricating a VLSI system that is anything other than correct. This holds especially for VLSI as a development medium for prototype or low-volume requirements.

Conventional approaches to VLSI synthesis are distinctly hit-and-miss in this respect. Often as much resource is spent on verification as on the design process itself, and just as often the design will not function correctly at the first attempt, for as we have stated previously VLSI design is a complex process. There may be many levels of representation, with scope for error in interpreting between each of them. The silicon compiler can avoid this situation by virtue of 'correctness by construction'.

There are two approaches to ensuring that chip designs are correct. One is to attempt a design and then test it, either by circuit extraction and simulation, or in the limit, by fabrication. If the result of the simulation (test) is unsatisfactory, the design is modified and this process is iterated until the simulated (tested) behaviour is correct. The cycle is illustrated in Figure 2.15. The scheme becomes practically unwieldy for VLSI systems because the data structures involved become extremely large, and the computational demands of whole-system simulation are prohibitive, if even possible. A more acceptable version of this is to design hierarchically and support the resulting structure with a series of extractor/simulators which verify behaviour between levels (see Lattin, 1982 for example). This technique has worked in practice for the correct design of complex circuits, but it is clearly costly to implement, and the many levels and iterations are demanding on expert skills, time and computational power.

The alternative approach is to use only techniques of construction that are known to be correct, and to complement these by automating their implementation and verifying this automation. Synthesis becomes automatic, rapid and correct, as in the silicon compiler. To ensure correctness therefore we need to verify our techniques and their implementation.

A model of the structure of FIRST is shown in Figure 2.16. We replace the requirement to verify the behaviour of each system (as above) by previously

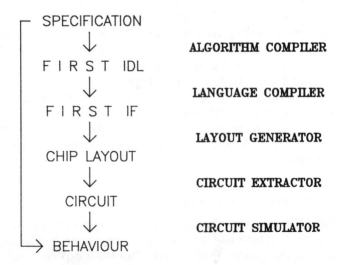

Fig. 2.15   A direct verification cycle.

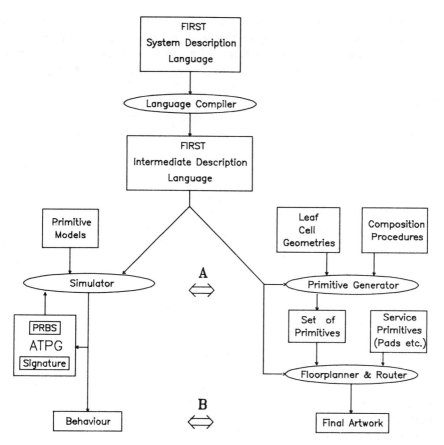

Fig. 2.16 Correctness by construction. We ensure an equivalence A (between system behaviour and physical description) by establishing a set of equivalences B which are independent of the specific system being implemented.

verifying a set of equivalences between the components of the physical design subsystem and the models and assumptions built into the simulator. These include:

the primitive leaf cell layouts
the primitive composition routines
the assumed interface conventions
the chip wiring routines
the behavioural primitive models.

Once the software and the data structures are validated, then we may be sure of each system that is composed by them. Validation of the primitive library is of particular importance, since this component is not fixed, as are the compiler, layout generator, and simulator. It is capable of expansion as required, or there may exist different versions for different technologies.

Briefly, we have carried out this validation through a benchmark test set. This contains examples of each primitive in alternative configurations, to test

different cases of the composition routines. This is compiled. Circuit extraction
and simulation is then used to validate the primitives, their interface
conventions, and the channel routing. A final proof is given by a fabrication-
test run imposed on any primitive before acceptance into the 'public' library.
Plate 2(b) is a microphotograph of such a primitive verification chip. Note that
several instances of any primitive may be required to test within the range of
parametric values. Ideally, every combination of parameters would be tested,
but in practice a judicious sampling must be taken from the parameter space.

2.8 Summary

In this chapter we set out to describe a complete environment in which VLSI
systems could be described at a high (structural) level and then automatically
synthesised down to the mask geometry level. To achieve this aim we have used
the concept of parameterised functional elements as building blocks and
ensured their correct interconnection by carefully defined interface protocols.
We chose to work with bit-serial architectures and with a simple, fixed
floorplan. As a reflection of the choices made along this route, the software
which automates the synthesis process is not especially lengthy or complex.
Also, because its creative tasks are relatively simple it runs very quickly; a four
thousand transistor LSI part may be compiled in a few CPU seconds on a
multiuser mainframe or super-mini computer. The same is not always true of
simulation; as much as one CPU hour may be required to simulate a large
recursive system (of the order of half a million transistors) for the equivalent
of seconds of real-time operation. During design, the simulator is often used
interactively, however, for smaller components and subsystems.

If there is a message from this work for those interested in other applications,
it must be the importance of architectural choice and constraint in simplifying
the synthesis problem. Probably the single most important feature is the
rigorously defined module interface. This clearly separates high-level function
from low-level circuit and layout issues and guarantees performance from the
outset, rather than addressing performance by post-layout design analysis. We
are grateful to R. F. Lyon for this insight. Another key to success has been
the application of modern software architectures to design automation. We are
grateful to N. W. Bergmann, J. P. Gray and I. Buchanan for assistance in this
area.

The field of silicon compilation is a topical one at present. An extended
bibliography, additional to the cited references, is appended for those with
special interest in this area.

References

Ayers, R. F., 'IC Design under ICL, Version 1', *Caltech SSP Report*, California Institue of Technology, 1978.

Batali, J., Goodhue, E., Hanson, C., Schrobe, H. E., Stallman, R. M., and Sussman, G. J., 'The SCHEME-81 Architecture – System and Chip', in: *Proceedings, Conference on Advanced Research in VLSI*, ed. P. Penfield Jr, pp 69–77, Artech House Inc., 1981.

Bergmann, N. W., 'A Case Study of the FIRST Silicon Compiler', in: *3rd Caltech Conference on VLSI*, ed. R. Bryant, pp 413–430, Computer Science Press, 1983.

Denyer, P. B., Renshaw, D. and Bergmann, N., 'A Silicon Compiler for VLSI Signal Processors', *Proc. ESSCIRC'82*, pp 215–218, Brussels, 1982.

Denyer, P. B. and Renshaw, D., 'Case Studies in VLSI Signal Processing Using a Silicon Compiler', *Proc. IEEE ICASSP'83*, pp 939–942, Boston, 1983.

Johannsen, D. L., 'Silicon Compilation', *Caltech SSP Report*, California Institute of Technology, 1978.

Johannsen, D. L., 'Silicon Compilation', PhD Thesis, California Institute of Technology, 1981.

Lattin, W. W., 'A Methodology for VLSI Chip Design', *VLSI Design*, vol. IIII (2), pp 34–44, 1982.

Locanthi, B., 'LAP: A Simula Package for IC Layout', *Caltech SSP Report*, California Institute of Technology, 1978.

Mead, C. and Conway, L., *Introduction to VLSI Systems*, Addison-Wesley, 1980.

Shrobe, H. E., 'The Data Path Generator', in: *Proceedings, Conference on Advanced Research in VLSI*, ed. P. Penfield Jr, pp 175–181, Artech House Inc., 1981.

Sherburne, R. W., Katevenis, M. G. H., Patterson, D. A. and Sequin, C. H., 'Data Path Design for RISC', in: *Proceedings, Conference on Advanced Research in VLSI*, ed. P. Penfield Jr, pp 53–62, Artech House Inc., 1981.

Siskind, J. M., Southard, J. R. and Crouch, K. W., 'Generating Custom High Performance VLSI Designs from Succinct Algorithmic Descriptions', in: *Proceedings, Conference on Advanced Research in VLSI*, ed. P. Penfield Jr, pp 28–39, Artech House Inc., 1981.

Bibliography

Anceau, F. and Schoellkopf, J. P., 'CAPRI: A Silicon Compiler for VLSI Circuits Specified by Algorithms', in: *VLSI Architecture*, eds. B. Randell and P. C. Treleaven, pp 149–154, Prentice-Hall, 1983.

Anceau, F., 'CAPRI: A Design Methodology and a Silicon Compiler for VLSI Circuits Specified by Algorithms', in: *3rd Caltech Conference on VLSI*, ed. R. Bryant, pp 15–31, Computer Science Press, 1983.

Ayers, R. F., *VLSI Silicon Compilation and the Art of Automatic Chip Design*, Prentice-Hall, 1983.

Benschop, N. F., 'Layout Compiler for Variable Array Multipliers', *Proceedings, Custom Integrated Circuits Conference*, 1983.

Bergmann, N. W., 'Idiomatic Integrated Circuit Design', PhD Thesis, University of Edinburgh, Computer Science Department, 1984.

Brebner, G. and Buchanan, D., 'On Compiling Structural Descriptions to Floorplans', *Proceedings, IEEE International Conference on Computer Aided Design*, 1982.

Buric, M., 'Microcomputers as Components of Custom ICs', *VLSI*, vol. V (5), pp 33–39, 1984.

Buric, M. R., Christensen, C. and Matheson, T. G., 'The Plex Project: VLSI Layouts of Microcomputers Genrated by a Computer Program', *IEEE International Conference on Computer Aided Design*, 1983.

Deas, A. R., 'The UNIT Silicon Compiler', MSc Thesis, University of Edinburgh, Computer Science Department, 1983.

Deas, A. R., 'Silicon Compilation: A VLSI Complexity Management Strategy', *Proceedings, Euromicro '84 Conference*, 1984.

Fox, J. R., 'The MacPitts Silicon Compiler: A view from the Telecommunications Industry', *VLSI Design*, vol. IV (3), pp 30–37, 1983.

Gray, J. P., Buchanan, I. and Robertson, P. S., 'Designing Gate Arrays Using a Silicon Compiler', *Proceedings, 19th Design Automation Conference*, pp 377–383, 1982.

Gray, J. P., Buchanan, I. and Robertson, P. S., 'Controlling VLSI Complexity Using a High-Level Language for Design Description', *Proceedings, International Conference on Computer Design*, 1983.

Johnson, S. C., 'VLSI Circuit Design Reaches the Level of Architectural Description', *Electronics*, pp 121–128, 1984.

Kowalski, T. J. and Thomas, D. E., 'The VLSI Design Automation Assistant: Prototype System', *Proceedings, 20th Design Automation Conference*, 1983.

Matheson, T. G., Buric, M. R. and Christensen, C., 'Embedding Electrical and Geometric Constraints in Hierarchical Circuit Layout Generators', *IEEE International Conference on Computer Aided Design*, 1983.

Newkirk, J. and Mathews, R., *The VLSI Designer's Library*, Addison-Wesley, 1983.

Peskin, A. M., 'Towards a Silicon Compiler', *Proceedings, Custom Integrated Circuits Conference*, 1982.

Pope, S. P. and Brodersen, R. W., 'Macrocell Design for Concurrent Signal Processing', in: *3rd Caltech Conference on VLSI*, ed. R. Bryant, pp 395–412, Computer Science Press, 1983.

Ruetz, P. A., Pope, S. P. and Brodersen, R. W., *Computer Generation of Digital Filter Banks*, University of California, Berkeley, 1984.

Rupp, C. R., 'Components of a Silicon Compiler', in: *VLSI 81: Very Large Scale Integration*, ed. J. P. Gray, pp 227–236, Academic Press, 1981.

Southard, J. R., 'MacPitts: An Approach to Silicon Compilation', *IEEE Computer*, pp 74–82, 1983.

Szepieniec, A. A., 'SAGA: An Experimental Silicon Compiler', *19th Design Automation Conference*, pp 365–370, 1982.

Thomas, D. E., Hitchcock, C. Y., Kowalski, T. J., Rajan, J. V. and Walker, R. A., 'Automatic Data Path Synthesis', *IEEE Computer*, pp 59–69, 1983.

Wallich, P., 'On the Horizon: Fast Chips Quickly', *IEEE Spectrum*, pp 28–34, 1984.

Werner, J., 'The Silicon Compiler: Panacea, Wishful Thinking, or Old Hat?', *VLSI Design*, vol. III (5), 1982.

Werner, J., 'Progress Towards the "Ideal" Silicon Compiler Part 1: The Front End', *VLSI Design*, vol. IV (5), pp 38–41, 1983.

Werner, J., 'Progress Towards the "Ideal" Silicon Compiler Part 2: Automatic IC Layout', *VLSI Design*, vol. IV (6), pp 78–81, 1983.

3

A System Description Language

3.1 Introduction

In Chapter 1 we encouraged the development of a structured design style for
bit-serial architectures. We emphasised the advantages of the technique as a
means of describing complex structures for signal processing. Here we define
a language to support such structured system descriptions. This forms an
appropriate system description language for use with the silicon compiler
discussed in the previous chapter.

Our intention is to give an introduction to the language and its capabilities.
This will form a useful guide as we later consider the construction of several
VLSI systems. In the following, keywords that have some special significance
in the language are given in upper case, although the compiler does not in
practice distinguish between upper and lower case.

3.1.1 Hierarchies and types

We suggested in Chapter 1 that systems should be constructed as a hierarchy
of connected functional elements. For convenience, we identify five types of
functional element, which delineate five level-types in the hierarchy, as
summarised in Figure 3.1. Only three have an obvious physical significance;
SYSTEM, CHIP and PRIMITIVE. The other two, OPERATOR and SUBSYSTEM, help
in structuring the definition of parts of the system between these physical

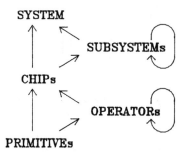

Fig. 3.1 A hierarchy of five types of functional element. Arrows indicate the legal call structure.

levels. Note that arbitrary hierarchies of OPERATORs and SUBSYSTEMs are possible, as shown by the looped arrows in Figure 3.1. These arrows indicate the legal call structure.

3.1.2   A case system

We illustrate the use of such a hierarchy by specifying an example 16-point FFT machine, shown in Figure 3.2. SYSTEM FFT is built from several SUBSYSTEMs,

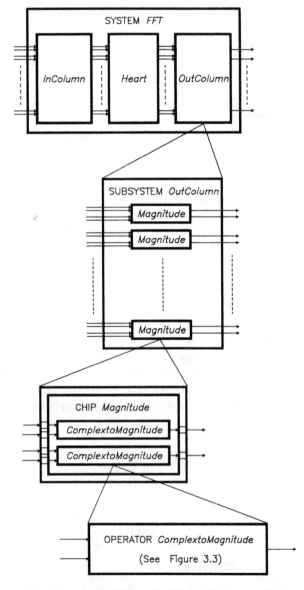

Fig. 3.2   An illustration of the use of full hierarchy in the definition of an FFT system.

the last of which is a column of complex-to-magnitude converters, SUBSYSTEM OutColumn. This SUBSYSTEM is in turn composed of several CHIPs. Each of these CHIPs is able to accommodate a pair of discrete complex-to-magnitude converters (two ComplextoMagnitude OPERATORs). These could be defined purely in terms of primitives, as in Chapter 1 or might be expressed using some degree of structuring, if this helps in representing the algorithm. Thus OPERATOR ComplextoMagnitude is built from OPERATOR SevenEighths and some direct primitives, shown in Figure 3.3. This flow-graph is essentially the same as that given in Figure 1.4, styled in a convention that we shall use for FIRST system descriptions. Operators are named, with parameter lists where appropriate (see below). Primitives are indicated by oblong or circular shapes, whereas higher-level operators adopt rectangular outlines.

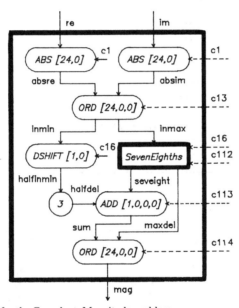

Fig. 3.3   Flow-graph for the ComplextoMagnitude problem.

We will study this elementary FFT machine in detail as one of the case studies in Part 2 of this book. The system is used simply for illustration in this chapter.

3.1.3   Names

Our primary task will be to define and link networks of functional elements. To help in this task we associate a name (or identifier) with each element and each node in the system. Examples of element names are: ADD, OutColumn, ComplextoMagnitude. Examples of node names are; sig23, filteroutput, vectormag, c13d1w2b. Element and node names are generally user-defined, except for the library of primitives, whose names are predefined, and for nodes VDD, GND and NC, which have predefined associations. All arbitrary character strings (up to 256 characters for FIRST) are legal names for alphanumeric user-defined objects, except for a list of reserved keywords which have special meanings. These include the functional element types and node names given above, as well as the predefined primitive names; lists are given in Tables 3.1 and 3.2. We cover the uses and meanings of these keywords as they arise.

Table 3.1   Keywords and reserved symbols

OPERATOR	PIN	=
CHIP	POUT	[
SUBSYSTEM	PCIN	]
SYSTEM	PCOUT	(
END		)
	VDD	,
SIGNAL	GND	
CONTROL	NC	->
		<-
PADIN	TIMES	+
PADOUT	THROUGH	−
PADORDER		*
	CONTROLGENERATOR	/
	CYCLE	
CONSTANT	EVENT	!
WORDLENGTH	ENDCONTROLGENERATOR	:
ENDOFPROGRAM		

Table 3.2   Primitive names

ABSOLUTE	ADD	BITDELAY
CBITDELAY	CONSTGEN	CWORDDELAY
DPMULTIPLY	DSHIFT	FFORMAT1TO1
FFORMAT2TO1	FFORMAT3TO1	FLIMIT
FORMAT1TO2	MSHIFT	MULTIPLEX
MULTIPLY	ORDER	SUBTRACT
WORDDELAY		

3.1.4   Syntactic niceties

To make sense of the examples that follow we need to cover some elementary syntax in relation to the input format used for FIRST.

Separators: Spaces, commas and new lines act as separators between statements.
Continuation: A dash at the end of a line implies continuation on the next line; where preceded by a comma the dash may be omitted.
Comments: Comment lines are prefixed by exclamation marks !

3.2   Syntax – Part I

FIRST syntax is closely related to the ideas of Buchanan (1982 a,b) on structural design languages. The syntax centres around the network of functional elements that we are trying to construct. A FIRST source file then is a sequence of statements about functional elements. In general these statements either define new functional elements (as networks of existing elements) or else call instances of existing elements. Statements of the first type are declarations, and those of the second type are instantiations. Generally functional elements must be declared before they are instantiated, except for primitives, which are all predefined.

3.2.1   Instantiating functional elements

Functional elements of all types are instantiated by a statement of the form:

    name [param list] (cntrl list) sig list

where
name is the name of the element; examples are Filter, ABSOLUTE, ADD.
param list is a list of integer values (or evaluatable expressions) which control attributes of the functional element; examples include the length of a delay primitive, the size of an FFT machine, etc.
cntrl list is a list of control node names of the form:
input list –> output list
sig list is a list of signal node names of the form:
input list –> output list.

For example, an instantiation of the primitive element ABSOLUTE in the OPERATOR ComplextoMagnitude is implemented as:

    ABSOLUTE [24,0] (c1) re –> absre

This has two parameters, one control input, no control outputs, one signal input and one signal output. The number and order of parameters and node names in the lists are determined by the declaration statements. Instantiations of given elements must have lists which match the declaration in number and type.

The notion of a connected network is realised by associating names with the input and output nodes of the functional elements. Connection is then implied between nodes that share a common name. This point is illustrated for the node **inmax** in the following description of the ComplextoMagnitude network of Figure 3.3:

    ABSOLUTE [24,0] (c1) re –> absre
    ABSOLUTE [24,0] (c1) im –> absim
    ORDER [24,0,0] (c13) absre, absim –> **inmax**, inmin
    DSHIFT [1,0] (c16) inmin –> halfinmin
    ADD [1,0,0,0] (c113) seveight, halfdel, GND –> sum, NC
    BITDELAY [3] halfinmin –> halfdel
    ORDER [24,0,1] (c114) sum, maxdel –> mag, NC
    SevenEighths (c16, c112) **inmax** –> seveight, maxdel

This is a list of instantiations of eight functional elements, which are either primitives, or else OPERATORs which have previously been declared (not shown here). Two of the network nodes have been emphasised in boldface to demonstrate the connection of output to input by the use of association through a single node name.

Notice how this example follows the syntax given above; for each functional element the list of parameters is in square brackets, the lists of control nodes are in round brackets and the lists of signal nodes are free; input lists are separated from output lists by right arrows, implying a flow of information through the element.

3.2.2   Declaring functional elements

New elements of all types (other than primitive) are declared by first assigning attributes, giving the element a name, some input nodes, output nodes, etc. Then all internal node names are declared, as lists of SIGNAL and CONTROL nodes respectively. The body of the declaration is given as a list of instantiations, like the one given above, and the whole declaration is finished with an END statement. The form of the total declaration is:

> type name [param list] (cntrl list) sig list
> > declaration of internal nodes
> > body of instantiations
> END

where *type* is one of the four element types; OPERATOR, CHIP, SUBSYSTEM, SYSTEM (but not primitive – these are all predeclared). Thus the declaration of a new OPERATOR called ComplextoMagnitude might be implemented as:

> OPERATOR ComplextoMagnitude [24] (c1,c13,c16,c112,c113,c114)
> re,im -> mag
>
> > SIGNAL absre, absim, inmax, inmin, halfinmin, seveight,
> > > sum, maxdel, halfdel
> >
> > ABSOLUTE [24,0] (c1) re -> absre
> > ABSOLUTE [24,0] (c1) im -> absim
> > ORDER [24,0,0] (c13) absre, absim -> inmax, inmin
> > DSHIFT [1,0] (c16) inmin -> halfinmin
> > ADD [1,0,0,0] (c113) seveight, halfdel, GND -> sum, NC
> > BITDELAY [3] halfinmin -> halfdel
> > ORDER [24,0,1] (c114) sum, maxdel -> mag, NC
> > SevenEighths (c16, c112) inmax -> seveight, maxdel
>
> END

The format of the first line of the declaration is important because this automatically becomes the format of the instantiation.

Because of their physical significance, any declaration of a CHIP or SYSTEM is automatically taken as both a declaration and an instantiation. It follows that CHIP and SYSTEM declarations do not take parameter attributes.

3.2.3 Declaring CHIPs

CHIP declarations differ from those of other functional elements in two ways. Firstly, the body of instantiations must include calls to the appropriate pad primitives; PADIN and PADOUT. These are the clocked input and output pads discussed in Chapter 2. They have the following syntax:

PADIN	(extnl cntrl –> intnl cntrl)
PADOUT	(intnl cntrl –> extnl cntrl)
PADIN	extnl sig –> intnl sig
PADOUT	intnl sig –> extnl sig

where the node names in *extnl cntrl* and *extnl sig* should appear in the node lists of the first line of the CHIP declaration (they are the set of interface nodes for this element), and the nodes in *intnl cntrl* and *intnl sig* are part of the internal node declarations.

These instantiations can lead to many pad statements in a chip definition. To avoid this situation a modified syntax is permitted which includes lists of input and output nodes within single statements. These are of the form:

PADIN (cntrl list) sig list

where the control and signal lists take their usual form. Association of node names on either side of the pads is in terms of the respective order of the lists. Thus:

PADIN (c1x,c2x –> c1i,c2i) s1x,s2x –> s1i,s2i

gives four clocked input pads; two control (c1 and c2) and two signal (s1 and s2). The external and internal nodes are post-fixed by x and i respectively. It follows that the input and output lists must contain the same number of identifiers so that a one-to-one association can be made.

Although the silicon compiler is not restrained on internal placement it is important that user should be able to control the resulting device pin-out. Recall that the chip floorplan includes predetermined placement of the VDD, GND and clock pads. This leaves three significant segments within the pad ring for signal and control pads. The PADORDER statement allows the user to define which pads are to appear in which segments, and the order in which they should do so:

PADORDER VDD, nodelist, GND, nodelist, CLOCK, nodelist

For example the complete CHIP definition for the FFT Magnitude chip is:

> CHIP Magnitude (pc1) pa1, pa2, pb1, pb2 –> pmag1, pmag2
>
>> SIGNAL a1, a2, b1, b2, mag1, mag2
>> CONTROL c1, c1c3, c1c6, c1c12, c1c13, c1c14
>>
>> PADIN (pc1 –> c1) pa1, pa2, pb1, pb2 –> a1, a2, b1, b2
>> PADOUT mag1, mag2 –> pmag1, pmag2
>> PADORDER VDD, pa1, pa2, pb1, pb2, pc1, GND, CLOCK, pmag1, pmag2
>>
>> ComplextoMagnitude [24] (c1,c1c3,c1c6,c1c12,c1c13,c1c14) – a1, b1 –> mag1
>> ComplextoMagnitude [24] (c1,c1c3,c1c6,c1c12,c1c13,c1c14) – a2, b2 –>mag2
>>
>> Cnetwork (c1 –> c1c3,c1c6,c1c12,c1c13,c1c14)
>
> END

3.2.4   The control generator

Each FIRST SYSTEM must contain one, and only one, control generator as the control data source. This provides nested cycles and events, as discussed in Chapter 1, from a set of counters. The control generator is built as a special OPERATOR with a reserved name (CONTROLGENERATOR), using primitives CYCLE and EVENT. The syntax of this structure also has a special form:

> CONTROLGENERATOR (eventrequest list –> inhibit, control list)
>> list of CYCLE [parameter] calls
>> optional EVENT after each CYCLE [parameter] call
>
> ENDCONTROLGENERATOR

where the *control list* consists of one node per CYCLE primitive, and optional EVENTs corresponding to nodes in the eventrequest list. EVENTs cause a synchronous event pulse, high for the period of the corresponding CYCLE primitive, to be generated in response to an asynchronous event request. The following code therefore defines a control generator to realise an LSB cycle (c1) of period 24 bits, plus a word level cycle (c2) of 32 words, plus an event (ev) to occur on request for a frame of 32 words:

> CONTROLGENERATOR (evreg –> inhibit, c1, c2, ev)
>> CYCLE [24]
>> CYCLE [32]
>> EVENT
>
> ENDCONTROLGENERATOR

3.3 Syntax – Part II

Apart from the main syntax given above, we include some additional features which greatly improve the expressive power and flexibility of the system description language. Without affecting the basic structure given above, each of these features is responsible for a significant simplification of the system description file.

3.3.1 Constants

So far in our example we have tied the system description to a wordlength of 24 bits. We declare this value as a parameter in most element instantiations, as shown in bold here:

> OPERATOR ComplextoMagnitude [**24**] (c1,c13,c16,c112,c113,c114) –
> re,im –> mag
>
> SIGNAL absre, absim, inmax, inmin, halfinmin, seveight,
> sum, maxdel, halfdel
>
> ABSOLUTE [**24**,0] (c1) re –> absre
> ABSOLUTE [**24**,0] (c1) im –> absim
> ORDER [**24**,0,0] (c13) absre, absim –> inmax, inmin
> DSHIFT [1,0] (c16) inmin –> halfinmin
> ADD [1,0,0,0] (c113) seveight, halfdel, GND –> sum, NC
> BITDELAY [3] halfinmin –> halfdel
> ORDER [**24**,0,1] (c114) sum, maxdel –> mag, NC
> SevenEighths (c16, c112) inmax –> seveight, maxdel
>
> END

We can make this system description more flexible by declaring a CONSTANT identifier for this parameter, using this identifier throughout. The new description looks like:

> CONSTANT swl = 24
> :
> :
>
> OPERATOR ComplextoMagnitude [**swl**] (c1,c13,c16,c112,c113,c114) –
> re,im –> mag
>
> SIGNAL absre, absim, inmax, inmin, halfinmin, seveight, sum,
> maxdel, halfdel
>
> ABSOLUTE [**swl**,0] (c1) re –> absre

ABSOLUTE [**swl**,0] (c1) im –> absim
ORDER [**swl**,0,0] (c13) absre, absim –> inmax, inmin
DSHIFT [1,0] (c16) inmin –> halfinmin
ADD [1,0,0,0] (c113) seveight, halfdel, GND –> sum, NC
BITDELAY [3] halfinmin –> halfdel
ORDER [**swl**,0,1] (c114) sum, maxdel –> mag, NC
SevenEighths (c16, c112) inmax –> seveight, maxdel

END

Now the information on system wordlength appears once only.[†] It may be altered easily, and on so doing all functional elements will automatically adjust to the new value.

In some of the examples given later in this text we use this CONSTANT assignment facility to alter loop delay lengths and so adjust the degree of computational multiplexing to suit differing real-time bandwidths.

3.3.2   Arithmetic expressions

The inclusion of a limited capability for handling arithmetic expressions is a very powerful feature to use in system description. Typically we use it to derive operator parameters as a function of a user-selectable system wordlength. Alternatively it enables us to write a filter description with filter length as an input parameter, or desired real-time sample rate, or both. In this way it is possible to write a filter description that can automatically select the correct degree of concurrency in the implementation, given the desired operation bandwidth.

FIRST supports the following integer arithmetic operations:

( )   brackets
–   unary minus
*,/   integer multiply, divide
+,–   integer add, subtract

The order of precedence is as given in the list, highest first.

We may form arithmetic expressions from these operators, bearing in mind that integer arithmetic is used throughout. Some example expressions from FIRST system description files are:

CONSTANT swl = 24, coef = 12
CONSTANT multdel = (3 * coef) / 2 + 2
BITDELAY [swl – 3] a –> b

This returns a value of 20 for *multdel*, and 21 for the parameter in BITDELAY.

---

†   In practice this declaration of the wordlength parameter has become a mandatory feature; it
    is used as a word formatting parameter in the FIRST behavioural simulator.

3.3.3   Shorthand for long signal lists

Frequently the designer specifies an object which is in turn composed of many identical objects working concurrently on a long input data list, producing a long output data list. The SUBSYSTEM Outcolumn in our example is one such object, taking in sixteen real and sixteen imaginary signals, and producing sixteen magnitude outputs. These lists can usually be named in a repetitive manner, and FIRST allows their representation in shorthand using the THROUGH statement. A nodelist of the form alphanumber, alphanumber+1,..., alphanumber+N may be represented by alphanumber THROUGH number+N. Thus:

sig31, sig32, sig33, sig34, sig35, sig36

may be represented by:

sig31 THROUGH 36

The first line of the declaration of Outcolumn, naming forty-nine nodes, looks like this in shorthand:

SUBSYSTEM OutColumn (c1) re1 THROUGH 16,
            im1 THROUGH 16 –> mag1 THROUGH 16

3.3.4   Shorthand for repeated instantiations and linear arrays

Modular architectures often require repeated instantiations of identical objects. FIRST provides a syntax for condensing such repeated instantiations into one statement. This is done by appending, to a normal instantiation, a phrase which defines the repetition and connection structure. The form of this phrase is as follows:

TIMES constant WITH cascade

where *cascade* is a phrase whose form and function is explained below. The full form of a repeated instantiation is:

name [param list] (ctrl list) siglist TIMES constant WITH cascade

The number of repetitions is defined by the value of *constant* and the different types of connection are defined by *cascade*.

Cascade can be a null string. In this case corresponding inputs and outputs of the repeated element are connected in common to the nodes named in the instantiation. An example of this is illustrated in Figure 3.4 and is represented syntactically as:

OPERATOR F1 in –> out
        BITDELAY [1] in –> out TIMES 3 WITH
END

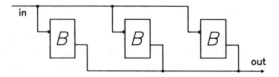

Fig. 3.4 OPERATOR F1, an example of repeated instantiation with global connections. (The globally connected outputs are not normally a valid construct.)

This syntax may describe a legal structure for inputs (though fanin may be a problem if the constant value is large) but the connection of more than one output to any node is not normally a legal construct. The mechanism for severing the corresponding output or input connections from this common node is a statement of *assignment replacement,* which follows the repeated instantiation. The form of this is:

name = list

where *name* is a node identifier (occurring in the repeated instantiation) and *list* is a list of the new node identifiers to be used as replacements. The effect of this statement is to replace each occurrence of *name* by the next name in the *list,* starting from the first occurrence and the first name. This substitution continues down to the assignment replacement statement or until the list is exhausted. An example of this type of connection of repeated elements is illustrated in Figure 3.5. The syntax for this is:

```
OPERATOR  F2  in1, in2, in3 -> out1, out2, out3
    SIGNAL in, out
    BITDELAY [1] in -> out TIMES 3 WITH
        in = in1, in2, in3
        out = out1, out2, out3
END
```

Thus we have a syntax for describing global and distinct connections in repeated instantiations. In order to describe other modes of connection for repeated elements it is necessary to use the *cascade* phrase. This allows the description of four different types of nearest-neighbour connection, one or more of which may be used. The types of connection available are:

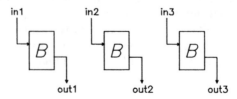

Fig. 3.5 OPERATOR F2, an example of repeated instantiation with separated connections.

(1) Forward
(2) Forward tapped
(3) Backward
(4) Backward tapped

The phrase *cascade* has four components, one for specifying the connections of each type. (Some or all may be empty, according to whether or not there are connections of the particular type.) Figure 3.6 illustrates each of these types of connection, and the corresponding syntax is as follows.

```
! Forward cascade
OPERATOR F3  in -> out
     BITDELAY [1] in -> out TIMES 3 WITH -
          out -> in
END

! Forward tapped cascade
OPERATOR  F4  in -> tap1, tap2, tap3
     SIGNAL out
     BITDELAY [1] in -> out TIMES 3 WITH -
     out => in = tap1, tap2, tap3
END

! Backward cascade
OPERATOR  F5  in -> out
     BITDELAY [1] in -> out TIMES 3 WITH -
          in <- out
END

! Backward tapped cascade
OPERATOR  F6  in -> tap1, tap2, tap3
     SIGNAL out
     BITDELAY [1] in -> out TIMES 3 WITH -
          in <= out = tap1, tap2, tap3
END
```

Each of the cascade phrases takes the form of lists of nodes on either side of the cascade assignment symbol (->, =>, <-, or <=). In the case of the simple forward and backward cascades the internal signal nodes are not externally named. However, a new set of nodes must be named for each of the tapped cascade configurations. This occurs through the phrase starting with the = symbol and followed by the list of nodes which are to be used for each of the tap points.

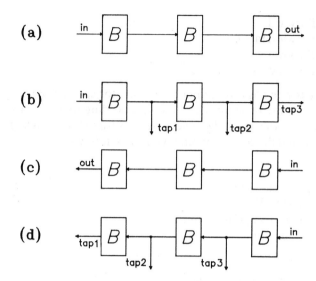

Fig. 3.6   Examples of four modes of cascaded connection:
(a)   Forward (OPERATOR F3)
(b)   Forward tapped (OPERATOR F4)
(c)   Backward (OPERATOR F5)
(d)   Backward tapped (OPERATOR F6)

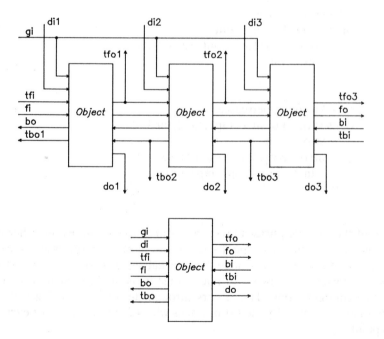

Fig. 3.7   OPERATOR F7, an example of various connection modes in one repeated structure.

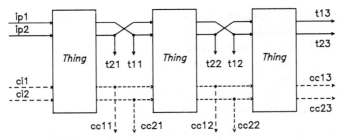

Fig. 3.8 OPERATOR F8, an example of more than one forward cascaded signal.

Figures 3.7 and 3.8 show two further examples which combine several different types of connection in one structure and two cascades of connection of the same type, respectively. The associated syntax follows.

OPERATOR F7 di1,di2,di3,gi,fi,bi,tfi,tbi –> –
    do1,do2,do3,fo,bo,tfi1,tfi2,tfi3,tbo1,tbo2,tbo3

SIGNAL di, do, tfo, tbo

Object [1] di,gi,fi,bi,tfi,tbi –> do,fo,bo,tfo,tbo –
TIMES 3 WITH –
  fo –> fi –
  tfo => tfi = tfi1, tfi2, tfi3 –
  bi <– bo –
  tbi <= tbo = tbo1, tbo2, tbo3
  di = di1, di2, di3
  do = do1, do2, do3
END

OPERATOR F8 (ci1, ci2 –> cc11 THROUGH 13, cc21 THROUGH 23) –
  i1, i2 –> t11 THROUGH 13, t21 THROUGH 23

SIGNAL o1, o2
CONTROL co1, co2

Thing [1] (ci1,ci2–>co1,co2) i1,i2 –> o1,o2 TIMES 3 WITH –
  (ci1, ci2 => co1 = cc11 THROUGH 13: co2 =cc21 THROUGH 23) –
    o1, o2 => i2 = t11 THROUGH 13: i2 = t21 THROUGH 23
END

Note that in the first of these examples the signal names have been chosen with a mnemonic letter code as follows.

gi   global input
di   distinct inputs
do   distinct outputs
fi   forward cascade input

fo   forward cascade output
bi   backward cascade input
bo   backward cascade output
tfi   tapped forward cascade input
tfo   tapped forward cascade outputs
tbi   tapped backward cascade input
tbo   tapped backward cascade outputs

In the second example there is more than one signal connected in the same cascade mode. All such signals must be named in the same phrase, as lists of nodes followed by corresponding lists of tap names. The lists of tap names are separated by the : symbol.

3.4 Summary

In this chapter, we have introduced a high level structural description language for bit-serial signal processing systems. The language is closely related to the physical structure of the system, but is technology independent. The systems designer may quickly produce FIRST source files to describe his system, and may iterate towards the optimal design using the floorplan layout and behavioural simulation output, both of which are automatically compiled from the source description. In later chapters we shall be looking at case-studies of complex signal processing systems described in this language.

References

Buchanan, I., 'SCALE – A VLSI Design Language', *Internal Report*, University of Edinburgh, Computer Science Department, 1982(a).

Buchanan, I., 'A Language for the Combined Physical and Structural Description of Leaf and Composition Cells', *Microelectronics '82*, pp 17–21, Institute of Engineers, Australia, 1982 (b).

4

Primitive Library

4.1 Introduction

In this chapter we list the elements of a bit-serial primitive library. Primitives are the lowest functional elements in the system hierarchy. They exist in hardware and all systems are constructed from them. In the abstract case it would be desirable to define a canonic or covering set of such primitives, which will deal with all problems. However, practical requirements often demand that special solutions be developed for particular applications. Thus, we have adopted the approach of building a library of primitives to cover the range of applications of most interest to us. Where no primitive exists to meet a requirement, then it may be necessary to design and verify one and then add it to the library. Our experiments in system design using the techniques outlined in this text demonstrate that a wide range of applications can be satisfied using a limited set of primitives. These are listed in Table 4.1, grouped according to membership of one of five categories.

Table 4.1 List of primitives

Arithmetic	Storage	Control	Format	Pads
ABSOLUTE	BITDELAY	CBITDELAY	FFORMAT1TO1	PADIN
ADD	WORDDELAY	CONTROLGENERATOR	FFORMAT2TO1	PADOUT
CONSTGEN		CWORDDELAY	FFORMAT3TO1	
DPMULTIPLY			FORMAT1TO2	
DSHIFT			FLIMIT	
MSHIFT				
MULTIPLEX				
MULTIPLY				
ORDER				
SUBTRACT				

Many of the primitives in this library may already be familiar. The primitives listed in the Format category largely perform conversions between multiple and single precision data with a complementary limit facility. Each is prefixed by F, which indicates that the operating parameters are fixed at design time. We envisage a subclass of Pformat primitives which might be end-user programmable to effect dynamic gain controls, etc.

It is a primary feature of this library that all of the composed primitives obey the geometric, electrical and signalling conventions set out in Chapter 1. The details of the design of each primitive are technology specific. As this text is an introduction to the design methodology and to the principles of system design that can be applied with it, we do not treat the technical circuit issues in detail here. An illustrative example of a complete primitive specification and implementation is given for the MULTIPLY primitive in the Appendix.

4.2   Primitive examples

The remainder of this chapter lists the library of primitives ordered into the five functional groups and alphabetically within the groups. The information on each primitive is presented in a stylised form for ease of reference. This contains definitions of the function, symbolic representation, syntax and latency of the primitive. We also give brief notes on the circuit architectures used to design the primitives. Casual readers need not be concerned with the formal details of syntax and function, but should familiarise themselves with the range of functions involved, to appreciate better some of the case studies presented in Part 2.

In what follows, the function of various primitives is illustrated by simulation in the form of sets of input and output data. Generally these are word-level interpretations plotted against time to give the impression of analogue data for ease of functional interpretation. This is not a valid representation for the control primitives, however, which operate strictly on binary signals. In these cases signals are shown with a binary interpretation which demonstrates their function.

As a guide to the relative areas occupied by members of the library, the reader is referred to the FIRST-compiled chips shown in Plates 1 and 3 which include instances of many of these primitives.

ABSOLUTE   *Group:* Arithmetic

ABSOLUTE performs the modulus (full-wave rectify) function on two's complement data. At its output, ABSOLUTE generates the input signal, if this is non-negative, or the inverted signal otherwise.

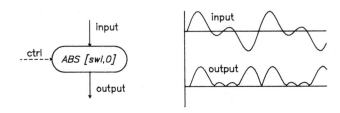

Syntax: ABSOLUTE [swl,del] (ctrl) input –> output

Parameters:

param	min	max	constraint	meaning
swl	6	32	integer	system wordlength
del	0	1	integer	predelay on input

Latency = (swl + 3) bits

Circuit Notes: This circuit includes a shift register to store the input word, a sign detect and programmable output inversion circuit, followed by an output drive stage. In the event of the input signal being negative, the output is a simple inversion of the input. Strictly, for a two's complement code a single least-significant bit should be added, although this accuracy is not required in any of the uses made of ABSOLUTE in this text.

ADD   *Group:* Arithmetic

ADD forms the bit-serial sum of two addends. The third input is an external carry, which is strobed at LSB time to initialise the adder. This input is normally connected to GND, but can be used to construct multiple precision adders (see below). A second output, the word of carry bits, is provided for the same purpose. ADD also contains a parameterised post-addition delay option, for adjusting latency. The latency of the sum output can have any user-chosen value in the allowed range.

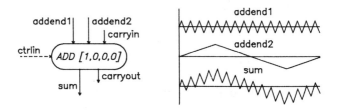

Syntax: ADD [latency,del1,del2,del3] (ctrlin) –
         addend1,addend2,carryin -> sum,carryout

Parameters:

param	min	max	constraint	meaning
latency	1	32	integer	latency of sum
del1	0	1	integer	predelay on addend1
del2	0	1	integer	predelay on addend2
del3	0	1	integer	predelay on carryin

Latency = user chosen value of parameter 1

Circuit Notes: The adder circuit uses pass transistor EXOR networks, giving minimum transistor count and power dissipation.

Double Precision ADD: (See Section 1.2.5 and Figure 1.10)

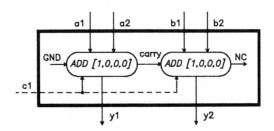

CONSTGEN   *Group:* Arithmetic

CONSTGEN is a one word bit-serial ROM. Each c1 cycle this primitive generates, LSB first, the m bits defined by parameter 2 (constspec), followed by (n − m) MSB repetitions to make up the full n-bit constant word. The use of CONSTGEN in fixed coefficient designs saves generating required constant values off chip.

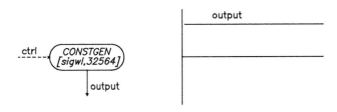

Syntax: CONSTGEN [sigwl,constspec] (ctrl) −> output

Parameters: Let n = swl, m = sigwl, k = constspec

param	min	max	constraint	meaning
sigwl	1	32	integer ⩽ swl	significant wordlength
contspec	*	*	integer	coded constant

* where the integer coding is as follows. The *output* is composed of the m bits of k right justified with n − m MSB repetitions (each identical to bit m of k) left justified to constitute an n-bit word.

Latency: = 1 bit

Circuit Notes: The constant generator consists of a parallel-load serial-output, m bit shift register, and control circuitry to govern the loading. The shift register has its parallel load inputs hardwired to correspond with the values of constspec, and the bit m is latched to generate the (n − m) bit repetitions.

DPMULTIPLY   *Group:* Arithmetic

DPMULTIPLY is a bit-serial multiplier which generates a double precision product on two wires (MSW and LSW). The entire product is right justified, with any remaining bits filled by sign extensions. The two parts of the product emerge separated by a delay of one word, in keeping with the double precision format (see Chapter 1). The product output can also be offset by the use of the addend input.

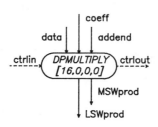

Syntax: DPMULTIPLY [coeffbits,del1,del2,del3] (ctrlin -> ctrlout)
                data,coeff,addend -> LSWprod,MSWprod

Parameters:

param	min	max	constraint	meaning
coeffbits	4	32	even integer	coefficient wordlength
del1	0	1	integer	predelay on data
del2	0	1	integer	predelay on coeff
del3	0	1	integer	predelay on addend

Latencies are as follows:
        ctrlout latency = coeffbits + 2
        LSWprod latency = coeffbits + 2
        MSWprod latency = swl + coeffbits + 2

Circuit Notes: The multiplier design is derived from the modified Booth serial-parallel multiplier used for the MULTIPLY primitive (see later entry). The hardware architecture of MULTIPLY forms all $(n + m - 1)$ bits of the double precision product internally, so that DPMULTIPLY includes some additional hardware to extract the lower order bits (which are otherwise removed in MULTIPLY) together with appropriate control and sign extend circuitry.

DSHIFT   *Group:* Arithmetic

DSHIFT implements an arithmetic right shift. The effect is the same as dividing the input signal by 2^p (where p is positive and integer) and then truncating to n bits.

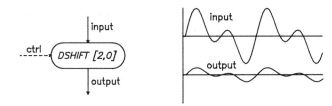

Syntax: DSHIFT [p,del] (ctrl) input -> output

Parameters: Let swl = n

param	min	max	constraint	meaning
p	1	n – 1	integer	power of 2 divide
del	0	1	integer	predelay on input

Latency = (p + 3) bits

Circuit Notes: DSHIFT is implemented as a latch in the signal path. This either passes the input signal to the output or latches a previous input. Circuitry for controlling this latch function consists of a cascadable control delay line, together with a distributed nor gate and inverter. Finally there is an initial input delay of one bit, and an output stage.

MSHIFT   *Group:* Arithmetic

MSHIFT implements an arithmetic left shift. The effect is the same as multiplying the input signal by 2^p, where p is positive and integer.

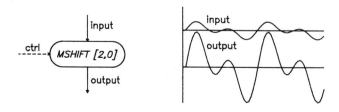

Syntax: MSHIFT [p,del] (ctrl) input -> output

Parameters: Let swl = n

param	min	max	constraint	meaning
p	1	n	integer	power of 2 multiply
del	0	1	integer	predelay on input

Latency = 1 bit

Circuit Notes: Several hardware architectures are possible. Two problems arise in deciding how to implement MSHIFT. The first concerns overflow, and the second latency. If overflow detection is omitted then a considerable reduction in circuitry is achievable. If, additionally, the output bits are made available with minimum latency then minimum hardware can be used. However, this gives rise to primitives which have zero or negative latency. MSHIFT has been implemented as a primitive with one bit latency and no hardware overflow detect, though the simulator gives warning of overflow. The circuit can then be implemented as a multiplexer with one input tied to ground and the other connected to the input signal. A control delay line and distributed nor gate then make up the internal control function.

MULTIPLEX   *Group:* Arithmetic

MULTIPLEX is a one-of-two select switch, controlled by c2 (or a higher cycle)

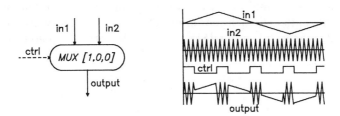

Syntax: MULTIPLEX [latency,del1,del2] (ctrlin) in1,in2 -> output

Parameters:

param	min	max	constraint	meaning
latency	1	32	integer	latency of output
del1	0	1	integer	predelay on in1
del2	0	1	integer	predelay on in2

Latency = user chosen value of parameter 1

MULTIPLY   *Group:* Arithmetic

MULTIPLY forms the truncated (or optionally the rounded) product of its two inputs. The input data word (multiplicand) is assumed to contain two guard bits (MSB repetitions). The coeffcient (multiplier) may be shorter than the multiplicand and is interpreted as the first (least significant) m-bits of the system wordlength. The delayed input data is available, synchronously with the product, as a second output. (See additional notes on the following page.)

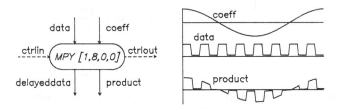

Syntax: MULTIPLY [type,coeffbits,del1,del2] (ctrlin –> ctrlout) –
       data,coeff –> product,delayeddata

Parameters:

param	min	max	constraint	meaning
type	0	1	integer	0=truncating, 1=rounding
coeffbits	4	24	even integer	coefficient wordlength
del1	0	1	integer	predelay on data
del2	0	1	integer	predelay on coefficient

Latency = (1.5*coeffbits+2)

Circuit Notes: The multiplier design is a variant of the modified Booth serial-parallel multiplier. It differs from the Lyon multiplier (Newkirk and Mathews, 1983) in respect of recoding and output scaling. Recoding is not performed in an explicit block at the input but is distributed throughout the multiplier cells. The scaling is adapted to preserve the arithmetic output format. The generaticn of the rounding signal is achieved using a shift register in the I/O channel, invisible to the system designer. The basic leaf cells are two bit multiplier cells, composed from a recoder cell, a programmable add-subtract cell and some shift register cells. The serial multiplier is naturally configured as a linear array, which in FIRST is folded at or near the half-way point so that data can enter and leave the primitive along a common waterfront.

Additional notes on multiplier function:

The precise arithmetic function of MULTIPLY produces:

product data*coeff*$2^{-(m-1)}$
delayeddata data

where data, coefficient and product are interpreted as integers, and m is the coefficient wordlength (coeffbits). Rounding is performed by adding $2^{-(m-2)}$ to the product before truncating.

If the data is interpreted as being fractional two's complement with 2 guard bits (sign repetition) and the coefficient is interpreted as being m bit fractional two's complement with the m-th bit as sign bit, then the product will be the same format as the input data: fractional two's complement with 2 guard bits. This corresponds to the form in which the multiplier is often most conveniently configured. In systems where the product scaling is not as required, either the data or coefficient must be scaled prior to multiplication or the product must be scaled subsequently.

ORDER   *Group:* Arithmetic

ORDER takes two input signals and orders them so that the larger is output on *max* and the smaller is output on *min*. The input data must be positive with two sign-bit extensions.

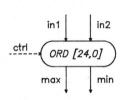
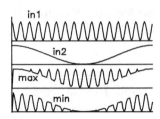

Syntax: ORDER [swl,del] (ctrl) in1,in2 -> max, min

Parameters: Let swl = n

param	min	max	constraint	meaning
swl	4	32	integer	system wordlength
del	0	1	integer	predelay on input

Latency = (n+3) bits

Circuit Notes: The circuit design of order requires two storage shift registers, output select circuitry and a detect and control latch circuit. Detection is achieved by a small finite state machine or serial decoder which determines which input is the larger.

SUBTRACT   *Group:* Arithmetic

SUBTRACT forms the bit-serial difference of the first two inputs. The third
input is an external borrow, which is strobed at LSB time. This input is
normally connected to GND, but can be used to construct multiple precision
subtracters. The second output, the word of borrow bits, is provided for the
same purpose. The latency of the difference output can have any user chosen
value in the allowed range.

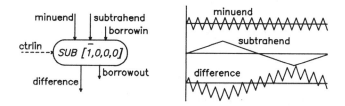

Syntax: SUBTRACT [latency,del1,del2,del3] (ctrlin) –
        minuend,subtrahend,borrowin –> difference,borrowout

Parameters:

param	min	max	constraint	meaning
latency	1	32	integer	latency of difference
del1	0	1	integer	predelay on minuend
del2	0	1	integer	predelay on subtrahend
del3	0	1	integer	predelay on borrowin

Latency = user chosen value of parameter 1

Circuit Notes: The SUBTRACT primitive is a minor modification of the ADD
primitive.

BITDELAY   *Group:* Memory

BITDELAY is a first in first out (FIFO) bit-serial memory, implemented as a shift register. The main system use of BITDELAY is for implementing compensating delay to synchronise signal data streams (cp. CBITDELAY).

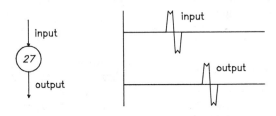

Syntax: BITDELAY [latency] input –> output

Parameters:

param	min	max	constraint	meaning
latency	1	32	integer	latency of output

Latency = user chosen value of parameter 1.

Circuit Notes: BITDELAY is implemented as a shift register with a six transistor per bit leaf cell. The input predelay is used as first cell in all instances of bit delay with latency greater than 1. The output buffer forms the last half cycle of delay.

WORDDELAY   *Group:* Memory

WORDDELAY is a word oriented FIFO, used to delay data by a
parameterised number of words. It is specially organised for efficient storage
of signals which utilise less than the full dynamic range of the system wordlength; for example coefficients which do not require full precision
quantisation. Word delay can be configured to store only the m least significant
bits of each input word. It assumes that bit m of the input word is the sign bit
and that the remaining bits are identical sign bit repetitions. It uses bit m on
output to replicate these sign bit repetitions.

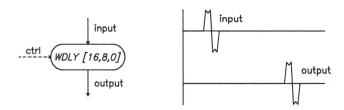

Syntax: WORDDELAY [words,sigbits,del] (ctrl) input –> output

Parameters:

param	min	max	constraint	meaning
words	8	–	integer	number of words storage
sigbits	1	swl	integer	number of significant bits
del	0	1	integer	predelay on input

Latency = (words*swl+1) bits

Circuit Notes: WORDDELAY is based on a three-transistor RAM design.
The memory block architecture consists of a serial to parallel input register,
a word organised block of RAM, and a parallel to serial output register. The
memory is organised as a FIFO with data items traversing the memory
locations. This obviates address generation and the control associated with
addressing. The input and output registers are clocked by c0, moving n bits
serially each word time. The internal RAM is clocked by c1, moving blocks
of words in RAM each bit time in such a way as to move all words one row
down the RAM each word time. The dynamic storage time is limited with this
configuration to one word time, regardless of the total length of the FIFO.

CBITDELAY   *Group:* Control

CBITDELAY is a first in first out bit-serial memory for control. The main system use of CBITDELAY is for implementing compensating delay to synchronise control streams. In particular, it is used to make delay lines from which appropriately delayed versions of control can be tapped.

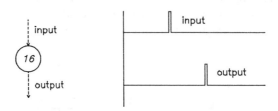

Syntax: CBITDELAY [latency] (input –> output)

Parameters:

param	min	max	constraint	meaning
latency	1	32	integer	latency of output

Latency = user chosen value of parameter 1.

Circuit Notes: CBITDELAY is implemented as a shift register. The input predelay is used as first cell in all instances of bit delay with latency greater than 1. The output buffer forms the last half cycle of delay.

CONTROLGENERATOR   *Group:* Control

Special purpose hardware is needed to generate the control pulses required to keep bits, words, multiplexing and initialisation operations, etc. in synchronisation. This is the function of the CONTROLGENERATOR primitive, which produces c1, c2, ... and event levels of control (see Chapter 1).

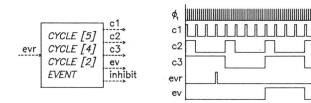

Syntax:
CONTROLGENERATOR (er1,er2,... -> INH,c1,e1,c2,e2,...)
          CYCLE [per1]
          EVENT
          CYCLE [per2]
          EVENT
              :
              :

ENDCONTROLGENERATOR

Note: Controlgenerator is a primitive with a variable number of inputs and outputs. Event request inputs er1, er2,... their associated outputs e1, e2,... and their associated event statement are optional. (To each er1, er2, er3,... there corresponds respectively e1, e2, e3,... and an event statement at the appropriate level. To each c1, c2,... there corresponds a cycle[per1], cycle[per2],... statement.) INH is an end of cycle signal for external interfacing (see Chapter 1).

Example
          CONTROLGENERATOR(evr -> INH, c1, c2, c3, ev)
                  CYCLE[5]
                  CYCLE[4]
                  CYCLE[2]
                  EVENT
          ENDCONTROLGENERATOR

Parameters:

param	min	max	constraint	meaning
period	2	256	integer	cycle length

Circuit Notes: CONTROLGENERATOR is based on a cascade of divide-by-n counters (where n is the count period) which are used to implement each cycle. The event control generation is achieved by use of a some detect circuitry, a latch and reset circuitry associated with the appropriate level of cycle.

CWORDDELAY   *Group:* Control

CWORDDELAY is a special bit-serial FIFO for word-oriented control delay.
It gives storage with a latency in 'guineas' (multiples of one word plus one bit).

Syntax: CWORDDELAY [m,del] (LSBctrl, ctrlin -> ctrlout)

Parameters:

param	min	max	constraint	meaning
m	1	–	integer	latency in 'guineas'
del	0	1	integer	predelay on input

Latency = $m(n+1)$ bits.
where n = system wordlength.

Circuit Notes: Because CWORDDELAY is designed for use with the periodic
waveforms generated by the control generator, it is not necessary for it to store
all the bits of each control word. By sensing the MSB of the previous control
word and latching it for one word time, the same function can be implemented
with much reduced hardware. This can be implemented by sixteen transistors
per guinea delay compared to $6(n + 1)$ transistors, where n = swl.

FFORMAT*x*TO1   *Group:* Format

This is a set of primitives which format multiple precision data into single precision form. They are *fixed* format primitives (as opposed to *programmable* PFORMAT primitives which might allow end-user gain control for example). The multiple precision data is deskewed and formed into a single long word. The single precision output word is selected from the long word commencing at the bit position indicated by parameter 3 (*shift*). Prior to this operation, the original data may have been limited (clamped) to any symmetric range ($\pm 2^m - 1$) where m is set by parameter 2 (*lim*) which points to the desired MSB of the clamped data.

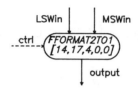

Syntax:
FFORMAT1TO1[swl,lim,shift,del] (ctrl) LSWin –> output
FFORMAT2TO1[swl,lim,shift,del1,del2] (ctrl) LSWin, MSWin –> output
FFORMAT3TO1[swl,lim,shift,del1,del2,del3] (ctrl)–
        LSWin, MSWin, HSWin –> output

Parameters:

param	min	max	constraint	meaning
swl	1	32	integer	system word-length
lim	0	63	integer	limit pointer
shift	0	63	integer	shift pointer
del	0	1	integer	predelays

Latency: (x^*swl +1) bits.

FORMAT1TO2   *Group:* Format

FORMAT1TO2 generates multiple precision data from a single precision source. The original input appears on LSWout with a latency of one bit. The MSB of each input is latched and output for a full c1 cycle and output on MSWout. Thus FORMAT1TO2 takes in a single precision format signal value and outputs the corresponding double precision format value, with a full word of MSB repetitions. It interprets the input as a two's complement number.

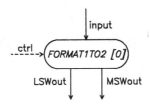

Syntax: FORMAT1TO2 [del] (ctrl) input -> LSWout, MSWout

Parameters:

param	min	max	constraint	meaning
del	0	1	integer	input predelay

Latencies: LSWout latency = 1 bit
             MSWout latency = (swl + 1) bits

FLIMIT   *Group:* Format

FLIMIT is used to constrain the range of single precision data. The desired range is set by a user-chosen parameter. If the input data exceeds this range then FLIMIT hard limits the output signal to the appropriate limit value. Otherwise the output value is the same as the input value. The maximum and minimum values are symmetrically placed about zero.

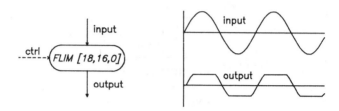

Syntax: FLIMIT [swl,lim,del] (ctrl) input -> output

Parameters: Let n=swl, let m=lim and iet k=2^{m-1}

param	min	max	constraint	meaning
swl	1	32	integer	system wordlength
lim	1	n-1	integer	limit position
del	0	1	integer	predelay on input

Latency = swl + 1

Circuit Notes: The circuit implementation of FLIMIT comprises the following components: a storage shift register, maximum and minimum value generation circuits, overflow detection circuitry and final output select and control circuits. Modularity ensures that these components can be assembled according to the user-chosen values of parameters 1 and 2 to carry out the defined function.

PADIN   *Group:* Pads

PADIN is the mechanism for getting signals and controls onto a chip and
provides the correct drive and buffering capability for doing this.
Communication between chips is pipelined, each chip boundary involving one
half phase of the bit clock for data transfer (see Chapter 2).

Syntax:
PADIN (c1 -> cc1)
PADIN s1 -> ss1
PADIN (c1,c2,... -> cc1,cc2,...) s1,s2,... -> ss1,ss2,...

Note: The first form is for a single control input: c1 is the off-chip, external
node name and cc1 the on-chip, internal node name. Similarly the second form
is for a single signal input, with s1 and ss1 corresponding to external and
internal nodes respectively. The third form is a condensed form for multiple
control and signal inputs (see Chapter 3).

Circuit Notes: The circuit design of PADIN is that of a Xerox-Parc input pad
(see Newkirk and Matthews, 1983), modified to include a clocked driver and
the necessary changes to metalisation to allow rotated placement.

PADOUT   *Group:* Pads

PADOUT is the mechanism for transmitting signals and controls off-chip and provides the correct drive and buffering capability. Communication between chips is pipelined, each chip boundary involving one half phase of the bit clock for data transfer (see Chapter 2).

Syntax:
PADOUT (cc1 –> c1)
PADOUT ss1 –> s1
PADOUT (cc1,cc2,... –> c1,c2,...) ss1,ss2,... –> s1,s2,...

Note: The first form is for a single control output: cc1 is the on-chip, internal node name and c1 the off-chip, external node name. Similarly the second form is for a single signal output, with ss1 and s1 corresponding to internal and external nodes respectively. The third form is a condensed form for multiple control and signal outputs (see Chapter 3).

Circuit Notes: The circuit design of PADOUT is that of a Xerox-Parc output pad (see Newkirk and Metthews, 1983), modified to include a clocked buffer and the necessary changes to metalisation to allow rotated placement.

4.3   Summary

In this chapter we have presented a bit-serial primitive element library. The scope of the library is sufficient to address a number of applications in signal processing. However, the set of primitives is not canonic. New applications may require additional primitives. The automatic generation and optimisation of new primitives is fertile ground for future research.

References

Newkirk, J. and Matthews, R., *The VLSI Designer's Library*, Addison-Wesley, 1983.

5

Algorithm to Architecture

5.1 Introduction

The preceding chapters have established tools and techniques to assist in the production of VLSI systems from functional flow graphs. The remaining problem is to generate a physical architecture that correctly represents the algorithm that is to be implemented. A major issue here is the provision and use of concurrency. In this chapter we develop ways in which to derive concurrent hardware architectures for a general class of real-time signal processing algorithms.

5.1.1 An example

By way of an introduction, and as an example of the type of problem to be tackled, consider the implementation of a programmable transversal filter, sometimes referred to as a finite impulse response (FIR) filter. This problem is less complex than many of the examples we shall demonstrate later, but it serves well to illustrate our approach. The transfer function of this type of filter can be formulated in terms of the z-transform (Rabiner and Gold, 1975) as:

$$H(z) = b_1 + b_2 z^{-1} + \ldots + b_M z^{-M+1} \qquad 5.1$$

Equivalently the filter can be specified in terms of its linear difference equation, which expresses the filter output sequence at times $t = nT$ in terms of its previous inputs and a vector of coefficients, b:

$$y(nT) = b_1 x(nT) + b_2 x(nT-T) + \ldots + b_M x(nT-MT+T) \qquad 5.2$$

The principal problem of implementation is to derive a computation scheme and a corresponding architecture which can eventually be expressed as a hardware flow-graph. For this particular problem there are many possible solutions, some of which are illustrated and discussed in this chapter.

5.1.2 Recurrence and concurrency

Our approach is to reformulate the linear difference equation or some equivalent representation of the problem as a *recurrence*. That is, we identify any set(s) of repeated operations (multiply/add in this case) within the formulation. We call each such operation an *iteration* within the recurrence. Recurrences are key to the major issue of concurrency and its responsible application. They permit a tradeoff between hardware (or silicon area) and bandwidth, because in general we may choose whether to implement them serially through one arithmetic unit (the *iteration processor*) or concurrently through many processors.

We are especially concerned to achieve specific real-time sample rates using adequate but not excessive arithmetic processing resources. The range of possibilities (in terms of processors per iteration) is as follows. Firstly, we could use only one processor, as in a von Neumann machine. We call this type of architecture *fully serial*. Secondly, we could use several processors, but fewer than there are iterations. We term architectures of this sort *multiplexed* architectures. Thirdly, we could use the same number of processors as there are iterations. We term these *full array* architectures. An example of a full array architecture is the systolic array. Finally, for very high speed applications, we might use more processors than there are iterations. We term these *hyperparallel* architectures.

Many of the real-time applications of interest to us can be implemented using multiplexed architectures. Thus, we shall work mainly in this area between the fully serial architecture and the full array architectures. Often neither of these extremes is optimal for a wide span of real-time applications and the most efficient choice is a multiplexed architecture.

From the time required by each processor to compute a single iteration, and given the input sampling frequency, it is possible to determine how many operations can be carried out in one unit of sample time, and therefore how many processors will be needed to evaluate the complete recurrence in real-time. This corresponds to finding a computation scheme which has the correct bandwidth for the application, so that the corresponding hardware will be capable of, but not greatly exceed, the required throughput rate. We term this *bandwidth matching*.

Suppose that we wish to construct a 256-point FIR filter. This filter can be implemented at one extreme with 256 multipliers and 256 adders, etc.; this would be a full array architecture. At the other extreme it can be implemented with one multiplier and one adder; this would be a fully serial architecture. Between these extremes there is a variety of choice, for example we could use 2, 4, 8,... multipliers and adders, which would give multiplexed architectures. Since the arithmetic elements have a fixed maximum operating speed, the choice of architecture limits the external bandwidth of the full function. Conversely, given a maximum sampling frequency for the filter, we can make the choice of how much concurrency to use.

5.1.3 Scope

This chapter has a generality which extends beyond the specific bit-serial constructions which are developed in the rest of the book. The architectures could be applied equally to bit-parallel or other implementations with different timing and communication protocols. However, we observe that the environment that we have so far developed essentially reduces the design task to that of synthesising a high level hardware network to implement particular signal processing functions, that is of mapping function, via computation scheme, into architecture: the remainder of the design task may be automated. It is possible to take an entirely *ad hoc* approach to this task, and then use a behavioural simulator of the type already described in Chapter 2 to verify and correct the design. However, such an approach is error prone and time consuming. This chapter proposes a systematic way of mapping function into architecture in such a way that it can be expressed conveniently and concisely as a hardware signal flow-graph. Chapter 6 is concerned with the subsequent issues of developing detailed hardware flow-graphs and summarises a methodology for system synthesis based on the material in this chapter but specific to bit-serial implementations.

The material developed here, together with an algorithm specification language, could form a basis from which to develop a next generation of silicon compiler with a higher, algorithmic level of input specification.

5.2   Mapping recurrences to concurrent architectures

In this section we consider the provision of an adequate set of concurrent processors with which to meet a desired real-time performance for a given recurrence.

5.2.1   Formulating the recurrence and the virtual machine

Consider the example FIR filter. There are several ways in which we might rewrite the linear difference equation as a recurrence (a repeated process or iteration). Each can lead to a different machine architecture in terms of the flow and timing of data. One possible recurrence formulation of (5.2) is:

For $i = 1$ to M: $x(0,t) = $ external input at time t
$$sum(0,t) = 0$$
$$x(i,t) = x(i-1,t-T)$$
$$sum(i,t) = sum(i-1,t-T) + b_i x(i,t) \qquad 5.3$$

Variables in this recurrence are indexed in iteration, i, and time, t. The primary iteration in this case is a multiply/accumulate function, plus a shift of signal x. As with many other such iterations, the importance of this formulation lies in its independence of a global store. Each iteration of the loop uses data only from nearby iterations in terms of indices i and t. In this case the iteration calls for three data sources; the value of 'sum' from the previous iteration this sample time, the value of 'x' from the previous iteration previous sample time, and a local constant, b.

Formulations of this type are disposed towards implementation in array architectures using near-neighbour communication paths only. Many

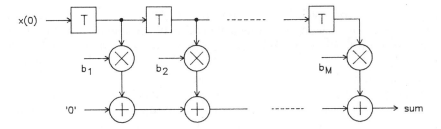

Fig. 5.1 Virtual machine architecture for the FIR problem

researchers have discovered the benefits of this factor, not least those concerned with VLSI implementation. This point is made clear in Figure 5.1, which is a literal interpretation of recurrence (5.3) as a fully parallel array. We call this representation the *virtual machine*. In the virtual machine, blocks marked T imply a delay of one recurrence cycle (equivalent to the external sample cycle), whilst all other elements act 'instantaneously'.

It is possible to use the virtual machine as a template for a physical machine. In general this leads to a large, fast array-like implementation. However, given a specific real-time application, it is unlikely that the speed of this processor will match the desired sample rate. Often it will be excessively fast, and consequently uneconomic compared with a custom machine that conserves space, cost and energy by using an appropriate, but not excessive number of processors. These optimised machines are our primary concern.

5.2.2 Introduction to multiplexed array architectures

Again we consider the example 256-point FIR filter. Between the fully serial (uni-processor) and full array (256 processors) architectures lies a spectrum of multiplexed architectures. For example, we might use eight processors which each effect 32 iterations during each recurrence cycle.

The concept of this multiplexed machine is shown in Figure 5.2. This comprises eight physical processors, each with local memory. The purpose of the memory is to store the state of the 32 virtual processes supported by each

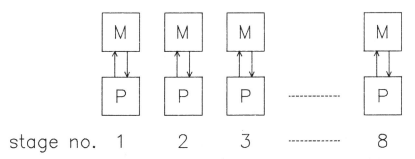

Fig. 5.2 Concept of multi-processor array architecture. Processors P and state memory M, form 8 stages of computation for the FIR problem. Each stage implements 32 iterations from from a total of 256 required each sample cycle.

physical processor. Each processor plus memory unit is termed a 'stage'. As yet we have not decided the detailed allocation of this memory, nor how the processors are to be connected together. These issues are determined partly by the form of the initial recurrence and partly by the pattern of computation that is adopted. One pattern of computation for example might have stage 1 evaluate iterations 1,2,3,..., stage 2 evaluate iterations 33,34,35,..., etc.

If we are to benefit from the use of parallel hardware, then it is important that the processors act concurrently. For the moment we suppose that it will be possible to have stages 1,2,3,..., evaluate iterations, 1,33,65,... in unison, then iterations 2,34,66,..., etc. In practice this implies some conditions on data flow in the machine. The management of this flow is considered shortly, and leads to the completion of the physical machine. For now we note that different recurrence formulations can lead to different physical machine architectures for the same problem. In particular, the amount of store required (and hence the size of the physical machine) can be minimised by an appropriate recurrence formulation and pattern of computation. Alternatively, resources can be wasted by an inappropriate formulation of the same problem.

To complete our terminology; we refer to the period between data samples presented to the iteration processors as the *word time*. In bit-serial systems this is the product of the system wordlength and the bit time; in bit-parallel systems it is usually the fundamental clock rate. The overall function of the array is to compute a full recurrence of M iterations each sample cycle. For example, in a speech application the sample rate may be 8 kHz, leading to a sample cycle of 125 μs. Normally the intention is to divide the M iterations between k physical processors, so that each computes m iterations per sample, where

$$mk = M \qquad\qquad 5.4$$

In our example $k = 8$, $m = 32$ and $M = 256$.

For the present we shall deal with those cases in which the array is clocked continuously and the sample cycle comprises exactly m word cycles. For each sample cycle the k processors together compute km iterations, which is one pass of the recurrence.

5.2.3   Selecting concurrency

Under these circumstances we can determine the degree of concurrency (the level of multiplexing) that should be applied in any given application. This is simply a function of the word rate W (computations per second) that can be sustained through the physical processors, the external real-time sample rate H (Hz), and the number of iterations, M, within the recurrence. The number of stages required to meet the real-time requirement is then;

$$k = MH/W \text{ stages} \qquad\qquad 5.5$$

Frequently W is constant in bit-serial systems, regardless of the complexity of the iteration processes. It is the maximum sustainable bit-rate divided by the system wordlength. In the case of bit-parallel architectures, W may be strongly dependent on the process complexity unless the processors themselves are uniformly pipelined.

5.3   Completing the physical machine

We can now complete the physical machine by specifying the processes to be implemented, the configuration of the stage memories and the interconnection of the stages. We define the physical machines in this section as compositions of three component types. These are: black-box processors that compute the iteration functions; FIFO delay registers that implement the state memory functions; and multiplex switches. We incarnate these components as bit-serial elements in Chapter 6. However, the architectures given below are independent of this form. Also for the purpose of this chapter we assume that the switches and processors act instantaneously, whilst the FIFOs delay data by integer multiples of the word-time (whatever this may be). This model is conceptually convenient, but physically simplistic. In practice it is a simple step to accommodate real (non-integer) delay in all components by adjusting FIFO lengths to absorb combined switch and processor latencies. This is covered in Chapter 6 for bit-serial systems.

5.3.1   Multiplexed uniprocessor arrays

We begin by considering multiplexed uniprocessor machines ($k = 1$) for one-dimensional recurrences (whose virtual machines are linear arrays) with degree 1 iteration dependencies (nearest-neighbour connectivity in the virtual machine). The development may be easily extended to more complex iteration forms; our concern here is restricted to an appreciation of the multiplex technique, and to extending the development to multiple-processor machines ($k > 1$). The restricted classes of recurrence of interest here are shown as virtual machines in the left-hand column of Figure 5.3. These are simple nearest-neighbour connected linear arrays, with and without sample delays between iterations. Data flows from left to right in these arrays, although this is not a condition of the following development. Various combinations of these recurrence modes may occur in any one application, including mixed left-to-right and right-to-left flows. Such machines can be built by independently implementing each flow path and combining the results.

It is possible to implement these recurrences as multiplexed single-processor machines. The processor in these cases is taken to be a custom implementation of the iteration process (IP), however elementary or complex this may be. There are two mappings of interest; one in which the processor steps 'forward' through the recurrence, evaluating iterations in the direction of data flow, and one in which the processor steps 'backward' through the recurrence, evaluating the sequence of iterations against the direction of data flow. The multiplexed uniprocessor machine architectures for each mapping are shown in the central and right-hand columns of Figure 5.3.

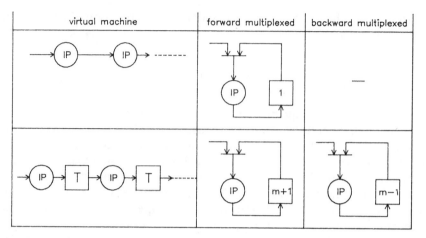

Fig. 5.3 Virtual and multiplexed uniprocessor arrays for first order recurrence types. IP = iteration process.

In each case the multiplexed machine cycle (corresponding to the total recurrence cycle) comprises M word cycles, during which the M iterations are computed. The state memory requirement in each case emerges as a FIFO structure which streams data resulting from each iteration back to the IP inputs at the appropriate moments within the recurrence cycle.

The various multiplexed machine architectures differ in the total delay around the multiplex loop. This is trivially one word in the forward multiplexed machine corresponding to no delay between iterations. In the multiplexed machines corresponding to delayed data flow, the loop length is one word greater or less than M word cycles. The effect of this is progressively to shift data in the loop by one iteration each recurrence cycle. The multiplex switch is activated for one word time in each cycle to grab the new external input sample.

Note that control in these machines is at the word-cycle level for the iteration processors and at the recurrence-cycle level for the multiplex switches.

Uniprocessor FIR example
In any given application we may mix several of these forms, depending upon the requirements of the recurrence in question. For the FIR filter defined as recurrence (5.3) and shown virtually in Figure 5.4(a), a forward multiplexed uniprocessor architecture is given in Figure 5.4(b). This simple example is worthy of closer study. The virtual architecture consists of a set of connected processes. The repeated process is a dotted box. It has three types of neighbour connection; forward delayed (the signal path), forward chained (the accumulator path) and constant input (the coefficients).

Figure 5.4(b) represents the multiplexed physical architecture, with the various connection modes mapped around it, using the standard forms given in Figure 5.3. The coefficients in this case are generated from a simple loop of length M words. The processor in this machine is identical to the iteration process marked in the virtual machine above.

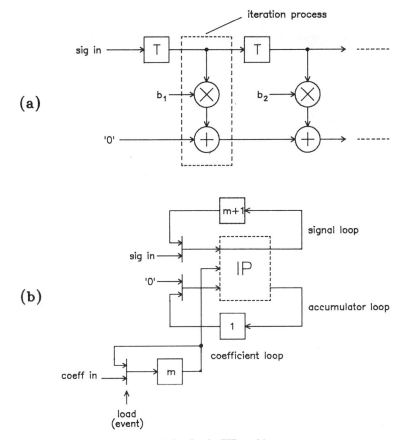

Fig. 5.4 Multiplexed uniprocessor solution for the FIR problem.
(a) the virtual machine architecture;
(b) the physical machine architecture.

5.3.2 Multiplexed multiprocessor arrays

In many real-time applications we require more than a single iteration processor in the multiplexed array. Normally, we build these arrays by cascading the single-processor stages given in the preceding section. We are here concerned with selecting the correct output node from the state loop to act as a cascade point.

Consider firstly the multiplexed equivalent of the forward chained recurrence shown in Figure 5.3(a). In practice it is not possible to cascade this stage and maintain the equivalent virtual machine architecture. This is because the result of the last iteration in stage 1, for example, is not available until iteration m is completed; at least m word times into the cycle. If we cascade these stages as shown in Figure 5.5, the equivalent virtual architecture now contains one sample cycle delay between stages. This is equivalent to *pipelining* the architecture. It adds additional latency to the realisation for the benefit of greater throughput via concurrent processing. In the event that the number of

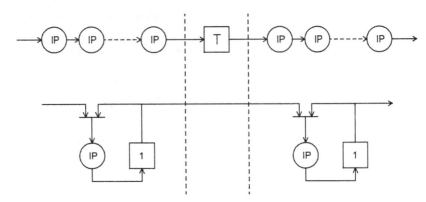

Fig. 5.5   The effect of cascading stages of the type given in Figure 5.3(a) is to introduce an interstage pipeline delay.

processors k is equal to M, there will be one physical processor per iteration and the architecture is fully pipelined.

Figure 5.6 shows cascade forms for both forward and backward multiplexed implementations of the delayed recurrence type. Each of these implementations faithfully preserves the timing of the virtual machine architecture. The backward multiplexed implementation appears to be

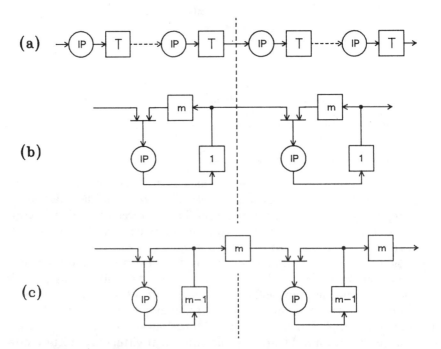

Fig. 5.6   Cascading stages of Figure 5.3(b) to preserve virtual machine timing
(a) virtual machine
(b) forward multiplexed
(c) backward multiplexed

relatively inelegant, since it requires the addition of an m-word delay element between stages. This requirement arises because the left-most iteration of the second stage is not computed until the end of the current cycle, but its input is derived from the right-most iteration of the first stage, which was computed at the beginning of the previous cycle, some $2m - 1$ word times previously. In practice only one useful datum is transferred through this interstage delay per cycle, so the m-word FIFO can be replaced by a one-word multiplexed loop that is timed to capture and hold the relevant sample. Better still, the introduction (below) of 'idle' time in the sample cycle can be used to gain an appropriate tap point in this loop with no interstage memory provision.

The enforced pipeline condition of Figure 5.5 occurs relatively frequently in the systems of interest to us. It is consequently of interest to find cascade connections in the complementary recurrence type to equalise this pipeline delay in parallel signal paths. Figure 5.7 illustrates configurations for these machines. Figure 5.7(b) is a forward multiplexed implementation that accommodates the additional pipeline delay. In contrast, the backward multiplexed implementation of Figure 5.7(c) effectively cancels this delay (or rather accommodates an interstage delay of $-T$) for applications where backward multiplexing is used with data paths that flow against the direction of the initial forward chained path of Figure 5.5.

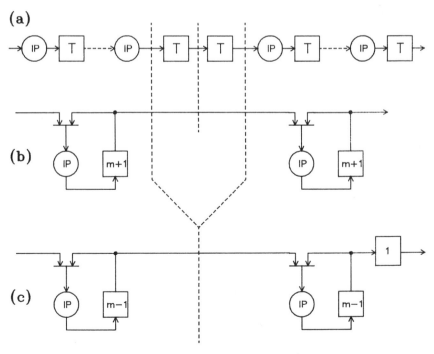

Fig. 5.7 Cascading stages of Figure 5.3(b) to compensate for stage pipelining
(a) virtual machine
(b) forward multiplexed incorporating interstage pipeline delay
(c) backward multiplexed incorporating interstage pipeline delay

Multiprocessor FIR examples
To demonstrate some of these issues, we show in Figure 5.8 a multiplexed multiprocessor array to implement the example FIR algorithm. The stages in this machine implement the forward multiplexed array form; that is each stage evaluates its series of iterations in left-to-right order. The delay-free forward accumulation path has become pipelined (as Figure 5.5) and the signal-shift path is cascaded using the form of Figure 5.7(b) to compensate. The latency of this machine is thus greater than implied in the original algorithm.

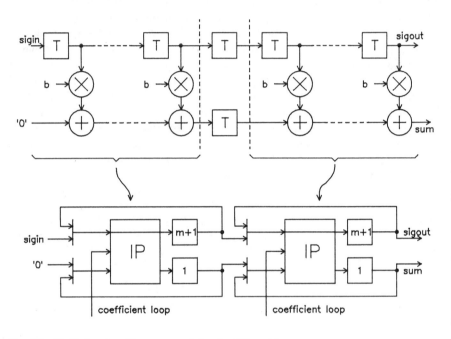

Fig. 5.8   Multiplexed multiprocessor solution for FIR problem.

An alternative configuration is shown in Figure 5.9. This preserves the ideal timing by altering the architecture to provide for the parallel accumulation of sums, as opposed to the series form. This is equivalent to rewriting the recurrence as:

$$\text{For } i = 1 \text{ to } M: \quad x(0,t) = \text{external sample input}$$
$$\text{prod}(i,t) = b_i x(i,t)$$
$$x(i,t) = x(i-1, t-T)$$
$$\text{Then:} \quad \text{sum}(t) = \Sigma \, \text{prod}(i,t) \qquad 5.6$$

For interest, the stages in this machine implement the backward multiplexed array form following the style of Figure 5.6(c); that is each stage computes its series of iterations in reverse order.

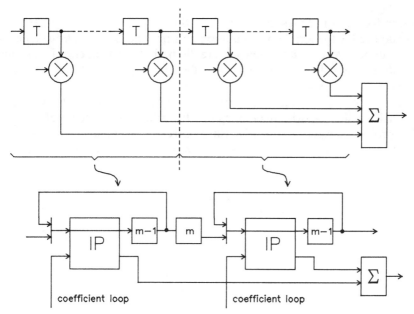

Fig. 5.9 Alternative (non-pipelined) formulation of the FIR problem.

5.3.3 More general machines and algorithms

Our interest in the preceding architectural forms stems from the common occurrence of the FIR algorithm, and others like it, in many signal processing applications. However, not all applications can be formulated as such a simple single recurrence. In general, algorithms may consist of many sets of computations; some interdependent and some independent. Concurrent architectural solutions are always possible wherever computation steps are independent of the results of other steps during a given sample cycle. The extent to which this potential is exploited depends upon the tradeoff between the desired sample rate and the relative cost of hardware (including monetary cost, physical size, power dissipation, etc.).

Where the computation steps are dependent but identical, as in the FIR example, it may be practically beneficial to implement a custom iteration processor and multiplex this to execute the steps in sequence. This is the basis of the multiplexed uniprocessor FIR machine of Figure 5.4. Furthermore, dependent computation steps can be isolated in some cases by delaying stages of computation by one or more sample cycles. This is the basis of pipelining, through which the newly independent stages may be implemented concurrently. Figure 5.8 gave an example of a pipelined, multiplexed multiprocessor FIR machine.

If it is not possible to avoid dependent computation steps there may be no efficient concurrent solution and the final machine must contain sequentially activated sub-machines. Where these sub-machines perform differing computations, we must make separate hardware provisions and accept that each sub-machine may be 'idle' for fractions of the sample cycle, while alternative sub-machines are 'active'. Ultimately, the algorithm may be so unstructured as to merit implementation only on a more general von Neumann architecture. Where dependencies are limited, however, custom machine hardware can still be attractive. A subsequent case study, the adaptive transversal filter, is one such case of interest.

This problem is considered as a case study later in the text; for the purpose of this discussion, we wish to demonstrate the principal architectural concepts. This problem resembles the FIR filter, except that we need to compute a second function following the FIR step, and return its result to the FIR sub-machine in time for the next recurrence cycle. The situation is described in Figure 5.10.

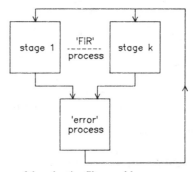

Fig. 5.10   Gross architecture of the adaptive filter problem.

In some applications it is possible to reinterpret the adaptive algorithm to admit a greater latency in the feedback path and this may be used to pipeline the physical machine. For the purpose of this discussion, however, we maintain the more severe condition that the 'error' function (as the second step is called) must be computed and returned during the same recurrence cycle. As a primary condition we note that a pipelined implementation of the FIR iteration is ruled out because the entire recurrence must be computed in one cycle.

For this reason we adopt the backward multiplexed array architecture of Figure 5.9. Clearly the first and second steps of the algorithm must be computed in sequence. This admits two possibilities: that the FIR sub-machine is used and then stopped while the second machine is active, or that the FIR sub-machine is run continuously but allowed to compute garbage for the second part of the cycle. Since our earlier conventions include a continuously running clock, we adopt the latter policy and divide the recurrence cycle into 'active' and 'idle' phases for the first sub-machine.

Suppose that the multiplexed FIR array completes in m word cycles (as before) and that we can build a machine to compute the error step in i word cycles. The total recurrence cycle now comprises m + i word cycles. Our concern is to realise a multiplexed array that successfully implements m iteration stages (with correct interstage data flow) while under the control of an m + i word recurrence cycle.

A successful arrangement for the FIR process is shown in Figure 5.11, corresponding to Figure 5.9 for the implementation with no idle cycles. The

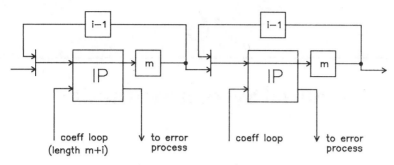

Fig. 5.11 Alternative formulation for FIR process of Figure 5.9 including provision for 'idle' phase of i word times.

state memory loops must be lengthened to m + i − 1 words, but only the first m words in each recurrence cycle are 'valid'. This lengthened memory loop removes the need for the inelegant interstage delay of Figure 5.9. Data precesses in the loop, which in this case retains the previous m + i − 1 signal samples. By cascading from a tap m words into the loop (which was previously impossible in a loop of length m − 1 words), we can transfer the correct datum between stages each sample cycle. The timing of this loop is further elaborated in Chapter 9.

5.4 Summary

In this chapter we have shown how signal processing algorithms can be restructured as recurrences. Such recurrences may be strongly iterative; often with local value passing between iterations. These properties lead naturally to pipelined array and systolic architectures.

Our major interest is in reducing the hardware cost of these arrays for real-time applications that demand some concurrency, but do not require the bandwidth of a full array implementation. We have addressed the multiplexing of custom iteration processors to achieve this aim in the case of linear arrays. Here the locality of communication results in FIFO-structured state-memory loops. We have provided for this as the predominant memory form.

We have dealt explicitly with simple examples and linear array forms, but stress that these techniques may be applied to more complex, higher-dimensional architectures. Further examples in this vein may be found in the case studies in Part 2 of this text. We would encourage the further development of these themes with the goal of realising higher forms of algorithm-to-concurrent-architecture compilers.

References

Rabiner, L. R. and Gold, B. *Theory and Application of Digital Signal Processing*, Prentice-Hall, 1975.

Kung, H. T. and Leiserson, C. E. 'Algorithms for VLSI Processor Arrays', in: *Introduction to VLSI Systems*, by Mead, C. A. and Conway, L., Addison-Wesley, 1980.

6

Serial System Synthesis

6.1 Introduction

In Chapter 5 we developed some target system architectures. Here we present methods to map these architectures into hardware flow-graphs. Our approach follows the well-known method of top-down design. Applied to the present problem, this approach expands algorithm to computation architecture, architecture to signal flow-graph, and flow-graph to primitive net list. Finally we are left with the problem of instantiating the structure; this is the process of bottom-up implementation.

Overview
Our plan is to build systems by identifying the target architecture, building arithmetic engines (processors), supporting the processors with state memory, and finally implementing the machine by instantiating the resulting hardware flow-graphs. The initial process of identifying the target architecture was considered in Chapter 5. The final process of instantiation by silicon compilation was covered in Chapter 2. This chapter deals with the intervening steps.

6.2 Implementing arithmetic engines

Custom processors are needed to execute the computational requirements of the algorithm to be implemented. As developed in the preceding chapter, these processors may be designed independently from the networks that support them. The responsibilities of data flow management and execution are independent; here we are concerned only with the latter issue.

Earlier parts of this text have demonstrated the ease with which such processes can be synthesised from a library of bit-serial primitives, using a functional design style. Ultimately the process must be realised as a flow-graph of simple functional elements from the base library. Where the process in question is complex, then hierarchical decomposition may assist its design.

Consider for example the implementation of the following recurrence, which defines part of an adaptive transversal filter:

$$y(i,t) = s(i,t).h(i,t)$$
$$h(i,t) = h(i, t - T) + u(t - T).s(i, t - T)$$
$$s(i,t) = s(i - 1, t - T)$$

6.1

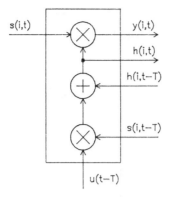

Fig. 6.1   A direct processor design for LMSPART.

A direct processor design (called LMSPART) for this task is shown in Figure 6.1.

6.2.1   Arithmetic aspects

Having decided a computation scheme for a given application, we must subsequently account for its arithmetic performance. The objectives of this task are to determine the appropriate scale factor and range of signals at each node in the system. At issue here is the provision of dynamic range such that the largest likely signals can be accommodated, and the smallest adequately resolved. Once the necessary range has been determined for each signal within the system, then we will be in a position to decide the system wordlength and to provide for signal scaling at appropriate points. These issues are the necessary consequences of fixed-point representations.

Commencing at the data input ports of the system, the incoming data streams will have a predetermined range (number of bits), and notional scale (position of the binary point). It is not usually possible to preserve this format at all subsequent nodes in the system. Arithmetic under- and over-flow both increase the range of representation. Of course all such forms of growth cannot be accommodated indefinitely, so it becomes necessary to limit and scale data at points within the system to retain a practical representation. Nevertheless the system wordlength and the notional scale factor for any signal usually differ considerably from those associated with the original data.

Theories to predict the processes of arithmetic growth, and techniques for its curtailment are treated elsewhere (see Jackson, 1970; Rabiner and Gold, 1975). We observe in general that bit-growth resulting from multiplication may be handled by rounding or truncation (or by preserving a multiple-precision format); all of these options are supported by the various multiply primitives described in Chapter 4. Bit-growth arising from addition or subtraction is usually accommodated by increasing the wordlength, scaling (down) the result, or clipping. The FORMAT, LIMIT and SHIFT primitives of Chapter 4 provide for the latter options.

Restrictions on data format imposed by the primitives themselves are a further consideration at this point. For example the ADD primitive expects to receive addend and augend bearing the same notional scale factor (equivalently positioned binary points). The multiplier primitive expects the multiplicand to contain two guard bits (sign extensions) in the most significant positions, and imposes a particular interpretation of scale factor on the coefficient.

To assist in tracking signal ranges throughout the system we advocate a notation for use on the hardware flow-graph, as demonstrated in Figure 6.2. This is a version of LMSPART which has been modified to include an FLIMIT primitive in the h loop to curb arithmetic growth. The number pair in single brackets at each node give respectively the maximum expected value and the minimum required representation, expressed as exponent powers of 2. These indicate the required range of representation for signal data at any node. This must be accommodated within the actual system wordlength interpreted by a notional scale factor at each node. This is indicated between the double brackets as the interpreted significance of the most and least significant bits of the actual system word at that point, again as exponent powers of 2.

If the statistics of signals throughout the system are known (or can be analysed), then it is possible to 'process' the range and scale data between nodes through the connecting primitives. This procedure provides a check on arithmetic growth throughout the system, which may be altered (through the addition of primitives to scale and limit data) to resolve the dynamic range requirements within the system wordlength. Often this is an *ad hoc* process for any system, and may result only in a draft design. Simulation is used subsequently to determine the signal ranges under typical operating conditions. The objective is always to preserve adequate dynamic range whilst minimising the system wordlength.

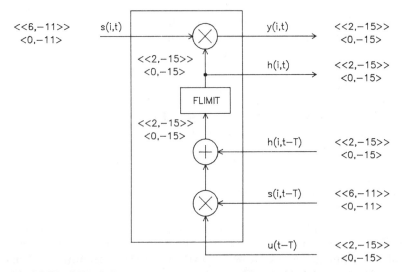

Fig. 6.2 LMSPART including limit primitive and target and real arithmetic ranges.

6.2.2 Maximal concurrency

The organisation of primitives within a processor should exhibit maximal concurrency. That is to say, we prefer to draw a fully concurrent flow-graph of the process, rather than multiplex primitive elements within it. This organisation maximises individual processor bandwidth and simplifies both the control structure and the problems of synthesis. It is possible to multiplex individual primitive elements in those applications where even a single custom processor is excessively fast; however, the increased hardware and control complexity reduce the tangible advantages. In these circumstances consideration should be given to the use of a conventional von Neumann machine.

6.2.3 Time alignment

The organisation of system architecture is simplified if all data entering and leaving each arithmetic processor is synchronous, or time-aligned. This requires an equal latency between all input and output ports. To satisfy this condition, equalising delay must be inserted into various signal paths within the system. Clearly it is desirable to make the overall processor latency as small as possible; that is, processors should incorporate only the unavoidable storage function associated with their pipelined computation. This convention considerably simplifies the initial stages of system synthesis at the possible expense of hardware optimisation. However, once a system design has been drafted and verified, this convention can be subsequently relaxed to reorder the timing and incorporate the optimal organisation. Figure 6.3 shows the

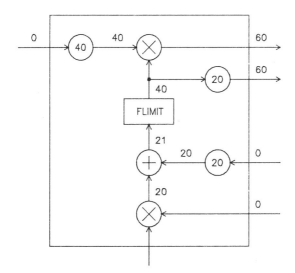

Fig. 6.3 LMSPART incorporating principles of time alignment and time tagging.

principle of time alignment applied to the LMSPART processor. With this configuration, all inputs and outputs are synchronous and the common processor latency is 60 bits, comprising 20 bits through each of the two multipliers, 19 bits through FLIMIT and 1 bit through the adder.

6.2.4   Time tagging

A demanding task in designing bit-serial arithmetic processors is that of accommodating latency through the various signal paths. Already our example processor has developed a reasonably complex timing chain. Time tagging helps to manage this process. We associate with each node in a net list a notional time tag. Time tags correspond to the arrival of new words at the hardware nodes. The tags are defined relative to some location chosen as the time tag origin and relative to some starting time.

The system time tag origin is usually taken at the control generator output. This corresponds to global tagging. Local time tag origins can be defined anywhere, for example at the inputs to a processor. A time tag is relative or absolute depending on its starting time, and local or global according to its origin.

The time tag of any node is simply its latency from the chosen origin. In other words, the time tag is the number of bit times required for the LSB-associated marker of a signal to travel from its origin to the node in question.

Time tags are used to keep account of data synchronisation during the design process and help later in generating the control network. Local time tags are usually used during processor design; changes of origin are easily accomplished during synthesis. Figure 6.3 also gives time-tag information (in bit-times) for LMSPART. In this example each multiplier has latency 20 bits (stems from 12-bit coefficient – see Chapter 4), the adder 1 bit, and FLIMIT 1 word and 1 bit. The wordlength in this case is 18 bits, giving an FLIMIT latency of 19 bits.

6.3   Setting the system wordlength

The arithmetic processes considered above set a lower bound on the system wordlength; call this LB(l). This may not always be the deciding factor. As discussed in Chapter 5, for processes that require the result of iteration $(i - 1, t)$ as input to (i,t), the processor latency, L, is also a lower bound on the system wordlength. Call this bound LB(L).

Once all the processors are designed we can choose the system wordlength as the greater of these lower bounds. Thus;

$$swl = greater\{LB(l), LB(L)\}$$

Note that if LB(l) is the greater bound (that is, the arithmetic consideration is overriding), then it may be possible to consider the provision of multiple precision formats at critical points in the system to reduce this bound and improve the processor bandwidth.

6.4   Implementing state memory, multiplexing and net synthesis

We can now fix the number of physical processors that will be needed by using the proposition of Chapter 5, together with the value for the system wordlength. This achieves the bandwidth matching necessary to give adequate performance with minimum hardware. Having designed the processors and determined the symbolic constant values, the system synthesis is completed by adding the required memory, multiplex switching and interconnections. A useful convention is to proceed as follows. Multiplexers are connected at relevant processor inputs. Recalling that the multiplex primitive has a latency of one bit, compensating delays are inserted into the other input paths, as necessary. Associate with each such processor the fixed amount of 'virtual' state memory required. This is the total memory required to make up the correct loop length. Implement this memory partially by the inherent processor latency and partially by the addition of word- and bit-delay primitives to make up the remaining virtual memory. Each processor output is then connected to this physical state memory and the state memory outputs are connected to the multiplexer inputs.

The interconnection of such processor, multiplexer, memory structures to each other is then achieved by tapping outputs from the processors, or from within the state memory, as developed in Chapter 5. Figure 6.4 details the implementation of the s loop for the example adaptive system following the style of Figure 5.11. The design of this machine calls for the processor to form a cascadable stage supporting m = 32 iterations, with an additional idle period of i = 7 words. This fixes the total s loop delay at (m + i − 1 = 38) words. The stage input is defined at the multiplexer and the processor operates one bit behind this origin. The correct tap point for the cascade connection in this case is (i − 1) words from the end of the loop. The principle of data precession within the loop may be exploited to derive s(i, t − T) from a tap one word ahead of s(i,t).

Following the complete design of the signal network at this point it may be possible to rationalise timing within the system by absorbing some delays and latencies into the state memory loops. This is an iterative process for any system; a useful example of its application in the adaptive transversal filter is discussed in Chapter 9.

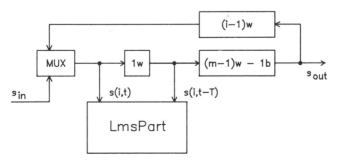

Fig. 6.4   Detail from implementation of s loop.

6.5 Implementing the control network

Thus far we have a system architecture, values for all the system parameters, designs of arithmetic processors and a primary network of signal nodes connecting processors, state FIFOs and multiplexing. Each primitive in this primary network has certain control requirements. These as yet undefined primitive inputs, together with the time tags associated with the corresponding signal nodes, implicitly define a secondary control network. This has no nodes in common with the signal network and may be viewed as an independent design exercise. The next task in the design process is to implement this network.

Time tagging for the signal network has already been dealt with in Section 6.2.4. The same process may be used with equal effect to assist the design of the control network. There is a hierarchy of control corresponding to the incidence of the start of a word (LSB), the start of a multiplex sub-cycle, the start and finish of an initialisation or test cycle, etc., at each node. Each level of control requires firstly a single source node from the CONTROLGENERATOR. Secondly, variously delayed versions of each level of control are required to synchronise with the primitives in the primary network of signal nodes.

We have already reviewed alternative implementations of the control network in Chapter 2. Figure 6.5 shows an example instantiation of the c1 control net within LMSPART. Here c1 enters the processor synchronously with the first-used data inputs. The first delayed version of c1 is generated through the lower multiplier, the next is an explicit delay by 1 bit to accommodate the ADD, and then a delay of 1 word plus 1 bit to equalise latency in FLIMIT. Here we note that delayed versions of any control cycle may be reduced modulo the cycle length. Thus the maximum delay necessary

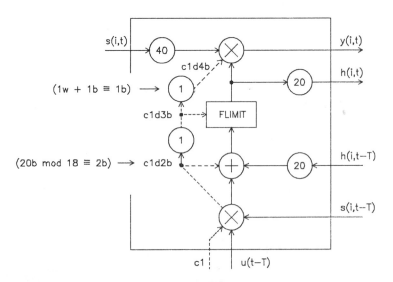

Fig. 6.5   Instantiation of control network in LMSPART.

for any level of control is always less than the cycle length for that level. An evident candidate here is the c1 delay of 1 word and 1 bit, which can be reduced to 1 bit. This and other tricks are developed further in Chapter 9.

6.6   Partitioning

We have not yet distinguished any physical boundaries in the system. Instead we have encouraged global system design, independent of such considerations. This is a feasible approach for bit-serial systems, where partitioning is possible in many ways due to the low overhead incurred when any signal path crosses a chip boundary.

In system design, chips are specified as a hierarchy of operators and primitives. The use of hierarchy eases the design task by allowing nested groupings of primitives to be specified, as appropriate to the system architecture. This feature serves design convenience and efficiency; the silicon compiler flattens out any hierarchy, and assembles the chip from an ungrouped list of primitives. Partitioning consists of determining which operators to place on each chip.

Partitioning is governed firstly by the maximum feasible chip size, which is in turn a function of process yield and packaging economics. Secondly it is influenced by the architectural groupings of primitives. In the early stages of design, floorplans may be generated in order to obtain likely chip sizes. These establish limitations on the architectural groupings of operators and primitives through chip size restrictions. This should be done at an early stage of design because partitioning involves a latency overhead. A latency of one bit is incurred in leaving one chip and entering another, by the principles outlined in Chapter 2. Thus, the location of a primitive on a chip places it inside communication boundaries. Primitives cannot be moved over these boundaries without modifying path latencies.

Efficient partitioning generally results from iterating floorplan trials throughout the design cycle. Initially, systems can be synthesised with architecturally grouped partitions. Generally the resultant system may contain oversize chips, or chips with unsuitable aspect ratios, prompting a redesign. This will require redistribution of primitives across chip boundaries. Even this is not usually a major task, and can normally be accomplished quickly. In the interest of modular design it is generally convenient to partition systems so as to include whole stages of recursive computation schemes within chip boundaries; this is exemplified by the examples in Part 2 of this book.

References

Jackson, L.B., 'On the Interaction of Roundoff Noise and Dynamic Range in Digital Filters', *Bell Sys. Tech. J.*, **49**, pp 159–184, 1970.

Rabiner, L.R. and Gold, B., *Theory and Application of Digital Signal Processing*, Prentice-Hall, 1975.

7

Testing and Self-Testing

Alan F. Murray

Department of Electrical Engineering
University of Edinburgh

7.1 Introduction

While specifying the silicon compiler in Chapter 2 we identified the testing and test-pattern generation processes as further candidates for a more structured approach. Here we develop such an approach and discover further advantages of bit-serial architectures. In particular, we find that bit-serial systems are inherently testable, are amenable to a simple design-for-test methodology and are also well suited for the inclusion of self-test circuitry on-chip at little extra cost. Each of these aspects is treated below. We first review the wider field of testability in order to identify the optimal approach for bit-serial architectures, and to justify its choice.

Testing a digital network involves applying a set of input patterns or *test vectors,* observing the resultant output patterns and comparing these with the known patterns for a 'good machine'. For SSI and MSI parts, exhaustive testing is often practical (all possible input patterns are applied and all possible internal states are probed). For LSI and VLSI components this is impossible in practice, as typical complexities and clock frequencies would lead to excessive test times. Methods have been developed which reduce the number of input vectors at the expense of fault coverage. It is the diversity of methods used, and their often limited applicability which makes testing a difficult business. For instance, the designer of test methodology for a microprocessor is faced with a very different set of problems from that seen by a memory designer. We are faced with a well-defined architecture and so can afford to analyse and enhance its testability in anticipation of gains to be made at the implementation stage.

In this chapter we explore the need for test and therefore testability, and examine briefly solutions adopted for different classes of circuit. From this we evolve a methodology for rendering bit-serial signal processing elements self-testing. This analysis will highlight the inherently high level of testability brought about by the bit-serial approach. We shall also describe the high level procedures which lead to a predictable rate of fault coverage.

7.2 Why test at all?

The answers to this question may seem self-evident, but we need to be very clear about the aims and purpose of 'design for testability'.

Figure 7.1 shows the life-cycle of a chip, along with the levels at which it may be tested both during manufacture and during its working life. If the system is a cheap digital watch, the consequences of missing out the tests performed by the system manufacturer may not be dire, as it may indeed be cheaper to throw away faulty watches than to test more fully. Furthermore, the effects of a cheap watch failing are not likely to be serious. If, however, the system is

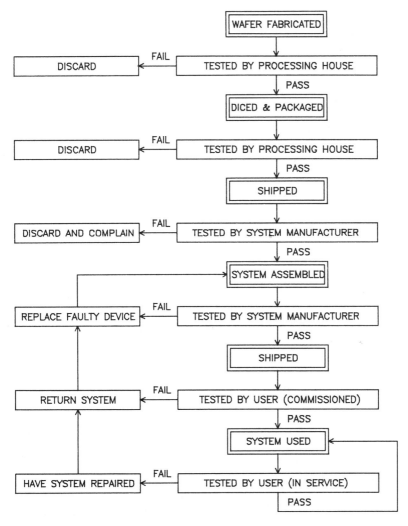

Fig. 7.1 Representation of the life-cycle of an integrated circuit.

a complex network of life-support equipment, everything must be tested rigorously at each stage and reliability in service is of paramount importance. In between these extremes there is a tradeoff between test effort and confidence level; between the desire to cut test time and cost and the need to avoid being submerged in a mountain of faulty parts. In addressing the problem of designing a testable chip we strive to enhance the testability of as many of the stages in the chip's evolution as possible. It is necessary, however, to identify the main goals of a scheme of testable design, as the optimal approach for improving the efficiency of wafer-level testing may have little relevance to in-service reliability.

In practice, we seek a test strategy giving a high level of confidence in the chip that can be performed without the need for expensive and bulky automatic test equipment (ATE). This enhances reliability by increasing serviceability 'in the field'. We may also contemplate including a self-test capability, which will avoid the exponential growth in complexity of automatic test equipment (and therefore its cost) as circuit complexity increases, by limiting the size and complexity of the module to be (self) tested. We will also avoid many of the problems inherent in using today's test equipment to test tomorrow's technology, particularly in respect of high speed testing, as self-test naturally proceeds at full system clock rate. This also provides a certain degree of parametric testing. If we can arrange that our design for testability fits in naturally to the framework of the silicon compiler, this will aid the system designer in the process of traversing from specification through compilation, fabrication and testing to obtaining good parts.

7.3   Approaches to test

7.3.1   The *ad hoc* approach

The least bothersome approach to design for testability from the designer's point of view is usually referred to as the *ad hoc* approach. This hardly deserves the title of an 'approach', as very little thought is given to test until the design is more or less complete. At this stage, some test points, observation points and perhaps a few gates may be added. The *ad hoc* approach leaves widespread problems for the test engineer faced with an essentially 'random' network from the test point of view. This approach may be discarded for future use, as it is out of keeping with current design philosophies, and will of necessity become more and more intractable as VLSI complexities increase. Worst of all, every new design requires a new *ad hoc* test modification.

7.3.2   Structured approaches

As the title implies, these methods are very much in keeping with the philosophy and methodology of VLSI design; for the same reasons they have traditionally been unpopular with the circuit designer. By their nature they impose restrictions on the designer, both in what he can and cannot do.

The foremost prerequisite for a VLSI design to be testable is that it be sensibly partitioned (in fact this is a prerequisite for any VLSI design). This is generally known as the 'divide and conquer' approach, and circumvents the problems of exponential growth of test time with circuit complexity. For instance, a 4n-bit counter requires 2^{4n} cycles to perform an exhaustive test. Partitioned into (say) $4 \times$ n-bit counters, only 2^n steps are required – a reduction by a factor of 2^{3n}, i.e. 4096 for a 16-bit counter.

The most common implementation of a systematic test strategy is the inclusion of a 'scan-path' (Eichelberger and Williams,1977). With this method the internal memory elements of a circuit can be reconfigured in 'test' mode to be chained together into a shift register, with the input and output of the register connected to a primary input and output respectively. The test proceeds as follows:

1. Test the latches by shifting a characteristic sequence through the scan-path.
2. Test the combinational circuitry by clocking through a test pattern fed in via the scan-path.
3. Shift out the resultant response vector and compare with 'good' result, while shifting in the next test vector.
4. Repeat from stage 2 until test coverage is sufficient.

When a scan-path approach is combined with a sensibly race-free design, the methodology known as level-sensitive scan design (LSSD) results.

This is the most common and useful means of rendering a complicated and large circuit testable by an automatic tester. The number of test vectors is reduced by this scheme, as only sections of combinational logic have to be tested, but the lengths of the sequences to be fed in and out of the scan-path continue to grow with VLSI complexity.

Scan-path design has historically been unattractive to designers, as it imposes strict constraints on their layout freedom. The solution to this problem is to make the circuit designer design the test program! In summary, the scan-path approach is a powerful generalised technique for enhancing the controlability and observability of large circuits, and has been adopted by many companies as a design 'rule', notably by the major computer manufacturers.

7.3.3   Self-test

Interest has been generated recently by a group of techniques which enable the philosophy of self-test or autonomous test (Sedmak, 1979, 1980). At any (or every) level in a system, self-test implies that test vectors are generated, and the resultant output data is analysed within the system, subsystem or chip. In this way, minimal external hardware is required (in particular, expensive ATE) to enable a system element to provide a 'go/no go' signal on execution of its self-test. Usually, only valid power supplies and clocks will be required, along with some means of initiating a test. The amenability of a circuit to self-test depends critically on its functionality, and different classes of system are best served by different forms of self-test. These are as follows:

Stored microprogram

In programmable systems, a test program can be stored in memory, and executed offline. In this way, a microprocessor can test its own memories, registers, etc., by executing a series of tests exercising different sections of its circuitry in a boot-strapped manner. If a high overhead can be tolerated, and the ultimate in reliability is required, redundant (duplicate) hardware can be added and a run-time test can be performed, with voting circuitry to take decisions on results from the redundant parts. This form of self-test can only be implemented for intelligent systems, and does not help in our search for a methodology for testability in signal processing parts.

Residue-3 or modulus-checking

This technique (Heckelman and Bhasvar, 1981), is suitable for systems involving linear arithmetic, although it presents formidable problems in implementation. The technique involves including redundant hardware to perform the system function in parallel, but to a different number-base (hence residue-3). The two answers to a computation are resolved to the common number base and compared online. A self-test is thus executed at run-time with no explicit test phase. Clearly, there is a significant overhead involved in implementing the redundant hardware, but this can be minimised by judicious choice of the second number base. From our point of view a more serious drawback is that the scheme cannot easily be made to accommodate nonlinear functions, such as those associated with rounding and truncation. These can lead to disagreements between the parallel systems when no fault exists. It is not easy to see how this can be avoided. The most that can be said at present is that this technique is likely to be viable only in specific instances of purely linear systems.

Random pattern stimulation with data 'hashing'

The most common and most generally useful technique for including self-test in non-microprocessor systems involves stimulation during an explicit test phase by pseudorandom patterns, which can be generated on-chip using linear feedback shift registers (LFSRs). This is an inexpensive means of generating large numbers of nondeterministic test vectors. By nondeterministic, we mean that the vectors are not selected algorithmically to sensitise particular faults, as are the vectors selected for ATE testing. Instead, we rely on their random nature and the large number applied to give a high quality test. The response data is also compressed or 'hashed' on-chip, and an offline self-test (in general) is thus performed. In fact, random pattern stimulation is often used in full offline testing using test equipment, as random patterns are generated much more cheaply than are deterministic test patterns. The data is then fully analysed or at least analysed using statistical or syndrome (Savir, 1980) techniques to give some diagnostic information. Self-test does not, in general, give any diagnostic information, but merely provides a go/no go decision.

There are two main forms of data compression used for self-test. These are transition counting and signature analysis (Frohwerk, 1977). Transition counting is fairly self-explanatory, involving the accumulation of a checksum representing the number of logic transitions on the output nodes for comparison with the known result (from simulation) for a fault-free system. Signature analysis is not so transparent and requires more detailed discussion. Details will be given later in this chapter, but for now we note that signature analysis is performed when the output data is exclusive-OR'ed into a linear feedback shift register, thus dividing the data by the characteristic polynomial of the LFSR generator. This reduces the data stream to an n-bit word or signature, where n is the LFSR length. The signature of a data stream is this n-bit word that is left in the LFSR at the end of a test sequence – a wrong data stream should lead to a wrong signature.

Clearly, some information is lost in the compression of an m-bit data stream to a number of transitions or an n-bit signature (if n<m). It is necessary to consider, therefore, the probability that a 'good' transition count or a 'good' signature results from a bad data sequence to give rise to 'fault masking'. In other words, what is the probability that a faulty system passed its own self-test? For transition counting this probability is (Frohwerk, 1977):

$$P_{TC} = 1 - \sum_{r=0}^{m} \frac{B_{mr}(B_{mr}-1)}{2^m(2^m-1)}$$

where

$$B_{mr} = \frac{m!}{(m-r)!r!}$$

for all errors, and

$$P_{TC} = \frac{m-1}{2m}$$

for single-bit errors.

For signature analysis, assuming all error patterns are equally likely, the probability that a fault will be detected is

$$P_{SA} = \frac{1-2^{-n}}{1-2^{-m}}$$

for all errors and

$$P_{SA} = 1$$

for m<n and single bit errors.

These results for transition counting and signature analysis are shown in Figure 7.2. Evidently, for general errors, signature analysis is superior for reasonable lengths of data stream if n>7. More importantly, the fault capture rate in signature analysis is insensitive to the length of the data stream for m>n, and the hardware required is similarly invariant. This cannot be said for transition counting, and longer transition counters are required for longer data sequences. It is desirable to be able to design for any given level of fault coverage without regard to data compressor hardware, so signature analysis is the better technique.

Some concern has been expressed over the ability of a signature analyser LFSR to capture different classes of fault. We can see from Figure 7.2 that the capture rate is 100% for one-bit errors. It is possible to envisage circumstances where errors may feed back to cancel a subsequent error (the multiple wrongs combining to make a right). More theoretical work is required to provide a definitive answer to this problem, but preliminary work suggests that the above result, derived from the rather simplistic assumption of random errors, is valid for evenly-spaced or 'repeated' errors provided a maximum length LFSR is used (Smith, 1980).

The effects of a failure to store errors are negligible compared with the effects of the less-than-perfect fault coverage by the pseudorandom test data which generally has to be tolerated if test time is to be kept to a reasonable level. We address this latter problem in Section 7.8.

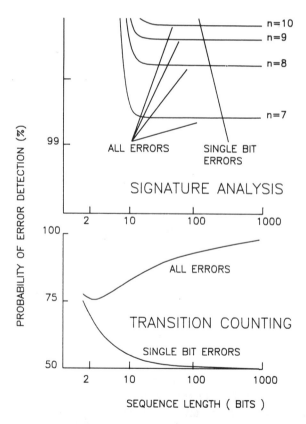

Fig. 7.2   Error detection probabilities for Signature Analysis and Transition Counting (n=LFSR length).

7.4   Towards a test methodology for bit-serial parts

We now need to state our goals for the introduction of a design for test methodology. We are not concerned with problems of design verification once a chip has been fabricated, as the methodology described in the preceding chapters should ensure that a design is functionally correct. Furthermore, we do not propose to address the problem of full parametric testing. We are only concerned with the detection of functional faults introduced during manufacture. We do not require diagnostic information to localise a fault within a single device, as once a faulty chip has been detected it will be discarded, or switched out (within a fault-tolerant system). It is clear that self-test is therefore a possibility in that it provides all the information required. Before committing to self-test, however, it is necessary to establish certain definitions and criteria for testability in general.

Fault coverage
To measure the degree of fault coverage by any set of input data it is necessary to decide what is meant by a fault. There are many mechanisms whereby a circuit's operation may be made faulty, such as open circuit, short circuit, uneven doping and oxide thickness, etc. At present no physically realistic method exists for examining the effects of such faults in complex circuits, and a simplified empirical fault model must be adopted. The accepted standard is at present the 'single-stuck fault' model. The coverage is measured by performing a large number of switch-level circuit simulations. First, a 'good machine' simulation must be performed with a particular set of input data to produce a set of good data for reference. Subsequent simulations are performed with stuck-at-one and stuck-at-zero faults injected at each circuit node in turn, and the same input data. A fault is said to be 'covered' by the given input stream if its injection causes the output data stream to differ from that of a good machine.

This procedure is computationally intensive and therefore very expensive and time consuming for all but the simplest circuits. Methods are being developed which will reduce this overhead by only injecting faults on 1000–2000 of the circuit nodes (Agrawal, 1981). This smaller number of simulations will still produce a highly accurate estimate of the fault coverage if the sample nodes are carefully chosen, but long simulation times are still required. Other concurrent techniques are based on assessing the probability that a fault on each circuit node is stimulated by random pattern inputs and subsequently propagated to an observable output point (Savir *et al.*, 1983; Savir and Bardell, 1983). These techniques are very promising as far as random pattern testability of general networks is concerned. For the particular case of bit-serial circuits, however, the operators exhibit a useful property which we can call *Propagative Randomness*. An operator with a random input data stream will produce a random output data stream. For instance, the product of two random numbers (both of which may be positive or negative) will be a random number, so a multiplier primitive has the property of propagative randomness. This property allows us to adopt a semi-statistical approach in keeping with the hierarchical compiler philosophy. With this proviso, coupled with the assumption that 'garbage in' means 'garbage out' for fault-free operators, we can summarise the response of 'good' and 'bad' operators to 'correct' and 'incorrect' random inputs as shown in Table 7.1.

Table 7.1 Response of primitive operators to different types of data.

Case	Operator	Input(s)	Output(s)
(A)	good	correct data	correct data
(B)	good	random and correct	random and correct
(C)	good	bad	bad
(D)	good	bad and multiple	good
(E)	bad	random and correct	bad
(F)	bad	bad	bad
(G)	bad	bad	good

Only cases D and G give cause for alarm in test mode, as they represent:

(D) The possibility that two erroneous test inputs may combine to give the correct answer. This is extremely unlikely to be a problem in bit-serial arithmetic systems but this issue, generally referred to as 'reconvergent fanout', is a significant cause for concern when using random patterns in large combinational networks.

(G) The possibility that an error caused by a fault in one operator may be corrected artificially by another fault in another operator. This second order effect is always a problem, as predicting the effects of multiple errors (even merely two at a time) increases the simulation times (i.e. the number of 'bad machine' simulations) intolerably. Fortunately, they account for a small percentage of faults in real systems.

7.5   The design-for-test methodology

We now state the design methodology to be imposed upon the designer in order that our design-for-test philosophy be workable. Firstly, it is essential that all looped data paths in the processor be openable in the test phase, to limit the sequential depth of the device to a few clock cycles. In fact, this requirement is usually met by the inherent control network, and never represents much of an overhead. Once loops are broken, the processor becomes a computational pipeline. Secondly, any primitive operators which do not obey propagative randomness must be readily configurable to do so in test mode (for example, by exclusive ORing the nonrandom outputs with a random stream). This is actually a requirement upon the designer of the primitives and will not concern the system designer. Finally the system designer must follow a series of fault coverage rules to ensure adequate confidence in the test. These will be described in Section 7.8.

As we have already suggested, a self-test capability satisfies the requirements we identified above for our testing scheme. The benefits of self-test are as follows (Sedmak, 1979):

1. The need for sophisticated and costly external, ancillary test equipment is eliminated. This removes an exponentially growing headache.
2. Test pattern generation is unnecessary.
3. Test proceeds at the system clock rate, and we remove the potential problems of testing tomorrow's technology with yesterday's.
4. The task of making the logic testable is necessarily part of the design process.
5. Fault-tolerance becomes a possibility, if the overhead of redundant hardware can be tolerated.
6. A system and/or its components can be verified almost anywhere, at any time, without the need for sophisticated test equipment, and without the need for the whole system to be operational or even present.

In the remainder of this chapter we shall demonstrate that self-test using random pattern stimulation and signature analysis can be achieved with an extremely high degree of coverage for bit-serial signal processing systems, and how it might be included as part of the design environment.

7.6   Realisation of signature analysis

The rate of fault capture by a signature analysis system has already been discussed in Section 7.3.3. In this section the building blocks in a signature analysis system are described, along with the system considerations which affect the details of the implementation.

The basic element in a signature analysis system is the linear feedback shift register or LFSR shown in Figure 7.3. The ten-bit register shown may be used as a signature analyser, when the input is the test response data to be compressed. With the input grounded it may be used as a pseudorandom sequence generator for input stimulation.

In many applications, distributed shift registers are more economical and versatile than compacted LFSRs, particularly when existing latches can be

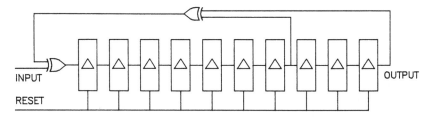

Fig. 7.3   Block diagram of a 10-bit maximum length Linear Feedback Shift Register(LFSR).

reconfigured to become elements of LFSRs (cf. scan path techniques). A reconfigurable latch known as the Built-In Logic Block Observer (BILBO) was developed for this purpose (Konemann *et al.*, 1979), and is now in common use in self-testing systems. A BILBO latch can be configured as either a normal circuit element, an element in a scan-path, a signature analyser element or part of a pseudorandom sequence generator. For the particular application of bit-serial signal processors it will be shown that this degree of versatility is neither necessary nor desirable. Furthermore, the distributed shift register arrangement is not appropriate. Accordingly, we have opted for compacted LFSRs for both input stimulation and signature analysis. To distinguish between these two, we shall refer to the input LFSR as a pseudorandom binary sequence register (PRBS), and the signature analyser as a feedback register output data observer (FRODO) (Tolkien, 1955).

The maximum length of pseudorandom pattern from an n-bit PRBS is $(2n - 1)$ bits. We have calculated the irreducible shift register polynomials (modulo 2) to degree 17, using a modified 'sieve' method (Golomb, 1967). In the interests of reduced layout complexity, we have also restricted the number

Table 7.2 Polynomials and sequence lengths for all maximum length linear feedback registers to order 16 with only two feedback taps

Number of LFSR stages	LFSR polynomial	Pseudorandom sequence length
2	111	3
3	1011	7
3	1101	7
4	10011	15
4	11001	15
5	100101	31
5	101001	31
6	1000011	63
6	1100001	63
7	10000011	127
7	11000001	127
7	10010001	127
7	10001001	127
9	1000010001	511
9	1000100001	511
10	10000001001	1023
10	10010000001	1023
11	100000000101	2047
11	101000000001	2047
15	1000000000000011	32767
15	1100000000000001	32767
15	1000000000010001	32767
15	1000100000000001	32767
15	1000000100000001	32767
15	1000000010000001	32767

of feedback taps to two. Table 7.2 shows the configurations of all such LFSRs up to order 16.

An important decision regarding test strategy at the system level is whether or not to make individual chips self-testing. We can represent the operation of a signature analysis system schematically as Figure 7.4. The decision to be made is whether the 'signal processor' is to be interpreted as a single chip or an entire system. In the interests of generality, and in anticipation of the effects on system and subsystem implementation of VLSI densities, we have chosen the former and implemented the self-test capability at the lowest sensible stage in the current system hierarchy by designing self-testing chips. This allows for in-system fault tolerance and fault pinpointing at the component level. We shall also show in Section 7.9 that system level self-test including test of the interchip wiring is also possible with this more versatile approach.

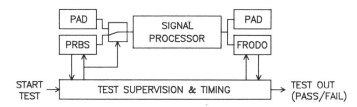

Fig. 7.4 Block diagram of a Signature Analysis self-testing system.

7.7 Implementation of self-test

In this section we will see how the inclusion of signature analysis with pseudorandom stimulation fits in neatly to a trial bit-serial VLSI design. We will discuss the decisions taken regarding how to place the extra circuitry and present a trial implementation, using a 64-point cascadable FIR filter as a test vehicle.

7.7.1 Operation of the self-test system

The hallmark of a successful methodology is that it can be easily understood and applied by system designers who are not expert in test/self-test methods.

The biggest attraction of our approach for the system designer is that the architecture and functionality of the central system are substantially unaltered.

Control signals are either operated in the normal mode or used to force open loops as described previously. Although this results in an incomplete test of the control circuitry, it is necessary to ensure a predictable state for the test to begin. We shall adopt the approach that test length, and therefore PRBS length, will be determined from high-level considerations in a manner similar to the construction of an operator or subsystem flow diagram.

There are two phases of the test. During the first phase, the processor is 'flushed-out' by PRBS stimulation to set all the internal registers to known states. On completion of this phase, the signature analysers are 'switched-on', and the actual test proceeds until fault coverage is adequate.

The test sequence length is determined by the computational latency of the processor (which impacts upon the 'flushing-out' time) and on the length of PRBS necessary to exercise the circuitry. The latency of our chosen test vehicle is thirty-two 14-bit words, so the flushing-out period must be greater than 448 cycles. In fact we will see that a ten-bit LFSR for both stimulation and signature analysis gives an adequate PRBS length (1023 bits for flushing out, and a further 1023 for the test proper), and a high rate of fault capture at the signature analyser (99.9%). It should be emphasised that this is merely a convenient length in this case, and in no way precludes the use of longer (or shorter) LFSRs in other applications.

The test phase is initiated by a positive transition edge, and proceeds as shown in Table 7.3.

Table 7.3   Operation of Test Cycle for 10-bit signature analysis system

Clock cycle	Event
3	PRBS generators reset, control inputs jammed to open any signal loops and thus reduce latency, output latch reset.
1027	Signal processing system is now in a known state – reset signature analysers.
2050	Test complete – check comparator outputs and set output latch if all signatures are good.

For a system clocking a bit rate of 8 MHz this represents a test cycle of 0.25 ms duration.

In Figure 7.5 we show in some detail how the chosen methodology has been implemented. This diagram is essentially an expanded version of Figure 7.4. It can be seen that a definite sequence of transitions (unknown 0 – 5 V) should result at the 'Test Out' output. This alleviates partially the problems of faulty test circuitry causing bad chips to appear to pass their self-test, although good devices with (say) a faulty flip-flop in the test circuitry may be rejected. As the self-test circuitry occupies only 4% of the chip area, the probability that a chip is good and the self-test circuitry is faulty is around 1% (for 30% overall yield). It has been assumed that the 'Test In' 0 – 5 V edge is asynchronous, to preserve generality.

The evolution of a complete, successful self-test sequence is shown in Figure 7.6. A failed self-test will occur if any one of the signatures at the output nodes does not match the expected signature. This will result in one of the nodes 28–33 (comparators from FRODOS) failing to be pulled up on cycles 2049. Failure of the test circuitry to produce a 'Test Complete' pulse will also result in a failed self-test. Grounding the 'Test In' pin puts the chip in 'run' mode. It would be possible to arrange for the test circuitry to be powered down in run mode, although its low power consumption scarcely warrants this extra complexity.

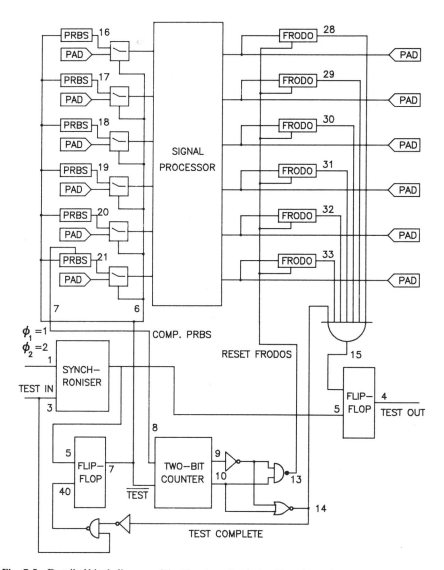

Fig. 7.5   Detailed block diagram of the Signature Analysis self-testing system.

7.7.2   The implementation

A gate level diagram of a PRBS or FRODO is shown in Figure 7.7. The correct signature for a FRODO or the decode state for a PRBS is encoded by selecting the appropriate connections for the pulldown transistors in the 10-input NOR gate.

It is a characteristic of bit-serial elements that the communication overhead is low and that the gate/pin ratio is consequently high. This often results in an area of unused silicon in the pad channel. We have therefore designed PRBS

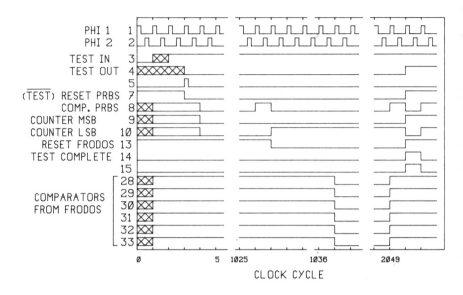

Fig. 7.6   Timing diagram for a successful self-test. Node numbers and names are given in Figure 7.5.

and FRODO elements and the timing logic in such a way that they can be placed in the pad channel. The timing circuit forms an extra entity to be inserted, but the PRBS and FRODO registers can be incorporated with minimal difficulty by simply redefining the signal input and output pads (for example Figure 7.8). The entire test circuitry can be placed in the pad channel of our trial design with ease (Figure 7.9). This single-chip filter is actually composed of two 32-point cascaded sections, each of which is represented by the operator flow graph of Figure 7.10.

7.8   Test coverage and cost

We have seen that random pattern self-test can be incorporated into bit-serial signal processing elements. In this section the benefits and costs of the inclusion of self-test will be examined, for this particular implementation.

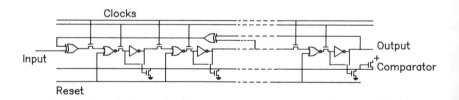

Fig. 7.7   Gate level implementation of a LFSR.

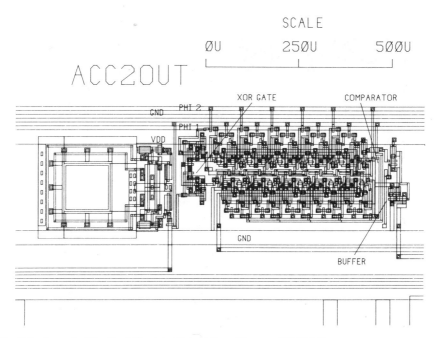

Fig. 7.8   Layout of Feedback Register Output Data Observer (FRODO).

We assert (in Section 7.4) that it is only necessary to ensure that individual operators are well tested by our chosen length of random pattern, and that the propagative randomness property is preserved. This impacts upon the design of the building blocks but does not restrict the system designer at all. The most complicated operator in the FIRST library is the multiplier, and we have chosen to study this in detail. In fact, it is clear that the delay operators (shift registers) in Figure 7.10 will be exhaustively tested in a short time by flushing with pseudorandom data. The only other nontrivial operator used is the adder, which is included as a subprimitive operator in the multiplier. We can therefore be sure that the fault coverage measured for the multiplier represents a lower bound on the coverage for our 64-point filter.

7.8.1   Fault coverage simulation results

We have chosen to use 10-bit LFSRs for both pseudorandom sequence generation and signature analysis rather than the more normal 16-bit length. This gives a pseudorandom sequence length of 1023 ($2^{10} - 1$) bits and a fault capture rate of 99.9% by the signature analyser. Even in the presence of elusive evenly spaced or 'repeated use' faults this high capture rate will be achieved due to the use of irreducible polynomials. The LFSR polynomials for coefficient and multiplicand generators in this simulation are 10000001001 and 10010000001 respectively. To give an insight into the nodal activity within a multiplier under pseudorandom stimulation, we present in Figure 7.11 the results of simulation measurements on 2, 4, 8 and 16 bit multipliers. The

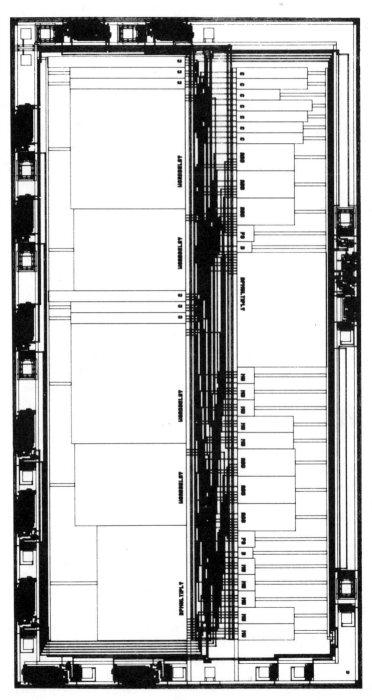

Fig. 7.9   Layout of self-testing Deltic section.

PROCESSING FUNCTION

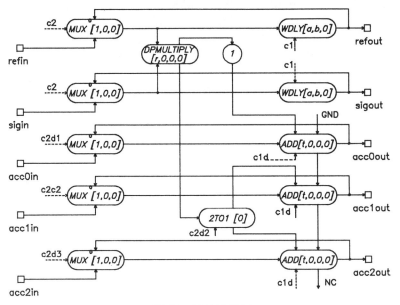

CONTROL FUNCTION

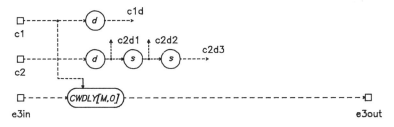

Fig. 7.10 Flow-graph of 32 point Deltic section.

vertical axis represents the percentage of all nodes which have toggled (undergone a change of state). The rapid rise between 0 and 20 cycles represents the 'flushing-out' of the shift registers and much of the adder circuitry, while the slower rise to 100% activation by 300 cycles (414 for the 16 bit operator) represents the exercising of the recoder logic, and its resultant effects on the adder. The similarity between these 'activation curves' for different multiplier lengths is striking, if not surprising in view of the aforementioned modulatory and propagative randomness property of the architecture. The major effect of increasing the multiplier length is to smooth the curve, as the presence of a larger number of nodes reduces the relative significance of any individual event. The similarity between these curves is very important as it allows us to draw conclusions from the more detailed simulation of a chosen length of multiplier which are relevant to all reasonable lengths of multiplier. It also confirms the propagative randomness property for a single multiplier stage, as any significant deviation from randomness at the input to any multiplier module would affect the activation curves of Figure 7.11 by changing the pattern of activity in subsequent modules. This would be manifest as a slowness, or even failure to reach the point where all the nodes have been toggled.

In Figure 7.12 we present a statistical picture of the nodal activity shown in Figure 7.11 in order to emphasise the insensitivity of average activity to multiplier length. From this figure we can also see that all nodes are toggled at least 6 times, and that a large percentage are toggled between 100 and 200 times. The nodes associated with the two-phase clock appear in Figure 7.12 as the small peak at 2000 – 3000 transitions (actually 2046). Once again we can see the striking similarity between the pattern of activity in different lengths of multiplier.

The fact that a given pseudorandom sequence causes a transition (or transitions) on a given node is a necessary but not sufficient condition for both types of stuck-at fault to be detected by the sequence. This is because there are, in general, 'don't-care' states with respect to any given node, and the effect of a fault may not be propagated to an output to appear as an error. We have therefore performed an exhaustive fault simulation for the 8-bit multiplier (a useful length, and one which yields tolerable simulation times). The coverage of single stuck-at faults is 100%.

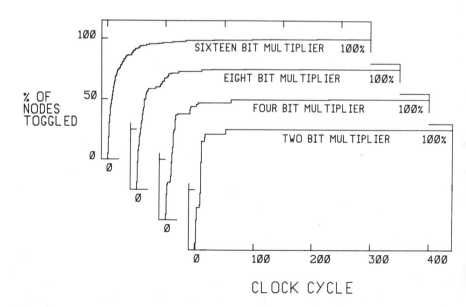

Fig. 7.11   Nodal activity in modified Booth's algorithm multipliers of different lengths.

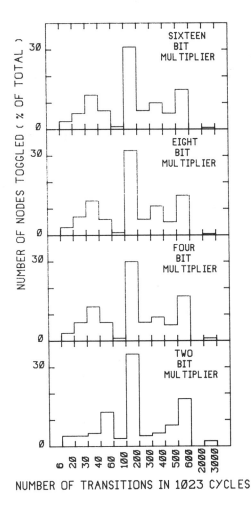

Fig. 7.12 Distribution of the number of nodes against the number of transitions for a 1023 bit prbs input sequence.

Clearly, this perfect fault coverage may not be achieved for all operators and all LFSR polynomials, but it is significant that it is achieved for the most random pattern resistant element within a comprehensive primitive set. With a 10-bit signature analyser the net rate of fault capture will be 99.9%.

We are committed, by our design-for-test methodology, to ensure that the property of propagative randomness is obeyed by all operators. If this is not the case, a minor reconfiguration of the operator is necessary in test mode to restore the randomness of its output. Armed with the further knowledge that wrong input to a fault-free operator yields wrong output, we can be confident that a single fault in (say) a multiplier will cause an error at the multiplier's output which will be propagated through subsequent fault-free operators (see Table 7.1) to show up as faulty data at the signature analyser.

In designing the test length, therefore, we need only consider the *most random pattern resistant* operator in the processor. This can be identified by studying a series of graphs (an example of which is shown in Figure 7.13), taken from full fault simulations of each operator, which show the clock cycle in which the single stuck faults actually appear at the operator's output. This form of representation is similar to that used by Williams and Eichelberger (1977). Although this resembles closely the activation curves of Figure 7.10, it actually represents a much more significant result (both computationally and in content). From the graph it can again be seen that the sequence length chosen (1023 bits) ensures 100% coverage of single-stuck-faults in the multiplier and thus a similar degree of coverage for the less random pattern constant elements. It can also been seen that considerably shorter sequences could be used (say 255 bits) if only 98.5% confidence is required. We have thus reduced the problem of test pattern design to that of assessing, from the testability graph for the most random pattern resistant operator in the processor (cf. Figure 7.13), the length of PRBS needed to provide any desired degree of coverage of that operator. The less random pattern resistant operators will be tested to an even higher degree of confidence. The testability issue can therefore be viewed at a system level, in a manner consistent with the steps involved in arriving at an operator network and flow diagram. The testability of each operator need only be measured once by full simulation to produce its testability graph, to which the system designer may then refer (Murray *et al.*, 1983).

7.8.2   Cost

We have shown that very high levels of fault coverage, and thence reliability, can be achieved. It remains to us now to count the cost.

Design difficulty
Design difficulty is not significantly increased since it is a simple matter to redefine the input/output pad cells to include PRBS/FRODO registers

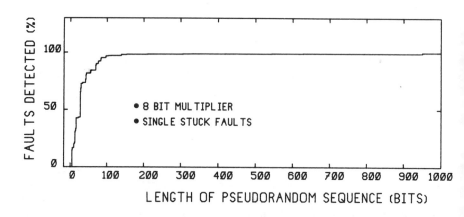

Fig. 7.13   Detection of single stuck faults in a multiplier (testability graph).

respectively, and to include a simply-connected timing cell. Only the test sequence length (and therefore the PRBS length) need to be determined by the procedures described above.

Silicon area and yield
We have seen that the overall chip area has not been increased at all by the inclusion of self-test, and that the active silicon area is increased by around 4%. This might be expected to decrease the yield by about 1%.

Power consumption
Each PRBS/FRODO register will have a worst-case power consumption (from analogue SPICE simulation) of 5 mW, and about 8 mW for the timing circuitry. The overall power overhead for the trial design is thus under 60 mW. With an estimated overall chip power consumption of 700 mW this represents a 9% overhead. This could be reduced at the expense of speed performance or by powering down the test circuitry in run mode, but it should be emphasised that this is a worst-case figure. Furthermore, a move to CMOS technology will allow reduction of the power consumption of the entire circuit.

System complexity
If the system does not have to be self-testing, no increase in system complexity is necessary, as the chip self-test may be initiated manually. In the more likely event that some degree of system self-test is required, a controller chip or module will be required, to define the mode of operation (test or run) and to act upon the results of the self-test. The details of this controller will depend upon the way in which the result of the test is to be used. The considerable benefits brought about by a small increase in system complexity will be discussed in Section 7.9.

7.9   System considerations

We have arrived at a methodology for including a reliable self-test capability in bit-serial signal processing elements with low design and implementation overheads. The test is essentially an offline test involving an explicit test phase of 0.25 milliseconds. So short is the test time, however, that it may be possible in certain applications to perform a pseudo-online self-test by 'cycle-stealing'. For instance, if in a sonar system the signal transmission period is 0.1–1 seconds, it is a simple matter to insert in a 0.25 milliseconds self-test between transmissions.

It is also possible to configure at least three different modes of operation within a multichip system using the existing hardware. These are illustrated in Figure 7.14(a),(b) and (c) and are 'run' or 'normal' mode, 'test chip' mode and 'test system' mode. In *run* mode, each device is set to 'run'. Real signals enter the pipeline via the system input(s) and are processed to produce signal outputs at the end of the pipeline. In *chip test* mode, each device in the computational pipeline is set to 'test' mode, and produces its individual 'good/bad' flag

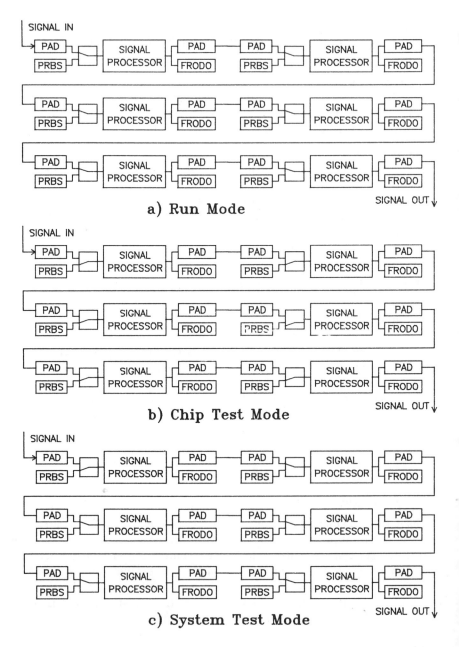

Fig. 7.14 A multichip signal processing system in 'RUN' mode (a), in 'CHIP TEST' mode (b) and in 'SYSTEM TEST' mode (c).

whereby faulty devices may be diagnosed. In *system test* mode (which may be entered once a successful chip test has filled the pipeline with known data), the first chip in the pipeline is set to chip test, and all the others to 'run' mode. In this mode pseudorandom data passes through the entire pipeline *including the inter-chip interconnections,* to produce a set of 'good/bad' flags at each inter-chip boundary. The enormous benefit of this hierarchically structured system test is that interconnect failures (which account for a large percentage of system failures) are tested.

By opting for self-test at the lowest sensible level in a system hierarchy (chip level), we have created a regime within which fault tolerance at the device level is a realistic possibility. If redundant elements are included in a system (at the board level), a voting arrangement can use the results of the self-test to switch in the redundant parts automatically when a failure occurs.

Yesterday's LSI boards are becoming today's VLSI chips, and there is no reason to suppose that this trend will not continue. This represents a severe problem for the proponents of scan-path design, and an insurmountable one for those relying on *ad hoc* measures. A scan path simply becomes longer, as do the associated test vectors, and simulation and test times increase accordingly. The *ad hoc* test designer is faced with a circuit with an increasing number of smaller nodes which are becoming progressively less accessible. By including a low-level self-test capability with the resultant hierarchical test capability, however, we have avoided one of the more significant problems of VLSI and beyond, as the hierarchy can be extended, in principle, *ad infinitum*. In other words, the devices we have implemented as self-testing chips could equally well be implemented as self-testing modules within a self-testing chip. In a similar manner, the self-test result could be used to configure (either dynamically or statically) a 'system-on-a-wafer', leaving out devices which have failed the self-test. In this way the expected yields for Wafer Scale Integration (WSI) can be enhanced to make WSI systems realistic when the ultimate in compactness, performance and reliability is required.

In summary, we have presented a generalised methodology for including hierarchically structured self-test in bit-serial parts. The confidence level is high and is determined without detailed simulation, while all costs are low. The method is also proof against obsolescence with improving technology, as far as one can guard against such a thing.

References

Agrawal, V. D. 'Sampling Techniques for Determining Fault Coverage in LSI Circuits', *Journal of Digital Systems*, **5**, pp 189–202, 1981.

Eichelberger, E. B. and Williams, T. W. 'A Logic Design Structure for LSI Testing', *Proc. 14th Design Automation Conf.*, pp 462–468, 1977.

Frohwerk, R. A. 'Signature Analysis, a New Digital Field Service Method', *Hewlett-Packard Journal*, 1977.

Golomb, S. W. *Shift Register Sequences*, Pub. Holden-Day Inc., San Francisco, 1967.

Heckelman, R. S. W. and Bhasvar, D. K. 'Self-Testing VLSI', *IEEE Solid State Circuits Conference*, pp 174–175, 1981.

Konemann, B., Mucha, J. and Zwiehoff, G. 'Built-In Logic Block Observation Techniques', *Proc. IEEE Test Conference*, pp 37–41, 1979.

Murray, A. F., Denyer, P. B. and Renshaw, D. 'Self-Testing in Bit-Serial VLSI Parts: High Coverage at Low Cost', *Proc. International Test Conference*, pp 260–268, 1983.

Savir, J. 'Syndrome testable design of combinational circuits', *IEEE Trans. Comput.*, **C-29**, pp 442–457, 1980.

Savir, J. and Bardell, P. H. 'On Random Pattern Test Length', *Proc. International Test Conference*, pp 95–106, 1983.

Savir, J., Ditlow, G. and Bardell, P. H. 'Random Pattern Testability', *Proc. 13th Int. Symposium on Fault-Tolerant Computing*, pp 80–89, 1983.

Sedmak, R. M. 'Design for Self-Verification: An Approach to Dealing with Testability Problems in VLSI Designs', *Proc. IEEE Test Conference*, pp 112–120, 1979.

Sedmak, R. M. 'Implementation Techniques for Self-Verification', *Proc. IEEE Test Conference*, pp 267–278, 1980.

Smith, J. E. 'Measures of the Effectiveness of Fault Signature Analysis', *IEEE Trans. Comput.*, **C29**, pp 510–514, 1980.

Tolkien, J. R. R. *The Lord of the Rings*, Allen and Unwin, 1955.

Williams, T. W. and Eichelberger, E. 'Random Patterns Within a Structured Sequential Logic Design', *Proc. Semiconductor Test Symposium*, pp 19–27, 1977.

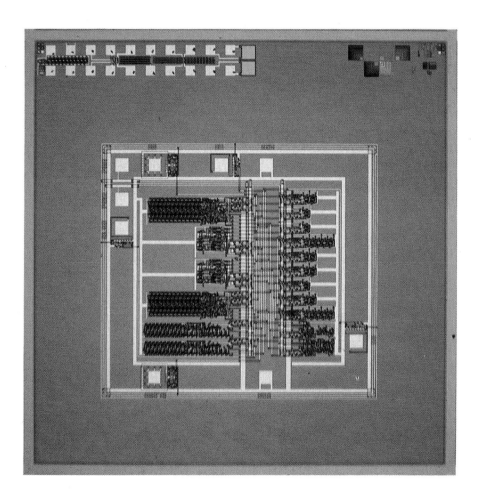

Plate 1   Photomicrograph of a FIRST compiled chip for the complex-to-magnitude problem (Chapter 1).

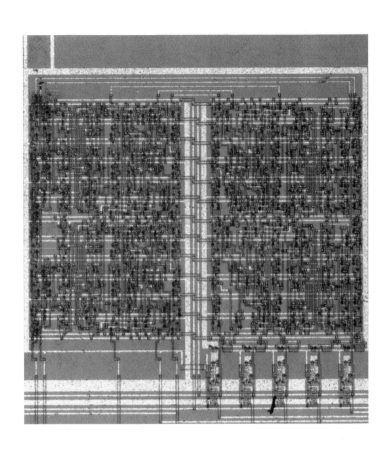

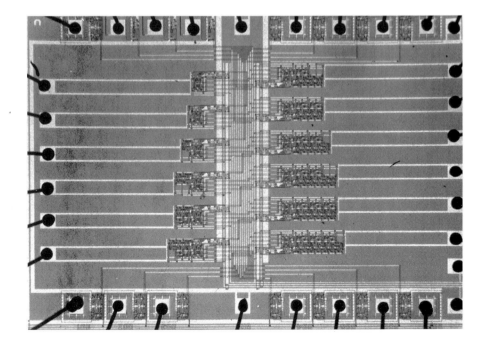

Plate 3 FIRST compiled FFT butterfly chip (Chapter 8).

Plate 2a Photomicrograph of an 8-bit MULTIPLY primitive including waterfront detail.

Plate 2b A primitive verification vehicle. This device tests differing compositions of the MULTIPLEX primitive corresponding to different latencies.

Plate 4   FIRST compiled layout for an adaptive LMS filter, featuring MULTIPLY and WORDDELAY primitives (Chapter 9).

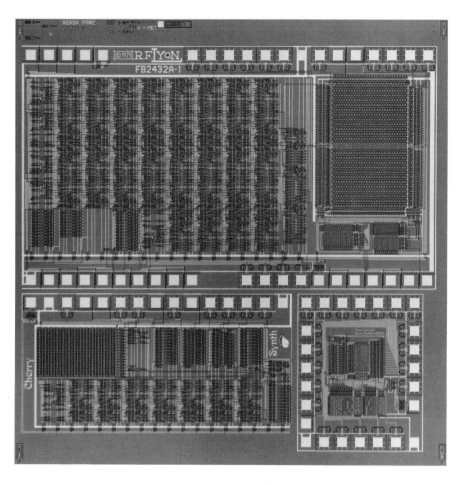

Plate 5   Lyon's 'Filters' chip is the upper part of this multi-project device (Chapter 11).

Plate 6 Lyon's 'SSP' chip (Chapter 12).

Plate 7 Wawryznek and Mead's chip integrating 10 UPEs (Chapter 13).

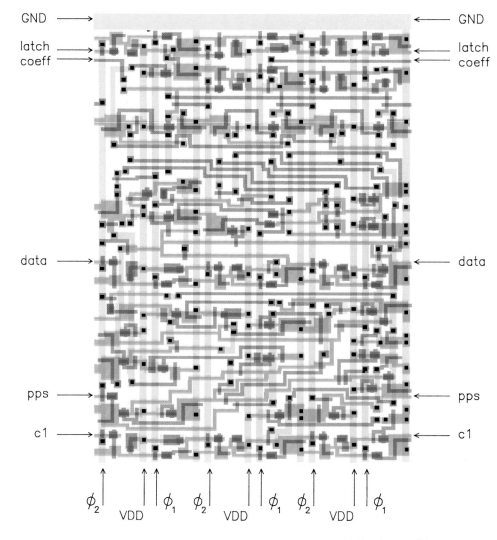

GND →   ← GND
latch →   ← latch
coeff →   ← coeff

data →   ← data

pps →   ← pps

c1 →   ← c1

ϕ_2 VDD ϕ_1 ϕ_2 VDD ϕ_1 ϕ_2 VDD ϕ_1

Plate 8   Layout of the principal leaf cell for the MULTIPLY primitive (Appendix).

Part 2
Case Studies

8

Fourier Transform Machines

Stewart G. Smith

Department of Electrical Engineering
University of Edinburgh

8.1   Introduction

As an introductory case study this chapter is somewhat more detailed than the
remaining studies. In part this reflects the importance of the Fourier transform,
in particular the Fast Fourier Transform (FFT), as a major field of application.
However, this chapter also offers some practical tuition on the use of FIRST
in constructing realistically large systems.

8.2   The Discrete Fourier Transform

The Discrete Fourier Transform (DFT) plays a significant role in the field of
spectral analysis, and is a common tool for mapping between time and
frequency domains in digital signal processing. The DFT transforms an N-
point sampled time series into an equivalent N-point frequency series.

Consider the k-th member of the output series, X(k). X(k) is constructed
by accumulating the element-by-element product of the input sequence x(n)
with the particular complex exponential weighting sequence which repeats
itself k times every N samples. In equation form, the value of the transform
X at the k-th frequency point, or 'bin', is given by:

$$X(k) = \sum_{n=0}^{N-1} x(n)e^{-j(2\pi/N)nk} \qquad\qquad 8.1$$

where both X(k) and x(n) are assumed periodic with period N (Rabiner and
Gold, 1975) and k ranges from 0 to N – 1. The factor $2\pi/N$ normalises the
argument of the complex exponential, allowing k to span (at discrete intervals)
the frequency range from zero up to, but not including, the sampling
frequency. The variable n represents time, and so the quantity nk represents
normalised angular displacement. As angles can be reduced modulo 2π, so can
normalised angles be reduced modulo N. The ability to reduce angles modulo
some sequence length is a cornerstone of the Fast Fourier Transform (FFT)
algorithm, as we shall see.

A unique property of the complex exponential function (of period N
samples) is that uniformly spaced samples form orthonormal sequences. Thus

the N complex exponential weighting sequences are mutually orthonormal over the transform length, and as such form the basis vectors of an N-dimensional transform space. The DFT consists of the projection of the input sequence on to each of these basis vectors. Alternatively, the DFT is the evaluation of the z-transform of the input sequence x(n) at N equally-spaced points on the unit circle in the complex plane. Whilst it is not absolutely necessary to absorb the underlying theory, the relevance of the unit circle to the DFT should not be missed.

Each complex exponential sequence may be realised by taking the unit vector in the complex plane, and repetitively rotating it by a constant angle until the N-point complex sequence has been generated. This process is carried out for the set of N different angles φ for which $N\varphi = 0$ modulo 2π. Any vector of unit length whose angle exhibits this property is an N-th root of unity. Then equation (8.1) can be expressed:

$$X(k) = \sum_{n=0}^{N-1} x(n)W_N^{nk} \qquad\qquad 8.2$$

where we take $W_N = \exp(-j2\pi/N)$ to be the principal N-th root of unity.[†] If we imagine the set of N-th roots of unity as forming the spokes of a wheel whose rim is the unit circle in the complex plane, then W is the clockwise neighbour to the spoke representing unity.

The input sequence to the DFT is assumed to consist of N rotating components, whose angular advances in one sample period (i.e. frequencies) correspond to the angles between the N wheel-spokes and unity. It is then periodic in N samples. Any component of normalised frequency k will be 'de-rotated' by the k-th complex exponential, and accumulation in the k-th bin will result in vector growth to a value proportional to the component.

Due to the orthogonality of the basis vectors, and the assumed orthogonality of the signal components, each signal component projects on to only one output bin. If the input signal is not periodic, it will contain components which project on to more than one basis vector, and the energy of such components will be distributed over several bins.

8.2.1   Some computational approaches to the DFT

To compute the DFT, we need only the operations of rotation and combination of vectors in the complex plane, which may be accomplished by complex multiplication and accumulation respectively. Computation of the DFT by straightforward means requires order (N^2) complex arithmetic operations (rotate-and-accumulates). This is equivalent to general matrix-vector multiplication. However, the DFT matrix may be factored in many ways, and if some combination is done before rotation, the amount of computation may be reduced.

[†] The reader should be aware of some inconsistency in the literature where the sign of the complex exponent is concerned. We follow the more usual convention $W_N = \exp(-j2\pi/N)$.

The Fast Fourier Transform (FFT) (Cooley and Tukey, 1965; Bergland, 1969) takes advantage of the properties of symmetry and periodicity of the DFT weights to reduce the computational complexity of the DFT to order(N log N).

Another class of DFT machines perform Number Theoretical Transforms (NTTs). These algorithms exploit number theoretical properties of either data or data addresses. The former class of algorithms treat data samples as elements in some finite computational structure, such as a field or a ring (McClellan and Rader, 1979). Hardware realisations make extensive use of residue arithmetic; for example Reed *et al.* (1983) detail a recent pipeline architecture for an NTT.

Examples of the latter algorithm class range from Rader's prime-length transform (Rader, 1968) to the Winograd Fourier Transform Algorithm (WFTA) (Winograd, 1978). The WFTA features a lower arithmetic complexity than the FFT, but at the expense of more complicated control arrangements. It is certainly a useful algorithm for computation of the DFT on mainframe computers, where complex data routing (still a matter of memory reads and writes) is almost free and multiplication is time-consuming. In VLSI, however, communication becomes a dominant algorithmic expense (Mead and Conway, 1980).

We restrict our studies to FFT and full DFT machines, staying within the mainstream of current systems implementation (Swartzlander and Hallnor, 1984; Linderman *et al.*, 1984). The first study consists of a full array realisation of a sixteen-point block FFT, using a constant geometry, decimation-in-time (DIT) radix-2 algorithm (Rabiner and Gold, 1975), but containing a hardwired shuffle to produce normally-ordered outputs. The use of multiplexing to reduce this machine to a single processor column is demonstrated, and partitioning issues are addressed to produce an optimised set of 4 chip types.

Next we describe a different multiplexing scheme, in the form of a radix-4, 64-point pipeline machine resembling that of McClellan and Purdy (1978) but with a shuffle network for output re-ordering. In contrast, our final study follows a modular, pipelined linear array architecture to compute the DFT as described by Allen (1984) after Kung (1980).

8.3 A DFT toolkit

It is normal design practice to specify from the top down, and implement from the bottom up. However, as this chapter serves to introduce the practical application of FIRST, we shall begin by creating some small modules which can be used later on to construct Fourier transform machines. This will necessarily lead to some 'acts of faith', as some computational elements are introduced before their theoretical background is discussed.

8.3.1 Vector rotation

It is clear from the preceding discussion that all Fourier transform machines require the operation of vector rotation. CORDIC (for Co-Ordinate Rotation DIgital Computer) hardware (Volder, 1959) is capable of either vector rotation or angle extraction, and has been used in the construction of FFT machines (Despain, 1974). However, being of iterative nature it is not well suited to bit-serial implementation.

The most common vector rotation element is the complex multiplier with unity-modulus coefficient. The FIRST primitive set outlined in Chapter 4 does not contain a complex multiplier *per se,* but its construction from real arithmetic elements is straightforward.

We need hardware to solve the following:

$$e + jf = (a+jb)(c+jd) \qquad\qquad 8.3$$

where $j^2 = -1$, i.e.

$$e = ac - bd, \qquad f = ad + bc \qquad\qquad 8.4$$

Equation (8.4) shows explicitly the requirements of complex multiplication using real arithmetic elements. We need four multipliers, an adder and a subtracter – all within the set of FIRST primitives. The code for this OPERATOR 'Xmult' is:

```
OPERATOR Xmult [coeff,lat] (cl -> clout) a, b, c, d -> e, f
!latency is (3*coeff) / 2 + 2 + lat, i.e. sum of multiplier and adder latencies

        SIGNAL ac, bd, ad, bc
        CONTROL cl1

        MULTIPLY [1,coeff,0,0] (cl -> cl1) a, c -> ac, NC
        MULTIPLY [1,coeff,0,0] (cl -> NC) b, d -> bd, NC
        MULTIPLY [1,coeff,0,0] (cl -> NC) a, d -> ad, NC
        MULTIPLY [1,coeff,0,0] (cl -> NC) b, c -> bc, NC
        SUBTRACT [lat,0,0,0] (cl1) ac, bd, GND -> e, NC
        ADD [lat,0,0,0] (cl1) ad, bc, GND -> f, NC

        CBITDELAY [lat] (cl1 -> clout)

END
```

This code declares an OPERATOR whose external input signal nodes a, b, c and d correspond to the initial variables of the right-hand side of equation (8.3); the elementary variables for the calculations. The external output signal nodes e and f represent the left-hand side of equation (8.3), which we wish to evaluate in terms of a, b, c and d. The internal signal nodes (ac, bd, etc.), on the other hand, are the intermediate terms in equations (8.4). We need neither remember how a complex multiplier works after we design it, nor have further dealings with internal nodes. These details are hidden in the hierarchy. We had a problem (equation 8.3), and now have a functional element (OPERATOR Xmult) to solve it.

The only significant feature of Xmult, apart from its function, is its latency; the time delay in bits between inputs and outputs. When Xmult is used at a higher design level, its latency must be known. It is good practice to include the latency in a 'comment'.

For future flexibility we have parameterised the coefficient wordlength used in the various multipliers, and the latency of the adder and subtracter. This allows the resolution and hence the accuracy of the vector rotator to be varied, while the adder latency may control its overall latency. We do not anticipate using the input predelay option, so all predelays are set to zero.

Control for the adder and subtracter is derived from one of the multipliers (the multiplier outputs control as well as data). The multiplier control output is further delayed to achieve synchronous control and data outputs from the OPERATOR. Figure 8.1 shows the flow-graph for Xmult.

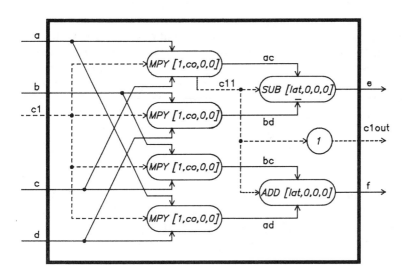

Fig. 8.1 Complex Multiplication OPERATOR 'Xmult'.

A better complex multiplier?

The components of Xmult are capable of generating the sum of one product pair and the difference of another. We have created a complex multiplier by cross-wiring the inputs. Just as the FFT uses the commonality of coefficients to make computational savings over the DFT by combining before rotating, so it is possible to perform addition before multiplication to reduce the number of real multiplies in the complex multiplier.

Using the commonality property, equation (8.3) may be expanded as:

$$e + jf = (ac-bd) + j((a+b)(c+d)-ac-bd)$$

or

$$e + jf = a(c+d) - d(a+b) + j(a(c+d)-c(a-b))$$

(Golub's method), or in the more specific case where $c = \cos\theta$ and $d = \sin\theta$ (vector rotation),

$$e + jf = (1+\cos\theta)(a-b\tan(\theta/2))-b + j((1+\cos\theta)(a-b\tan(\theta/2))\tan(\theta/2)+a)$$

(Buneman's method (Despain, 1974)).

Each expression involves only three multiplies, and five (Golub) or three (Buneman) add/subtracts. In terms of silicon area, these seem to be more attractive options. However, there are penalties to be paid for these savings.

Firstly multiplier coefficients have been allowed to exceed unity; some extra shifting must be incorporated to re-align products. Initial addition causes words to grow by one bit, causing loss of coefficient resolution which can only be regained by increasing the size and latency of the multipliers. The same loss (of a bit) applies to the data, and thus the system wordlength must be increased by one bit to compensate. Finally we must include some control delay primitives, as we cannot derive control output from an adder. These features make the three-multiplier rotators somewhat less attractive in this case.

The best of all solutions is to engineer a dedicated complex multiplier primitive. Murray *et al.* (1984) report an example of a bit-serial, modular design. Here advantage is taken of commonality of coefficients to produce a compact linear array complex multiplier, cascadable to any desired coefficient size.

8.3.2   Short DFT machines

Another building block common to most Fourier transform machines is the short DFT. This is used in the construction of 'butterflies' of various radix (Rabiner and Gold, 1975). A radix-2 butterfly, so called because of its conventional graphic representation (Figure 8.2), realises either:

$$v = y + wx \qquad \text{and} \qquad u = y - wx$$

if decimating in time (DIT), or

$$v = y + x \qquad \text{and} \qquad u = w(y-x)$$

if decimating in frequency (DIF) (Rabiner and Gold, 1975).

Here y and x are complex inputs, v and u are complex outputs, and w is a complex weight of unity magnitude, known as a 'twiddle factor' (Gentleman and Sande, 1966) – realisable using OPERATOR Xmult. Decimation in time (or frequency) is so called because the input (or output) sequence is split into R sub-sequences of 1/R times the original length in the process of replacing an N-point transform by R of length N/R, R being the machine radix (Rabiner and Gold, 1975). We discuss this later.

The radix-2 butterfly performs a 2-point DFT, with a twiddle (or vector

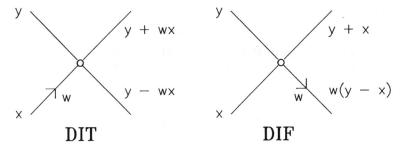

Fig. 8.2   Radix-2 DIT and DIF butterfly representations.

rotation) carried out on either the lower input (if DIT), or lower output (if DIF), leg. We have seen that an N-point DFT requires the generation of N distinct, equally-spaced unit vectors in the complex plane (recall the wheel-spokes analogy). Here N = 2, and the vectors are simply 1 and –1. Thus no multipliers are required for a 2-point DFT. We need only add

$$e + jf = (a + c) + j(b + d)$$

and subtract

$$g + jh = (a - c) + j(b - d)$$

the two complex data inputs. Once again, we need to implement some complex arithmetic elements – call them 'Xadd' and 'Xsub'. Figure 8.3 shows OPERATOR Xadd.

OPERATOR Xadd [lat] (c1) a, c, b, d –> e, f
!latency is lat

        ADD [lat,0,0,0] (c1) a, c, GND –> e, NC
        ADD [lat,0,0,0] (c1) b, d, GND –> f, NC

END

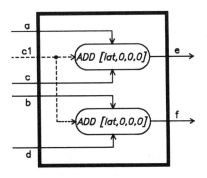

Fig. 8.3   Complex Addition OPERATOR 'Xadd'.

OPERATOR Xsub [lat] (c1) a, c, b, d –> g, h
!latency is lat

      SUBTRACT [lat,0,0,0] (c1) a, c, GND –> g, NC
      SUBTRACT [lat,0,0,0] (c1) b, d, GND –> h, NC

END

We can now design a 2-point DFT machine, and call it 'Dft2' (Figure 8.4):

OPERATOR Dft2 [lat] (c1) a, c, b, d –> e, g, f, h
!latency is lat

      Xadd [lat] (c1) a, c, b, d –> e, f
      Xsub [lat] (c1) a, c, b, d –> g, h

END

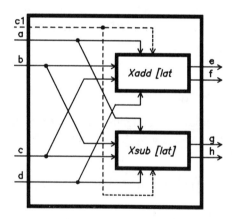

Fig. 8.4 2-point DFT OPERATOR 'Dft2'.

Here we have used the same parameter and node names in the declarations as in the instantiations. FIRST does not require this – however, it helps to clarify the mapping of 'algorithm' into FIRST source code. We leave the simulation of Dft2 until later.

Butterflies of any radix normally have twiddle-free top legs. Data on this leg must be delayed to compensate for the latency of any twiddles. Before constructing a radix-2 butterfly, we encapsulate Xmult and some delay to make a time-aligned twiddling block called 'Twiddle2', shown in Figure 8.5. The expression for compdel derives from the latency formulae for multiplier and adder in Xmult.

OPERATOR Twiddle2 [coeff,lat] (c1 –> c1o) rin1, rin2, iin1, iin2, wre,
              wim –> rout1, rout2, iout1, iout2
!latency is compdel (see CONSTANT declaration below)

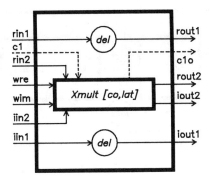

Fig. 8.5 Radix-2 twiddling OPERATOR 'Twiddle2'.

CONSTANT compdel = (3 * coeff)/2 + 2 + lat

BITDELAY [compdel] rin1 –> rout1
BITDELAY [compdel] iin1 –> iout1
Xmult [coeff,lat] (c1 –> c1o) rin2, iin2, wre, wim –> rout2, iout2

END

It is now possible to construct both DIT and DIF radix-2 butterflies; called 'Rad2Dit' (Figure 8.6) and 'Rad2Dif' (Figure 8.7) respectively:

OPERATOR Rad2Dit [coeff,lat1,lat2] (c1) rin1, rin2, iin1, iin2, wre,
            wim –> rout1, rout2, iout1, iout2
!latency is compdel (see CONSTANT declaration in Twiddle2) + lat2

    SIGNAL r1, r2, i1, i2
    CONTROL c11

    Twiddle2 [coeff,lat1] (c1 –> c11) rin1, rin2, iin1, iin2, wre, wim –> r1,
        r2,i1, i2
    Dft2 [lat2] (c11) r1, r2, i1, i2 –> rout1, rout2, iout1, iout2

END

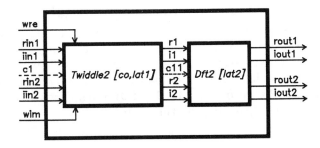

Fig. 8.6 Radix-2 DIT butterfly OPERATOR 'Rad2Dit'.

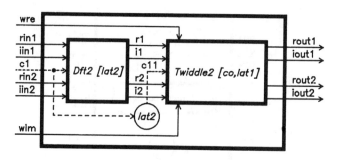

Fig. 8.7   Radix-2 DIF butterfly OPERATOR 'Rad2Dif'.

OPERATOR Rad2Dif [coeff,lat1,lat2] (c1) rin1, rin2, iin1, iin2, wre,
            wim –> rout1, rout2, iout1, iout2
!latency is lat2 + compdel (see CONSTANT declaration in Twiddle2)

    SIGNAL r1, r2, i1, i2
    CONTROL c11

    Dft2 [lat2] (c1) rin1, rin2, iin1, iin2 –> r1, r2, i1, i2
    Twiddle2 [coeff,lat1] (c11 –> NC) r1, r2, i1, i2, wre, wim –> rout1,
        rout2, iout1, iout2

    CBITDELAY [lat2] (c1 -> c11)

END

These OPERATORS have time-aligned inputs and outputs (see Chapter 6). Whilst this makes them conceptually easier to handle later on in the design process, they contain delays which may impair their efficiency. It may be desirable to optimise these elements for a particular design.

Notice that we require a CBITDELAY in Rad2Dif, as we cannot take advantage of a control output from Dft2. Also the CBITDELAY primitive in Xmult is redundant here – a penalty of time-aligning.

8.3.3   A radix-4 DFT

The radix-2 machine Dft2 performs a parallel DFT on 2 points of complex data. It requires no multipliers because internal rotations are through 0 and 180 degrees only, which can be accomplished by adding and subtracting. The step to a radix-4 butterfly, which involves angular shifts of 0, 90, 180 and 270 degrees – none of which require multipliers – is a logical one. Furthermore, we can build a 2×2 array of Dft2 OPERATORS to implement 'Dft4', a little 4-point FFT machine. This is depicted in Figure 8.8.

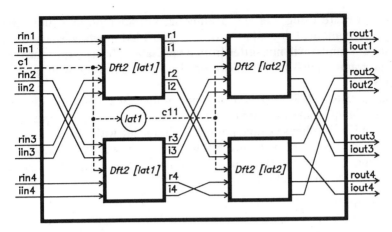

Fig. 8.8 4-point DFT OPERATOR 'Dft4'.

OPERATOR Dft4 [lat1,lat2] (c1) rin1 THROUGH 4, iin1 THROUGH 4 –
      –> rout1 THROUGH 4, iout1 THROUGH 4
! latency is lat1 + lat2

      SIGNAL r1 THROUGH 4, i1 THROUGH 4
      CONTROL c11

      Dft2 [lat1] (c1) rin1, rin3, iin1, iin3 –> r1, r2, i1, i2
      Dft2 [lat1] (c1) rin2, rin4, iin2, iin4 –> r3, r4, i3, i4
      Dft2 [lat2] (c11) r1, r3, i1, i3 –> rout1, rout3, iout1, iout3
      Dft2 [lat2] (c11) r2, i4, i2, r4 –> rout2, rout4, iout4, iout2

      CBITDELAY [lat1] (c1 –> c11)

END

Note the use of the shorthand THROUGH statement (Chapter 3) to avoid naming long node lists explicitly. The delays lat1 and lat2 are parameterised for the present, and the required control delay is built in to synchronise the second column of processors. The tortuous routing around the last Dft2 operator is to effect a premultiplication by –j, an internal 'twiddle' in the 4-point FFT machine.

Simulation
The structure has now become sufficiently complicated to merit simulation. We must create a simulation environment for Dft4. This entails creation of a SYSTEM containing a CHIP with Dft4 connected to a CONTROLGENERATOR primitive, and of course the inputs and outputs of Dft4 connected to pads.

Here we are using 'perfect' arithmetic, i.e. addition and subtraction, in which no numerical degradation occurs (provided overflow is avoided), and the input samples will not suffer from quantisation, being either zero or some constant amplitude. Therefore we need not be concerned with quantisation effects.

The OPERATOR Dft4 is a 4-point parallel DFT machine. Let us input parallel signal blocks of length 4 samples, containing single frequencies of 0, $\pi/2$, π and $3\pi/2$ radians/sample period, each starting with zero phase, and with some space between. In Figure 8.9 we see the response to each frequency appearing only in the correct single output wire (or bin), and the four distinct phases of each sample block.

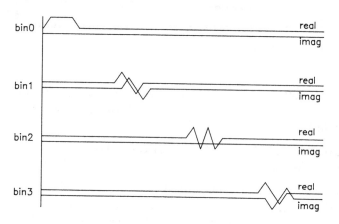

Fig. 8.9   Simulation of 'Dft4', showing complex amplitude response to stimulus at distinct output frequencies.

8.3.4   A radix-4 butterfly

To construct a radix-4 butterfly, we must add twiddles, just as in the case of radix-2. All but the top leg of the butterfly contain twiddles. Here we require a block of 3 Xmult operators and the compensating delays for the top (untwiddled) wire. We already have the components for this – Twiddle2 and Xmult. So the code for 'Twiddle4' (Figure 8.10) is:

```
OPERATOR Twiddle4 [coeff,lat] (c1 -> c1o) rin1 THROUGH 4,
        iin1 THROUGH 4, wre1 THROUGH 3, wim1 THROUGH 3 -> -
        rout1 THROUGH 4, iout1 THROUGH 4
!latency is constdel (as defined in Xmult) + lat

        Twiddle2 [coeff,lat] (c1 -> NC) rin1, rin2, iin1, iin2, wre1, wim1 -> -
                rout1, rout2, iout1, iout2
        Xmult [coeff,lat] (c1 -> c1o) rin3, iin3, wre2, wim2 -> rout3, iout3
        Xmult [coeff,lat] (c1 -> NC) rin4, iin4, wre3, wim3 -> rout4, iout4

END
```

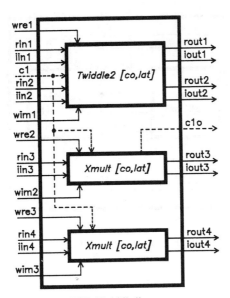

Fig. 8.10 Radix-4 twiddling OPERATOR 'Twiddle4'.

and 'Rad4Dif' (Figure 8.11) follows on easily:

OPERATOR Rad4Dif [coeff,lat1,lat2,lat3] (c1 –> c1o) rin1 THROUGH 4,
     iin1 THROUGH 4, wre1 THROUGH 3, wim1 THROUGH 3 –> –
     rout1 THROUGH 4, iout1 THROUGH 4
!latency is constdel (as defined in Xmult) + lat2

     SIGNAL r1 THROUGH 4, i1 THROUGH 4
     CONTROL c11

     Dft4 [lat2,lat3] (c1) rin1 THROUGH 4, iin1 THROUGH 4 –> –
       r1 THROUGH 4, i1 THROUGH 4
     Twiddle4 [coeff,lat1] (c11 –> NC) r1 THROUGH 4, i1 THROUGH 4,
       wre1 THROUGH 3, wim1 THROUGH 3 –> –
       rout1 THROUGH 4, iout1 THROUGH 4

     CBITDELAY [lat2 + lat3] (c1 –> c11)

END

'Rad4Dit' is constructed by cascading the two components of Rad4Dif in
reverse order.

8.3.5 Windowing

The DFT operates on blocks of data. A block of data can be imagined as an
infinite time series pointwise multiplied with a unit rectangular window
function, that is a function which is zero outside some range, else unity. Since

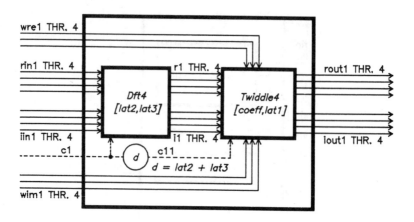

Fig. 8.11   Radix-4 DIF butterfly OPERATOR 'Rad4Dif'.

pointwise multiplication in the time-domain is equivalent to convolution in the frequency-domain (Rabiner and Gold, 1975), we find that the DFT output is convolved with the spectrum of a rectangular window, whose amplitude function is of the sin(x)/x type (Harris, 1978). Although it has value zero at all discrete observation frequencies, and accordingly does not affect on-bin components, this function has a symmetrical series of off-axis peaks (sidelobes).

A related problem in analysis of finite length sequences is that any signal components which are not periodic in the block length exhibit discontinuities at the boundaries of the observation, resulting in what is known as 'spectral leakage'. When a non-periodic component is convolved with the window spectrum, the result is a spread of energy over the range of bins. The normal solution to this problem is to window the input sequence with some function whose sidelobe behaviour in the frequency domain improves on that of the rectangular window.

All window design is an application-dependent compromise. Harris (1978) summarised many of the alternatives, and Nuttall (1983) reduced the design criteria to two parameters – sidelobe decay and mainlobe to peak-sidelobe ratio.

For now we will consider the design of a programmable window processor – we can worry about window functions later. The twiddles preceding the first column are trivial in the case of a DIT FFT, and non-existent in the case of DIF, so we can take advantage of this by building in the window multipliers instead of the twiddles. The window function has identical weights for real and imaginary signal components, leading to some sharing of coefficients. All that is required is a real weighting OPERATOR 'Xweight2' (Figure 8.12) which performs four real multiplications with two shared coefficients on two complex data points:

OPERATOR Xweight2 [wcoeff] (c1 -> c1o) rin1, rin2, iin1, iin2, w1,
          w2 -> rout1, rout2, iout1, iout2
!latency is 3/2 * wcoeff + 2

    MULTIPLY [1,wcoeff,0,0] (c1 -> c1o) rin1, w1 -> rout1, NC
    MULTIPLY [1,wcoeff,0,0] (c1 -> NC) rin2, w2 -> rout2, NC
    MULTIPLY [1,wcoeff,0,0] (c1 -> NC) iin1, w1 -> iout1, NC
    MULTIPLY [1,wcoeff,0,0] (c1 -> NC) iin2, w2 -> iout2, NC

END

Again we defer simulation – the effects of window type, quantisation, etc., can only be properly studied in the context of a real system simulation. The first-column processor 'Window2' will consist of Xweight2 and Dft2 in cascade:

OPERATOR Window2 [wcoeff,lat] (c1) rin1, rin2, iin1, iin2, w1,
          w2 -> rout1, rout2, iout1, iout2
!latency is 3/2 * wcoeff + 2 + lat

    SIGNAL r1, r2, i1, i2
    CONTROL c11

    Xweight2 [wcoeff] (c1 -> c11) rin1, rin2, iin1, iin2, w1, w2 -> r1, r2,
        i1, i2
    Dft2 [lat] (c11) r1, r2, i1, i2 -> rout1, rout2, iout1, iout2

END

The OPERATORs Window2 (not illustrated) and Rad2Dit are functionally dissimilar, but topologically identical.

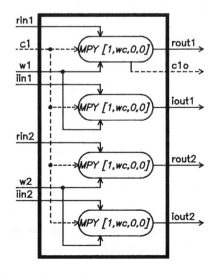

Fig. 8.12 Weighting OPERATOR 'Xweight2'.

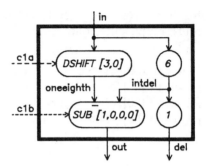

Fig. 8.13   7/8 scaling OPERATOR 'SevenEighths'.

8.3.6   Complex-to-magnitude conversion

In many cases only the magnitude output of an FFT processor is required. The magnitude of a complex number is the root of the sum of the squares of its components. There exist many approximation algorithms, summarised by Filip (1976), the simplest of which has already been introduced in Chapters 1 and 3. We structure the OPERATOR to show explicitly how the fraction 7/8 is realised. OPERATOR SevenEighths (Figure 8.13) is the time-aligned

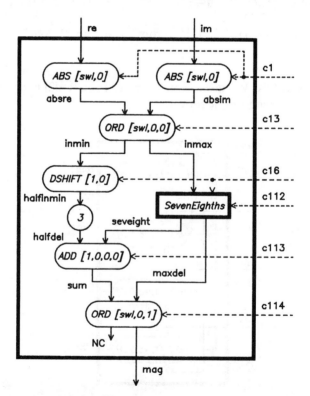

Fig. 8.14   OPERATOR 'ComplexToMagnitude'.

component which executes the 7/8 function. The two BITDELAYs compensate for the latencies of the DSHIFT and SUBTRACT primitives.

OPERATOR SevenEighths (c1a, c1b) in -> out, del
!latency is 7

    SIGNAL oneeighth, intdel

    DSHIFT [3,0] (c1a) in -> oneeighth
    SUBTRACT [1,0,0,0] (c1b) intdel, oneeighth, GND -> out, NC
    BITDELAY [6] in -> intdel
    BITDELAY [1] intdel -> del

END

The full OPERATOR ComplexToMagnitude (Figure 8.14) contains OPERATOR SevenEighths. Note that use has been made of input predelay in the final ORDER primitive, allowing time aligning of SevenEighths outputs at no expense in waterfront. ComplexToMagnitude is an example of an OPERATOR which contains a mixture of elements at the same level and at the adjacent lower level in the hierarchy. FIRST allows infinite nesting of those levels of hierarchy (OPERATOR and SUBSYSTEM) which have no direct physical significance.

OPERATOR ComplexToMagnitude [swl] (c1, c13, c16, c112, c113, c114) re,
                                     im -> mag
!latency is 3 * swl + 17

    SIGNAL absre, absim, inmax, inmin, halfinmin, seveight, sum,
           maxdel, halfdel
    ABSOLUTE [swl,0] (c1) re -> absre
    ABSOLUTE [swl,0] (c1) im -> absim
    ORDER [swl,0,0] (c13) absre, absim -> inmax, inmin
    DSHIFT [1,0] (c16) inmin -> halfinmin
    ADD [1,0,0,0] (c113) seveight, halfdel, GND -> sum, NC
    SevenEighths (c16,c112) inmax -> seveight, maxdel
    BITDELAY [3] halfinmin -> halfdel
    ORDER [swl,0,1] (c114) sum, maxdel -> mag, NC

END

Simulation
We use the ComplexToMagnitude OPERATOR to evaluate the amplitude of a complex signal. We input a signal of the form $\exp(-(a + jb)t)$, where $a < 1$. This signal consists of a complex sinusoid with an amplitude envelope $\exp(-at)$, which we may extract with ComplexToMagnitude. Figure 8.15 shows the result. Note the delay in response due to the OPERATOR latency.

With this addition to the toolkit, we may consider it complete enough to start looking at some DFT systems.

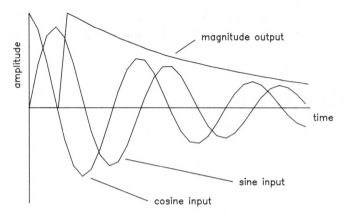

Fig. 8.15 Simulation of 'ComplexToMagnitude', showing response to a decaying complex exponential input.

8.4   FFT machines

For tutorial purposes, we commenced design in a bottom up manner; now we shall start to specify systems from the top down. The DFT toolkit is ready for the construction of an actual FFT machine. We have a vector rotator, and radix-2 and 4 DFT machines, which may be used to build the butterflies which are germane to the FFT computation. We also have windowing and magnitude conversion blocks for front and back end processing.

Before we can build an FFT machine, however, we must know a little more about the operation of the FFT. Those readers who are already familiar with the FFT, or indeed those who don't wish to be, may skip the next section. Alternative derivations and explanations abound in the literature (see References).

8.4.1   Indexing and shuffling in the FFT

It is instructive to investigate two types of shuffling transformation which occur naturally in the FFT. The first is the ideal, or perfect shuffle (Stone, 1971). A radix R, order M perfect shuffle σ_M has the effect of interleaving elements of a data sequence of length $N = R^M$ in such a manner as to bring together elements spaced apart by P samples, where $P = N/R = R^{M-1}$. The second shuffle is the digit reversing shuffle – the result of repeated application of M perfect shuffles of descending order.

Having defined R as a radix,[†] we may index data sequences in terms of R, giving an M-digit index. These shuffles serve to transform the indices of data sequences – the latter in a rather obvious manner. The effect of a perfect shuffle of order m is to circular left-shift the m least-significant digits of the index (Stone, 1971). Note that significance, or weight, of digits remains constant throughout transforms.

[†] Here R is constant throughout the transform, although mixed-radix transforms are possible (Rabiner and Gold, 1975).

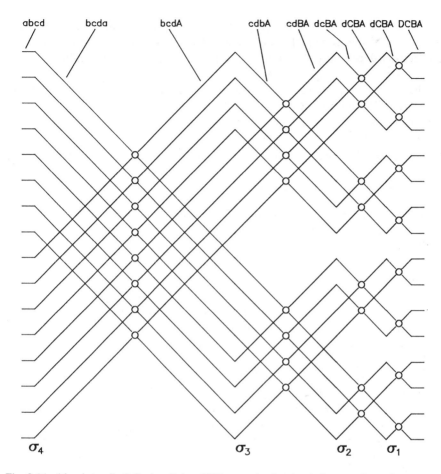

Fig. 8.16 16-point radix-2 Cooley–Tukey FFT network, showing index transformations across the array.

Figure 8.16 shows a network for computing the Cooley–Tukey FFT (Cooley and Tukey, 1965), with R = 2 and M = 4. The key property of this network is that each point in the input sequence is able to communicate through a radix-R, depth-M tree structure with each point in the output sequence. We refer to this property as 'universal connectivity'.

Digit reversal
Although the input sequence is correctly ordered, the topology of the network effectively perfect shuffles the sequence, bringing together elements spaced apart by P = 8 samples into groups of R = 2 before the first column of the machine. After the first column, we have R groups of P/R samples, which are in turn perfect shuffled by the network topology. The order of the perfect shuffle here is one less than before. The effect on the data index of repeated, decreasing order perfect shuffles at the column interfaces is shown along the top of Figure 8.16.

It is important to note that the digit reversing shuffle inherent in the FFT is a result of the universal connectivity of the network, and nothing else. If correctly ordered output is required, a further digit reversing shuffle must be performed at some stage in the transform.

The butterflies have no topological effect (they are horizontally symmetrical), and only serve to alter the interpretation of the stage digit from time to frequency indexing (see lower and upper case letters in Figure 8.16). Each butterfly carries out a local R-point DFT on a time sub-sequence, summing over the stage digit, for all combinations of the other digits.

8.4.2   The Cooley–Tukey FFT algorithm

So far we have described a network which offers a constant, minimum length path from any input point to any output point, given a radix R. We have yet to implement the arithmetic which occurs in the nodes and branches of the network, although we hinted at its function.

The FFT can be described in theory as successively fracturing one-dimensional sequences into equivalent two-dimensional sequences (Gold and Bially, 1973). This can be done in several ways, the two most common of which are decimation in time (DIT) and in frequency (DIF) (Rabiner and Gold, 1975). As we develop the two algorithms below, their similarity will become obvious.

Either DIT or DIF algorithms may be implemented on the network of Figure 8.16. A right-to-left mirror image of Figure 8.16 will produce correctly ordered output from digit-reversed input, again using either DIT or DIF. The algorithms and topologies merely decide the location and value of twiddle factors. The networks exhibit isomorphism (they are all different layouts of the same radix-R, universally connective tree structure). From a functional point of view they are identical.

Using the shorthand notation

$$z'_m = \sum_{i=0}^{m} R^i z_i$$

we index the input series $x(n)$ and output series $X(k)$ with

$$n = \sum_{m=0}^{M-1} R^m d_m = d'_{M-1} \qquad k = \sum_{m=0}^{M-1} R^m c_m = c'_{M-1}$$

With this indexing notation in mind, we may now develop the FFT algorithm. We start with the DFT equation:

$$X(k) = \sum_{n=0}^{N-1} x(n) W_N^{nk}$$

Expressing n in terms of its component digits d_m allows splitting of the summation into M sums, each over R terms.

$$X(k) = \sum_{d_0=0}^{R-1} \sum_{d_1=0}^{R-1} \ldots \sum_{d_{M-1}=0}^{R-1} x(n) W_N^{nk} \qquad\qquad 8.5$$

The advantage in splitting into a nest of sums over R terms is that, if a rotation factor can be found which is periodic in R, the basic computational unit at each network node can be realised by an R-point DFT machine, which we have already seen to be a fast and compact unit (at least for R = 2 and 4). The mechanism of the FFT algorithm may now be revealed, as we manipulate the W term.

As a completely general algorithm development would lead to some rather unwieldy expressions, we shall develop the DIT and DIF algorithms in parallel. In the text, references to variables will appear in the form DIT {DIF}. Equations are in pairs, DIT first.

First of all we separate the component digits of n {k}.

$$W_N^{nk} = W_N^{d_0k} W_N^{Rd_1k} \ldots W_N^{R^{M-1}d_{M-1}k}$$

$$W_N^{nk} = W_N^{R^{M-1}c_{M-1}n} W_N^{R^{M-2}c_{M-2}n} \ldots W_N^{c_0n}$$

then we use the periodicity property to cancel powers of R in the exponent of W at each stage, thereby 'coarsening' its angular range where possible.

$$W_N^{nk} = W_N^{d_0k} W_{R^{M-1}}^{d_1k} \ldots W_R^{d_{M-1}k}$$

$$W_N^{nk} = W_R^{c_{M-1}n} W_{R^2}^{c_{M-2}n} \ldots W_N^{c_0n}$$

Next we resolve k {n} into its component digits, noting that only those digits whose weight is less than the periodicity of W are effectively non-zero (again due to the periodicity property):

$$W_N^{nk} = W_N^{d_0c'_{M-1}} W_{R^{M-1}}^{d_1c'_{M-2}} \ldots W_R^{d_{M-1}c'_0}$$

$$W_N^{nk} = W_R^{c_{M-1}d_0} W_{R^2}^{c_{M-2}d_1} \ldots W_N^{c_0d'_{M-1}}$$

and finally we separate terms involving d {c} into a part which is periodic in R, and a part which isn't:

$$W_N^{nk} = W_R^{d_0c_{M-1}} W_N^{d_0c'_{M-2}} W_R^{d_1c_{M-2}} W_{R^{M-1}}^{d_1c'_{M-3}} \ldots W_R^{d_{M-1}c_0}$$

$$W_N^{nk} = W_R^{c_{M-1}d_0} W_{R^2}^{c_{M-2}d'_0} W_R^{c_{M-2}d_1} \ldots W_N^{c_0\, d'_{M-2}} W_R^{c_0d_{M-1}} \qquad 8.6$$

Substituting equation (8.6) into equation (8.5) gives the DIT expression

$$X(k) = \sum_{d_0=0}^{R-1} W_R^{d_0c_{M-1}} W_N^{d_0c'_{M-2}} \sum_{d_1=0}^{R-1} W_R^{d_1c_{M-2}} W_{R^{M-1}}^{d_1c'_{M-3}} \ldots \sum_{d_{M-1}=0}^{R-1} x(n)W_R^{d_{M-1}c_0}$$
$$\qquad 8.7$$

and the DIF expression

$$X(k) = \sum_{d_0=0}^{R-1} W_R^{c_{M-1}d_0} W_{R^2}^{c_{M-2}d'_0} \sum_{d_1=1}^{R-1} W_R^{c_{M-2}d_1} \ldots W_N^{c_0d'_{M-2}} \sum_{d_{M-1}=0}^{R-1} x(n)W_R^{c_0d_{M-1}}$$
$$\qquad 8.8$$

The reader should attempt to establish a link between these equations and the topology of the FFT network. At each stage of the machine, a summation is performed over the associated index digit. This summation is performed for all combinations of the other digits, leading to an N/R by M array of processors. Each butterfly column effectively transforms the interpretation of the stage digit from the time domain to the frequency domain. As butterfly inputs and outputs are characterised by the stage digit, the 'span' of each column, i.e. the distance between these elements, equals the weight of the stage digit.

The rotation factors which are not periodic in R are the twiddle factors employed in network branches of the transform. Those which are periodic in R serve to complete the DFT definitions, whose necessity was underlined earlier. Wherever d $\{c\} = 0$, the twiddle factor corresponds to a multiplication by unity, and is omitted – hence the twiddle free input {output} top leg on all butterflies.

Whatever the geometry used, any twiddle factor may be evaluated by tracing connections to any elements in transform input and output sequences, and evaluating at the relevant stage in equation (8.7) {(8.8)}. Finally, note that both transforms render twiddle factors unnecessary outside the DFT columns – a fact which is often overlooked in the literature.

8.4.3   The constant-geometry algorithm

Many other topologies exist to satisfy the needs of FFT users. Constant geometry algorithms (Rabiner and Gold, 1975) allow one column of processors to be repeated across the array, thus allowing a standard part (whether a chip or a circuit board) to be used throughout the transform. The cost of this modular approach is the inclusion of trivial rotations by W^0 before the first (in DIT realisations) or after the last (in DIF) column, or some extra control and switching circuitry for their obviation.

To implement a constant-geometry algorithm, we must ensure that the spacing between elements in sequences (i.e. span) remains constant across the array. This may be achieved by including an order-M perfect shuffle after each stage. Figure 8.17 (a) and (b) illustrates (explicitly and implicitly) the right-hand side of one such stage, showing the action of the perfect shuffle. Spans are increased by a factor of R, which cancels the reduction by R inherent in the Cooley–Tukey FFT. The effect on DIT twiddles is merely to perfect shuffle them as well – this has the beneficial effect of ordering them correctly down the columns (cf. digit reversal in the Cooley–Tukey DIT FFT).

Note that in this network M extra shuffles are performed. They have no overall effect, as this corresponds to a complete circular shift of the index back to its original state. Given N and R, all FFT networks are isomorphous and differ only in the employment of twiddles and shuffles throughout. For instance, normally-ordered output can be produced from the mirror image of the network implied by Figure 8.17, if the input sequence index is digit-reversed. The perfect shuffles of the network, both inherent (for universal connectivity) and additional (for constant geometry), are in this case inverse shuffles, or 'unshuffles'.

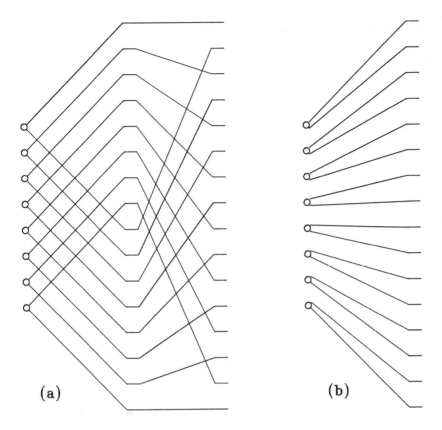

Fig. 8.17   Right-hand side of constant-geometry FFT stage, showing (a) explicitly and (b) implicitly the action of the additional order-M perfect shuffle.

We now have the tools and the knowledge to proceed with the design of an FFT machine.

8.5   The full array FFT machine

Our first exercise is a 16-point full array FFT machine with programmable input data windowing, implemented on the inverse constant-geometry network just described and operating on 12-bit data words. We include a hard-wired shuffle on the inputs, and arrange for the output of the machine to appear in magnitude form.

The heart of an N-point FFT machine may be represented at the highest level by a block with N time-domain inputs and N frequency-domain outputs. However, the input signal is normally a word-stream (e.g. the output from an A/D converter), and so we employ a corner-turning memory to load a block of N samples, and output each sample on its own wire (or wire pair if the input signal is complex). Although the inverse of this process can be performed on the transformer output, converting N parallel words into a block of N contiguous frequency-domain samples on one wire, we choose to leave the transform output in word-parallel form. Figure 8.18 shows the high level system plan.

The corner-turning memory has not been studied as part of our methodology, but it is clear that this is no more than a sophisticated input primitive. The corner-turning memory is the word-stream equivalent of a serial-to-parallel converter (SIPO) acting on a bit-stream. Garverick and Pierce (1983) report the design of such a memory. For the purpose of this study we restrict ourselves to the main computational engine.

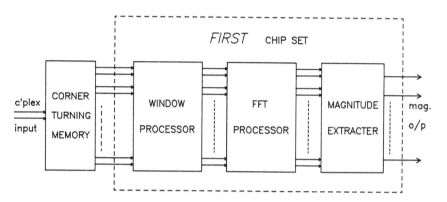

Fig. 8.18   High-level system plan of parallel FFT machine.

8.5.1   Preliminary architectural decisions

We wish to realise a 16-point FFT machine, containing a minimal number of different chip types. For the purpose of simulation, we shall create notional chips for generation of constants (window coefficients and twiddle factors – see below), and for the input corner-turning memory. The heart of the machine, in slightly expanded form, will consist of an array of 8 by 4 radix-2 'butterfly' processors. The 16-point complex output will feed a column of complex-to-magnitude converters.

As we saw earlier, twiddle factors in the first column are not required, and the correspondingly reduced butterfly can be combined with the windowing coefficients and the data shuffling to form a first-column processor. The remaining three columns then consist of regularly connected butterfly processors. The block diagram for the target system is detailed in Figure 8.19.

Word ranges and precisions
Due to the additions and subtractions inherent in the butterfly, word growth occurs in the FFT as computation proceeds across the array. As this array consists of 4 columns, we need 4 guard bits on top of our system wordlength to accommodate word growth. This is a simpler approach, although one very slightly inferior in terms of noise performance, to any form of truncation within the process (Oppenheim and Weinstein, 1972). We also must observe the

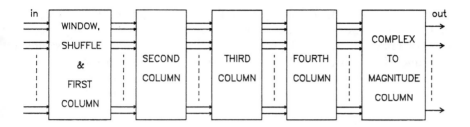

Fig. 8.19   Block diagram of parallel FFT machine.

requirement for the customary 2 guard bits in the data input to all multipliers, which ensure their correct operation.

The fact that the final butterfly stage follows the final multiplier in the data path allows us to 'steal' one of the two guard bits, potentially reducing the system wordlength swl by one bit. Although the magnitude converter can cause growth by one bit, given full-scale signals on both real and imaginary inputs, we feel that this is a sufficiently unlikely situation to warrant an extra bit of system wordlength. Thus swl must be at least five bits greater than the input signal wordlength s.

We present here a fully concurrent implementation of the FFT algorithm. The transform rate r_t for the block FFT is thus equal to the word rate, which we recall is the ratio of process clock rate r_p (8 MHz here) to system wordlength, i.e.

$$r_t = \frac{r_p}{s+5}$$

The latency of a butterfly processor will depend on the resolution of the coefficients. This resolution is a fundamental system parameter. As our transform is a very short one (the wheel spokes are sparse), a considerable amount of coefficient inaccuracy can be tolerated. In any case, the 3% tolerance of the magnitude converters introduces a considerable amount of noise into the output. As 8-bit multipliers are physically compact, we select an 8-bit coefficient wordlength.

For a 8-bit coefficient, the minimum butterfly latency is 16 bits, the objects in the data path being an 8-bit multiplier (latency 14 bits), and two adders or subtracters (latency a minimum of 1 bit each). If, as seems likely, a chip boundary is to be included, this figure rises to 17. Happily, a 12-bit input signal wordlength requires at least a 17-bit system wordlength, as explained earlier. For a system wordlength of 17 and a bit-rate of 8 MHz, the word rate will be 471 kHz. Assuming this is adequate, we set the system wordlength at 17 bits, thereby forcing word synchronism between columns as well as rows in the array, which greatly simplifies control.

Thus the 16-point demonstration machine will perform block transforms at 471 kHz, on data sampled at 7.53 MHz. If this data rate seems unspectacular, it should be noted that throughput here is proportional to transform length.

Thus, by merely instantiating more identical processors, extending the rows and columns of the machine according to their formulae given above, we could commission a 256-point FFT processor capable of transforming data sampled at frequencies exceeding 80 MHz. In this case, the 8-bit coefficient word would severely degrade numerical accuracy, and an increase to 12 bits might be called for. The cost of this ploy would be increased chip area and transform latency, and the loss of column synchronism.

8.5.2   A twiddle factor strategy

We are using a fractional two's complement number system to implement twiddle factors, to 8-bit accuracy. This approach suffers from the inability to express unity, which is outside the range of the number system. Most rotations suffer from inaccuracy due to quantisation errors, but we can always choose a complex coefficient which is within 0.707 of a bit of its correct value in the complex plane (consider any point within a unit square, and its distance from the nearest corner of the square). When attempting to represent unity (or for that matter j), however, we must accept a constant 1-bit error in the representation, which notably degrades accuracy at short coefficient lengths. Alternatively, we can seek a method of avoiding unity in either real or imaginary coefficients, noting that the number -1 is exactly represented in fractional two's complement.

The transform is a parallel one, and reads all elements of its input vector simultaneously. In that case, it is a simple matter to reverse the input sequence to the transform, thereby replacing the sequence by its conjugate (the real part is an even function, the imaginary part odd). This conjugation can be cancelled by replacing all twiddle factors by their conjugates. Although this means that the transform output appears in conjugate form, this phase error is of no concern as we are extracting output magnitude. Commonality of real and imaginary twiddle coefficients has now increased, and the number -1 is no longer required as a coefficient.

We wish to avoid unity (not -1), so the next step is to negate the conjugate twiddle factors. The effect of this step can be immediately cancelled by adding instead of subtracting, and vice versa, in OPERATOR Dft2. Rather than disturb the low-level OPERATOR Dft2, which is useful in its own right, we create the modified OPERATOR Dft2Swap, which we subsequently use in Rad2Dit and Window2. We are making one declarational change, and two instantiational changes, but only from the point of view of renaming constituent elements of OPERATORs. This means that the topology of the machine remains undisturbed.

To sum up, by reversing the input sequence, replacing all twiddle factors by their negative conjugate, and effectively swapping the adds and subtracts in the 2-point DFTs, we may maximise coefficient commonality and represent unity in exact manner. Such a strategy is only feasible in parallel transforms, and only necessary where coefficient resolution is poor.

8.5.3   Implementation

We have completed the design of arithmetic elements to be employed, and have made the decisions on numerical issues. Now we can implement the remainder of the machine.

As stated earlier, our architecture is based on the use of regular columns of processors. This immediately suggests a SUBSYSTEM corresponding to each column. The machine then consists of one windowing and shuffling column, three butterfly columns, and one complex-to-magnitude column in cascade.

Estimates on chip sizes, based mostly on multiplier content, indicate that for a 5 μm nMOS process, one butterfly processor will fit on a chip, one windowing processor likewise, while two of the magnitude processors may share a chip. This means that the first column, the three central columns and the final column each contain 8 chips, making 40 chips in all. (It is reasonable to assume that each of these columns could fit on one chip using a more advanced technology with around 2 μm feature sizes.) We now formally specify the three CHIPs.

The CHIPs
To create the CHIP Bfly2 we have to encapsulate Rad2Dit in a CHIP, and assign values to the various parameters using the CONSTANT statement.

CHIP Bfly2 (pc1) prin1, prin2, piin1, piin2, pwre, pwim –> prout1,
          prout2, piout1, piout2
!latency is 17 bits

        SIGNAL rin1, rin2, iin1, iin2, wre, wim, rout1, rout2, iout1, iout2
        CONTROL c1

        PADIN (pc1 –> c1) prin1, prin2, piin1, piin2, pwre, pwim –> rin1,
            rin2, iin1, iin2, wre, wim
        PADOUT rout1, rout2, iout1, iout2 –> prout1, prout2, piout1, piout2
        PADORDER VDD, pc1, prin1, prin2, piin1, piin2, GND, pwre,
                pwim, CLOCK, prout1, prout2, piout1, piout2

        CONSTANT coeff = 8, lat1 = 1, lat2 = 1

        Rad2Dit [coeff,lat1,lat2] (c1) rin1, rin2, iin1, iin2, wre, wim –> rout1,
            rout2, iout1, iout2

END

Plate 3 is a photomicrograph of CHIP Bfly2 (here parameter lat2 = 2, and coeff = 12). Such a device might form a computational node in a much larger transform, e.g. 256-point. The CHIPS 'Window' and 'Magnitude' are equally easy to implement – Window contains one Window2 OPERATOR, and Magnitude two ComplexToMagnitude OPERATORs. As before, this task is merely one of encapsulation and parameter assignment.

rc1 THROUGH 8

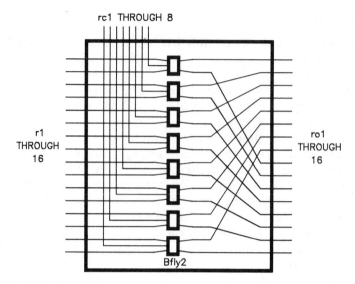

r1
THROUGH
16

ro1
THROUGH
16

Bfly2

Fig. 8.20 Main butterfly processor column SUBSYSTEM 'MainColumn', showing perfect unshuffle on output. All data lines are complex.

Now we have the three chip types which we require to build the full array FFT. Our only remaining task is to implement the network topology in the SUBSYSTEMs.

The MainColumn and Heart subsystems
The Bfly2 CHIPs connect together in the constant-geometry FFT architecture depicted in Figure 8.20 to form the SUBSYSTEM MainColumn.

SUBSYSTEM MainColumn (c1) r1 THROUGH 16, i1 THROUGH 16,
            rc1 THROUGH 8, ic1 THROUGH 8 –> ro1 THROUGH 16,
            io1 THROUGH 16

SIGNAL yr, xr, yi, xi, wr, wi, yro, xro, yio, xio

Bfly2 (c1) yr, xr, yi, xi, wr, wi –> yro, xro, yio, xio – TIMES 8 WITH
yr = r1, r3, r5, r7, r9, r11, r13, r15
xr = r2, r4, r6, r8, r10, r12, r14, r16
yi = i1, i3, i5, i7, i9, i11, i13, i15
xi = i2, i4, i6, i8, i10, i12, i14, i16
wr = rc1 THROUGH 8
wi = ic1 THROUGH 8
yro = ro1 THROUGH 8
xro = ro9 THROUGH 16
yio = io1 THROUGH 8
xio = io9 THROUGH 16

END

This code uses the shorthand TIMES statement, with assignment-replacement to wire up the Bfly2 chips. The network topology is contained in the ordering of the replacement lists following the TIMES statement. The list of internal nodes declared in the SIGNAL statement are in fact dummy nodes – they are replaced by the corresponding element of the list as the chips are instantiated. Every node here is distinct (no nodes connect to more than one chip). TIMES syntax allows many more connection types, as we saw in Chapter 3.

As we selected a constant-geometry algorithm, the SUBSYSTEM Heart may be constructed by simply cascading three MainColumn SUBSYSTEMs. Here the appropriate twiddle factors must be routed to the butterflies. In practice we would store these in ROM, but for the purpose of simulation we create a chip which contains CONSTGEN primitives for each numerically individual coefficient.

```
SUBSYSTEM  Heart (c1) r1 THROUGH 16, i1 THROUGH 16,
               wre0 THROUGH 7 – ro1 THROUGH 16, io1 THROUGH 16

    SIGNAL rc1 THROUGH 8, ic1 THROUGH 8

    MainColumn (c1) r1 THROUGH 16, i1 THROUGH 16, rc1 THROUGH 8,
        ic1 THROUGH 8 – ro1 THROUGH 16, io1 THROUGH 16 –
        TIMES 3 WITH ro1 THROUGH 16, io1 THROUGH 16 –
        r1 THROUGH 16, i1 THROUGH 16
        rc1 wre0, wre0, wre0
        rc2 wre0, wre0, wre1
        rc3 wre0, wre2, wre2
        rc4 wre0, wre2, wre3
        rc5 wre4, wre4, wre4
        rc6 wre4, wre4, wre5
        rc7 wre4, wre6, wre6
        rc8 wre4, wre6, wre7
        ic1 wre4, wre4, wre4
        ic2 wre4, wre4, wre3
        ic3 wre4, wre2, wre2
        ic4 wre4, wre2, wre1
        ic5 wre0, wre0, wre0
        ic6 wre0, wre0, wre1
        ic7 wre0, wre2, wre2
        ic8 wre0, wre2, wre3

END
```

Note the extensive use of assignment-replacement in Heart (Figure 8.21), to route the appropriate twiddle factors to the Bfly2 CHIPs. We take full advantage of commonality between real and imaginary twiddle components.

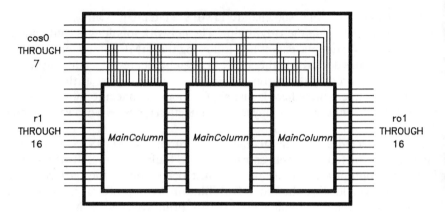

Fig. 8.21 SUBSYSTEM 'Heart', showing routing of twiddle factors. All data lines are complex.

Cascading is realised by the syntax immediately after the TIMES statement, which specifies how outputs of one column connect to the next. Any node not mentioned in either the cascading syntax or the assignments is connected globally – for instance the c1 inputs to these SUBSYSTEMs. Thus all output nodenames must appear in the syntax which follows the TIMES statement, if node conflicts are to be avoided.

The InColumn SUBSYSTEM
The construction of the SUBSYSTEM InColumn (Figure 8.22) is a more complex problem, as it is here that the index bit-reversal is implemented. We further complicate matters by using the symmetry of the windowing function to reduce the number of coefficient lines into the SUBSYSTEM. Again we use

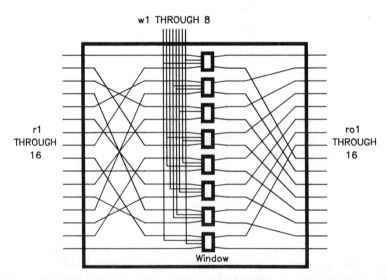

Fig. 8.22 Windowing SUBSYSTEM 'InColumn', showing bit-reversing shuffle on input and perfect unshuffle on output. All data lines are complex.

assignment-replacement for coefficient routing.

Here we are using a truly symmetric window, and not a DFT-symmetric window (Harris, 1978). The axis of symmetry of the latter falls on sample $N/2$, while that of the former falls half a sample period earlier. The DFT symmetric window requires one extra coefficient to be generated, increasing pin count, and the improvement in performance (over true symmetry) predicted by Harris is unlikely to be significant, given the noisy nature of our transform.

```
SUBSYSTEM  InColumn (zc1) r1 THROUGH 16, i1 THROUGH 16,
                  w1 THROUGH 8 -> ro1 THROUGH 16, io1 THROUGH 16

    SIGNAL yr, yi, xr, xi, wy, wx, yro, xro, yio, xio

    Window (zc1) yr, xr, yi, xi, wy, wx -> yro, xro, yio,
        xio TIMES 8 WITH
        yr = r1, r5, r3, r7, r2, r6, r4, r8
        xr = r9, r13, r11, r15, r10, r14, r12, r16
        yi = i1, i5, i3, i7, i2, i6, i4, i8
        xi = i9, i13, i11, i15, i10, i14, i12, i16
        wy = w8, w4, w6, w2, w7, w3, w5, w1
        wx = w1, w5, w3, w7, w2, w6, w4, w8
        yro = ro1 THROUGH 8
        xro = ro9 THROUGH 16
        yio = io1 THROUGH 8
        xio = io9 THROUGH 16

END
```

The OutColumn SUBSYSTEM

Recall the OPERATOR ComplexToMagnitude from Chapter 3, which was duplicated and integrated on CHIP Magnitude. The construction of SUBSYSTEM Outcolumn (Figure 8.23) then consists of 8 distinct instantiations of Magnitude. The wiring topology used is somewhat arbitrary, as any scheme which maintains consistency of in, out and mag node numbering will do.

```
SUBSYSTEM  OutColumn (c1) re1 THROUGH 16,
                im1 THROUGH 16 -> mag1 THROUGH 16

    SIGNAL rea, reb, ima, imb, maga, magb

    Magnitude (c1) rea, reb, ima, imb -> maga, magb TIMES 8 WITH
    rea = re1 THROUGH 8
    reb = re9 THROUGH 16
    ima = im1 THROUGH 8
    imb = im9 THROUGH 16
    maga = mag1 THROUGH 8
    magb = mag9 THROUGH 16

END
```

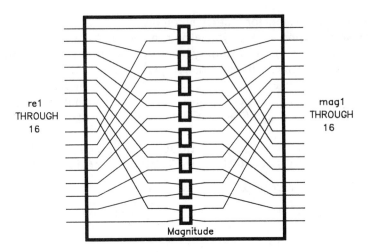

re1
THROUGH
16

mag1
THROUGH
16

Magnitude

Fig. 8.23 Magnitude extraction SUBSYSTEM 'OutColumn', showing necessary symmetry. Input lines are complex, output real.

The FFT SYSTEM

We have now arrived at the top (SYSTEM) level in the hierarchy. The power of hierarchy lies in the ability of the designer to hide detail in lower levels. This we have already done within SUBSYSTEMs (topological details), and CHIPs (computational details). Thus putting together the SYSTEM FFT (Figure 8.24) is merely a matter of cascading the SUBSYSTEMs InColumn, Heart and OutColumn in a regular manner, and requires little effort.

```
SYSTEM FFT rin, iin -> out1 THROUGH 16
    SIGNAL rin1 THROUGH 16, iin1 THROUGH 16,
        r1 THROUGH 16, i1 THROUGH 16, ro1 THROUGH 16,
        io1 THROUGH 16, cos0 THROUGH 7, w1 THROUGH 8
    CONTROL c1

    Corner rin, iin -> rin1 THROUGH 16, iin1 THROUGH 16
    Twiddles (c1) -> cos0 THROUGH 7
    HamCoeffs (c1) -> w1 THROUGH 8
    Cgenerate (-> c1)

    InColumn (c1) rin1 THROUGH 16, iin1 THROUGH 16,
        w1 THROUGH 8 -> r1 THROUGH 16, i1 THROUGH 16
    Heart (c1) r1 THROUGH 16, i1 THROUGH 16,
        cos0 THROUGH 7 -> ro1 THROUGH 16, io1 THROUGH 16
    OutColumn (c1) ro1 THROUGH 16, io1 THROUGH 16 -> -
        out1 THROUGH 16

END
```

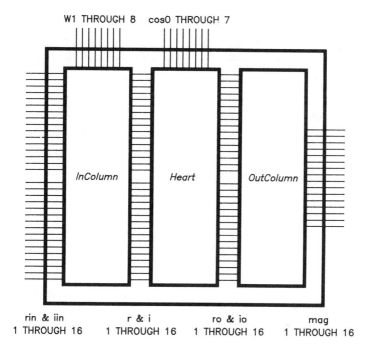

W1 THROUGH 8   cos0 THROUGH 7

InColumn   Heart   OutColumn

rin & iin   r & i   ro & io   mag
1 THROUGH 16   1 THROUGH 16   1 THROUGH 16   1 THROUGH 16

Fig. 8.24 SYSTEM 'FFT'.

8.5.4 Simulation

The Fourier transformer is a machine which allows decomposition of a signal into an arbitrary number of spectral components or 'bins' – in this case 16. Windowing is performed prior to FFT processing to minimise the effects of 'off-bin' components on non-related bins. We employ Hamming and Blackman windows (Harris, 1978) to effect windowing.

To demonstrate the use of windows, we illustrate a simple two-tone detection problem. One tone is at full-scale amplitude, and the other is at 1% of this (i.e. 40 dB down). Figure 8.25 shows the log-magnitude output of the processor when both tones are at discrete observation frequencies, on bins 7 and 12. We observe the 40 dB difference between these bins, and note that transform noise due to poor arithmetic accuracy almost masks the minor tone. The worst offender is the partner tone to the dominant – this is bin 15 (7 + the span, which is 8 here). This bin accumulates energy (and errors) in identical manner to the dominant until the last butterfly column, where it is uniquely identified. The 6 dB loss of dynamic range necessary for correct multiplier operation can be seen in the dominant tone. The energy in bins 2, 6, 10 and 14 corresponds to one bit.

Next we move the dominant tone on to a position between bins, the new normalised frequency being 6.5. The spread of energy over the other bins is apparent, and the minor tone is no longer detectable (Figure 8.26).

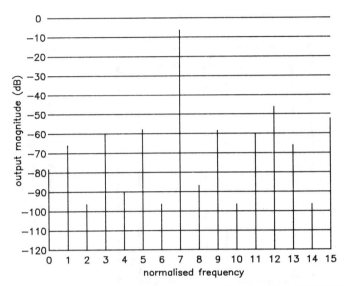

Fig. 8.25 FFT simulation, showing response to tones on bins 7 and 12, with 40 dB difference, no window used.

Introduction of the Hamming window, shown in Figure 8.27, reduces the leakage to a great enough extent to reveal the minor tone once more – a good 14 dB above its neighbours. The Blackman window has a wider main lobe, and lower sidelobe energy than the Hamming window. Its detection characteristics are displayed in Figure 8.28, showing higher energy in immediate neighbours of the two tones, but less in other bins.

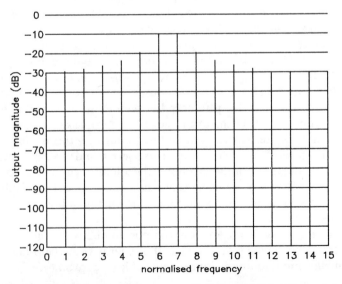

Fig. 8.26 Result of moving dominant tone to a mid-bin position (bin 6.5), no window used.

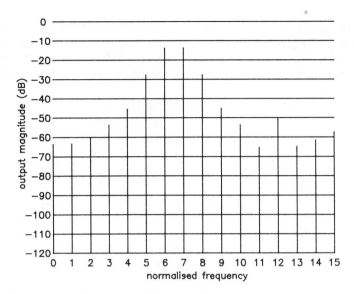

Fig. 8.27 Introduction of Hamming window reveals minor tone once more.

8.5.5 Some communications issues

The full array FFT machine is capable of one transform every word-time. If the input word rate to the entire machine – corner-turning memory included – is equal to the processor word-rate, then such a machine performs a 'sliding transform' on the input data. Each incoming word participates in N transforms before expiring, and the maximum amount of processing is carried out on the

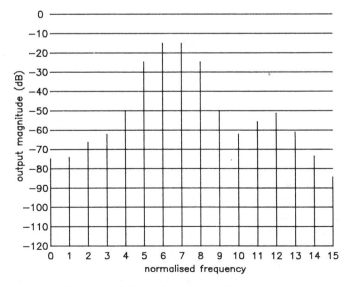

Fig. 8.28 Response of Blackman window in the same experiment.

input sequence. A sliding transform of the type just described, where phase information is neglected, can also be realised recursively by a column DFT machine with only order(N) processors (Ting, 1980). Although this machine accumulates an output phase error, this is of no importance if only output magnitude is of interest.

A more common transform is the 'block transform', whereby a block of entirely new samples is presented to the machine every word-time. Each input word then participates in just one transform. However, for such a scheme to be effective, the input word-rate should be N times the processing word-rate. Even for a modest machine such as the one just described, the input word-rate is 7.53 MHz. Higher transform lengths lead to unattainable input data rates, despite the ability of the processor to deal with the data once input. In/out bandwidth limits performance in this case.

A common compromise between the computational burden of the sliding transform and the communications burden of the block transform is the 'overlapped transform' (Rabiner and Gold, 1975). This is accomplished through the multiplexing technique described in Chapter 5, allowing matching of in/out and processing bandwidths. Alternatively, block transform machines may be realised with in/out data rates less severe than that of the parallel machine.

The FFT being implemented on a rectangular array of processors, two multiplexing schemes suggest themselves – a row scheme and a column scheme. We investigate both, but only produce a chip set for the former machine.

8.6   The column FFT machine

We mentioned earlier that the constant geometry network would allow one column of processors to be repeated spatially, i.e. cascaded, to implement the transform. If the repetition is made temporal rather than spatial, then only one physical column of processors is required. We are trading time against silicon area – a common technique in systems optimisation.

It is fortunate that in the case $N = 16$ (giving $M = 4$ for radix-2), the sub-block length ($= N/M, = 4$) is an integer. Thus we process 4 samples at a time, and carry out block transforms at a quarter of the rate of the full array machine, using approximately a quarter of the hardware. We say 'approximately' because the area-time tradeoff is more than just a matter of dividing down the hardware of the full array machine – some delay and switching elements must also be introduced for correct operation.

A further penalty, as mentioned earlier, is that we must implement the 'trivial' twiddles of the first column, as the same hardware realises all columns of the machine. Thus we cannot combine windowing with the first column as before. Not only is this wasteful of silicon, but it also causes arithmetic degradation due to the fact that unity cannot be represented. One way round this would be to negate all twiddle factors, and swap the complex adders and subtracters in the butterflies (one of the tricks used in the full array machine).

Hardware overview

Our initial concept of the column machine is a single column of butterfly processors, like MainColumn of the full array study, with a windowing front end and a magnitude-extracting back end. The front end can be a set of simple weighting blocks, like Xweight, and the back end can contain elements like ComplexToMagnitude. As the in/out data rate is one-quarter of that of the full array machine, only four instantiations of these OPERATORs are required. The corner-turning memory takes four samples from the input word-stream, and outputs them on four wire-pairs. Figure 8.29 shows a high level system plan.

Some design problems manifest themselves as we consider the operation of the butterfly column, and how it communicates with the front and back ends. This column must read in its 16-point windowed data block, then recirculate its outputs three times before reading the next block. Its inputs and outputs are 16-point, while the interfaces to the front and back ends are 4 x 4-point (i.e. four sequential blocks of four). Two actions are required from the designer.

Firstly we must 'time align' the four sub-blocks which are output sequentially from the weighting block. Similarly we must 'de-align' the column outputs, for correct presentation to the magnitude-extraction block. Secondly we must ensure that the column and the back end 'read' the correct data at the correct time.

The former strategy can be implemented using 'wedges' of delay – in the case of the front end interface with common inputs, and in the case of the back end with distinct inputs (Figure 8.30). The front end wedge is arranged to perform the required bit-reversing shuffle on the 4 × 4-point signal block. The technique employed minimises the number of crossovers in signal paths, at no greater hardware cost than a hardwired shuffle.

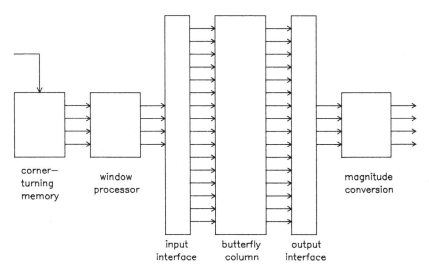

corner–
turning
memory

window
processor

input
interface

butterfly
column

output
interface

magnitude
conversion

Fig. 8.29   Column FFT machine plan.

The latter strategy is accomplished by employing MULTIPLEX primitives – at the front end interface to read a valid input block once in four cycles, and at the back end to select one from four sub-blocks, ensuring both that selection order is correct, and that the valid machine output is read and not some intermediate inter-column result. The signals are passed by the MULTIPLEXers when valid (as shown by the node numbers in time sequences in Figure 8.30).

Another issue is the sharing of multiplier coefficients in the weighting block and in the FFT column engine. We must realise a memory loop of length 4 words for each processor, containing a MULTIPLEX switch to read in coefficients on start up. The coefficients will subsequently recirculate indefinitely, appearing in the correct time-slot at the multiplier. Thus the machine must run in two modes – start up and steady state.

Initial hardware decisions
We now have a much clearer idea of what comprises the column machine, and can commence its design. Much of this work has already been done in the full array study – we need only add the wedges, switches and memory loops described above. The front end wedge can be included at the outputs of each windowing multiplier, at the cost of increasing pin count on that chip. The back end wedge, having distinct inputs and outputs, should inhabit the same chip as the '1 from 4' data selector used by the magnitude extractors, thereby minimising the number of pin-expensive 16 channel transfers between chips.

The butterfly chips can be the same as used in the full array study, with the addition of MULTIPLEX primitives for input data selection, and memory

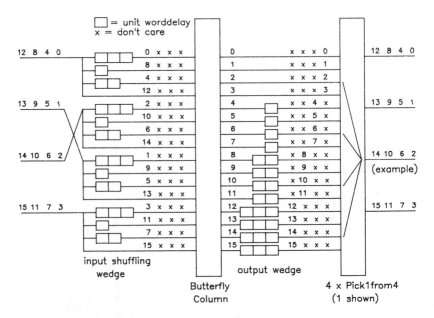

Fig. 8.30   Action of input and output interfacing wedges.

loops for storing real and imaginary coefficients. Note that the inclusion of MULTIPLEX in the signal path increases the swl by one bit, as the swl has a minimum value decided by the latency of the BFLY2 chip (for synchronisation reasons). Thus swl = 18 bits here. Finally the Magnitude chip, being small, can support the system CONTROLGENERATOR (CG).

Control and multiplexing issues
In the full array study, we ensured a simple control system by making all columns of the machine word synchronous. All we then needed to do was supply a c1 signal to each chip in the system. Here we are involved with a more complicated control network, and some care must be taken in the design process.

We are using a multiplexing regime, and accordingly must employ higher levels of control than c1. MULTIPLEX primitives are situated at the column inputs, and at the back end inputs. In the former task, they select one from two signals, recirculating outputs back to inputs for 3 out of 4 word cycles. This suggests a c2 CYCLE, or 'frame', of length 4. In the latter task they select one from four, in a cyclic fashion.

As we only have one-from-two MULTIPLEX primitives available to us, we could construct a one-from-four selector as a binary tree of three MULTIPLEXers. This necessitates a c2 CYCLE of 2 words and a c3 CYCLE of 2 frames, yielding a 2-bit control code for selection control. Unfortunately this compromises our earlier scheme for the butterfly data recirculation, and, as it is the latency of this loop which will decide our minimum system wordlength, we must seek another solution for the one-from-four selector. Figure 8.31 shows a scheme which employs a c2 CYCLE of 4, and a c3 CYCLE of 2.

We must also provide the facility for catching multiplier coefficients described earlier. A MULTIPLEX switch can be programmed to allow the coefficients to be loaded into the loop on start up. This action is under the

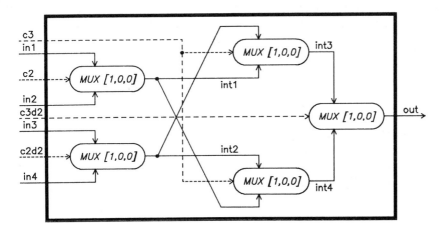

Fig. 8.31   Output selection OPERATOR 'Pick1from4'.

control of an event pulse, of length 4 words (the frame length), and thus we associate the EVENT with CYCLE c2.

A final design issue is the control timing. We maintain c1 synchronism at chip level throughout, at the cost of a 4-bit CBITDELAY on Magnitude CHIPs (which in turn allows some cyclic c1 optimisation on Magnitude). We have hidden c1 details in the hierarchy.

The next control level, c2, decides when the butterflies read the new input vector. As we are not concerned about how the input data stream is sectioned into blocks, we can treat the inputs to the Column SUBSYSTEM as a temporal 'reference point' (RP), and design the control network from there on. The controls input to OPERATOR 'Pick1from4' are word synchronous, and in fact are c2-frame synchronous as well (the Column output is valid at the same time as it reads its new input). Thus the control implementation of 'Pick1from4' reduces to the problem of wiring up its 4 input lines – see code and Figure 8.31.

```
OPERATOR Pick1from4 (c2, c2d2, c3, c3d2) in1 THROUGH 4 -> out
!latency is 3

    SIGNAL int1 THROUGH 4

    MULTIPLEX [1,0,0] (c2) in2, in1 -> int1
    MULTIPLEX [1,0,0] (c2d2) in4, in3 -> int2
    MULTIPLEX [1,0,0] (c3) int1, int2 -> int3
    MULTIPLEX [1,0,0] (c3) int2, int1 -> int4
    MULTIPLEX [1,0,0] (c3d2) int3, int4 -> out

END
```

The event pulse for coefficient catching should be in synchronism with other control signals. Synchronism may be maintained by setting the latency of OPERATOR 'CofCatch' to swl, via the MULTIPLEX latency parameter. (Signals passing through MULTIPLEX are delayed by at least 1 bit, thus 1 word is the cost of maintaining synchronism.) Now we must ensure that coefficients are presented to CofCatch in such a fashion as to coincide with the desired data samples at the multipliers.

```
OPERATOR CofCatch [swl] (e3) in -> out
!latency is swl

    SIGNAL s1 THROUGH 3

    MULTIPLEX [swl,0,0] (e3) s3, in -> out
    BITDELAY [swl] out -> s1
    BITDELAY [swl] s1 -> s2
    BITDELAY [swl] s2 -> s3

END
```

Hardware partitioning

The description contains 4 SUBSYSTEMs, each of which contains multiple instances of a unique CHIP. Figures 8.32–8.35 show the floorplans of the four CHIPs employed.

The windowing CHIP Windo contains 4 multipliers, 4 wedges, and 4 CofCatch OPERATORs. The wedges, consisting of BITDELAYs of length 1, 2 and 3 words, are decomposed into 6 equal-length BITDELAYs to reduce chip height. Similarly CofCatch is partitioned into 4 word-sized blocks.

The butterfly CHIP Bfly is much the same as the parallel version, but includes 2 CofCatch OPERATORs, 4 MULTIPLEX primitives and output recirculation. The MULTIPLEXs are combined with Xmult to make the time-aligned block 'PickAndTwiddle' (like Twiddle2 of the previous study, with selection on all 4 inputs). Note the 1-bit predelay on all multiplexers, to compensate for pin delay. This is necessary because synchronous data recirculation is internal to the CHIP, and does not incur a pin delay. Delays required in the twiddle-free top leg are realised in the MULTIPLEX latency parameter.

OPERATOR PickAndTwiddle [coeff,lat] (c1, c2 –> c1o) rin1, rin2, iin1, iin2,
          rb1, rb2, ib1, ib2, wre, wim –> rout1, rout2, iout1, iout2
!latency is compdel + 1 (see expression below)

    SIGNAL r, i

    CONSTANT compdel = $(3 * coeff)/2 + 2 + lat$

    MULTIPLEX [1 + compdel,1,0] (c2) rb1, rin1 –> rout1
    MULTIPLEX [1 + compdel,1,0] (c2) ib1, iin1 –> iout1
    MULTIPLEX [1,1,0] (c2) rb2, rin2 –> r
    MULTIPLEX [1,1,0] (c2) ib2, iin2 –> i
    Xmult [coeff,lat] (c1 –> c1o) r, i, wre, wim –> rout2, iout2

END

We partition the SUBSYSTEM WedgePair in a different manner from the rest of the machine - we separate real and imaginary parts, as this is the only form of symmetry displayed by the SUBSYSTEM. SUBSYSTEM WedgePair consists of two OutWedge CHIPs, one each for real and imaginary signals. OutWedge in turn consists of 4 Pick1from4 OPERATORS, and a wedge made with 6 DelayBlock OPERATORs, DelayBlock being a 4 channel parameterised delay element. We call DelayBlock 6 times, not 3, in order to restrict BITDELAYs to a size commensurate with the rest of the chip, just as in Windo and CofCatch.

Finally the Magnitude CHIPs are implemented much as before, but with the inclusion of a CONTROLGENERATOR primitive, and a 4-bit CBITDELAY to maintain c1 synchronism at chip level (4 bits is the latency of the previous CHIP in the path, OutWedge). The CG must be isolated from the rest of the chip, as FIRST allows the use of only one CG per system. Internal control on Magnitude is brought in via its pins.

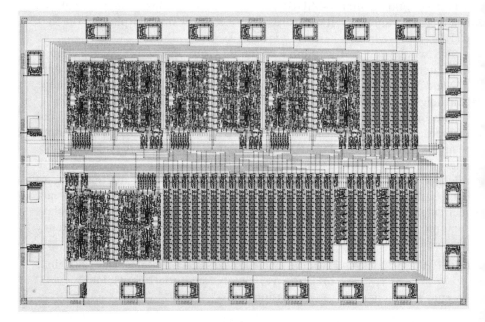

Fig. 8.32 Floorplan of input weighting CHIP 'Windo'.

Fig. 8.33 Floorplan of butterfly processor CHIP 'Bfly'.

Fig. 8.34   Floorplan of output wedging and selecting CHIP 'OutWedge'.

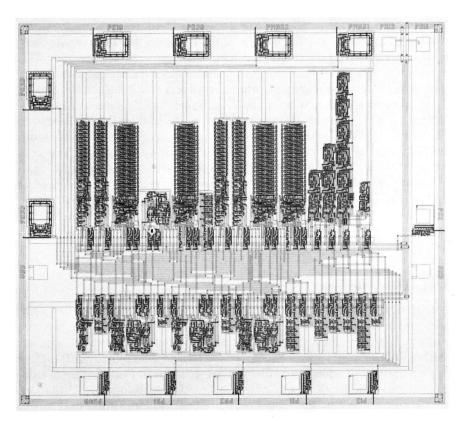

Fig. 8.35   Floorplan of magnitude extraction and control generation CHIP 'Magnitude'.

Figures 8.32 – 8.35 show the chips used – their sizes are as follows:

Chip	Width (λ)	Height (λ)	Aspect Ratio
Bfly	2461	1645	1.50
Windo	2657	1666	1.59
OutWedge	2237	1314	1.70
Magnitude	1691	1337	1.26

This study has shown that many design issues arise after floorplans have been produced, and some iteration is normally required to optimise any chip set. The silicon compiler lets the designer successively refine his work, allowing physical, as well as functional, considerations to come to bear on the design. We oversimplified the physical design issues in the full array study – it is unusual to compile and use an OPERATOR 'toolkit' without any regard to physical implications.

8.7   The pipeline FFT machine

We have seen (for radix-2) how the FFT can be implemented in a fully parallel manner, using a large number – $(N/R)\log_R N$ – of butterfly processors, where N is the transform length and R is the radix. It follows that the hardware cost is of order $(N/R)\log_R N$ (there are $\log_R N$ columns, each containing N/R processors). The parallel structure is capable of block transforms in unit word time. The area-time product is therefore also of order $(N/R)\log_R N$.

We have also seen how area could be traded against time to realise the column machine. When N is large, this scheme still leads to fast but hardware-intensive systems. A more common area-time tradeoff is to divide area, and multiply time, by N/R, i.e. to employ a multiplexing level of N/R. The same transform may then be performed in a word time of N/R, using only $\log_R N$ processors. This is in effect implementing just one row, and multiplexing down the columns. The resulting machine is a pipeline FFT (McClellan and Purdy, 1978), and the most advanced FFT machine known to the authors employs this architecture (with radix R = 4) to realise 4096-point transforms on 40 MHz data (Swartzlander and Hallnor, 1984).

8.7.1   Some radix issues

A radix-R DFT is capable of processing R points of complex data at a time, and a radix-R butterfly uses (R – 1) twiddles. An N-point radix-R full array machine requires $(N/R)\log_R N$ butterflies, while an equivalent pipeline machine needs $\log_R N$ stages of processors (Rabiner and Gold, 1975). If we neglect the cost of adders, and also 'trivial' columns of twiddles (usually one column is twiddle-free), we can state that a radix-R machine will yield a factor of R/2 improvement in throughput over a radix-2 machine, whilst only costing $(R-1)/\log_2 R$ times more hardware.

It would seem from these figures that if the ratio of throughput to hardware cost were proposed as a figure of merit for FFT machines, then we should choose as high a radix as possible. This leads us to expose the fallacies of the approximations we made. At radices higher than 4, using standard arithmetic, the DFT machines used in the butterflies require internal multipliers, for instance 2 in the case of radix-8. It seems that radix-4 is in some sense optimal for long transforms on pipeline machines (McClellan and Purdy, 1978), and this is the radix we choose.

We shall demonstrate here a fairly modest machine; a 64-point, radix-4 transform. In this instance we omit the details of physical implementation, i.e. the partitioning of the system into chips.

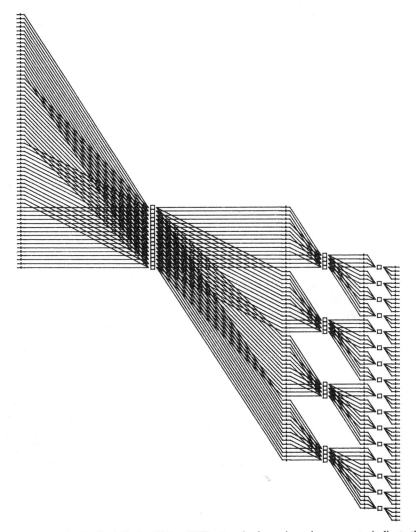

Fig. 8.36 64-point Radix-4 Cooley–Tukey FFT network, drawn in such a way as to indicate the position and size of delays in the equivalent pipeline machine.

8.7.2   Architecture

The area-time tradeoff mentioned above is a little more complicated in reality, as we neglected the cost of storage in the pipeline FFT. Storage is required as a result of the non-local routing in all FFT algorithms. We choose a network which has maximal locality of routing, and correspondingly requires minimal storage. This network implements the radix-4 Cooley–Tukey FFT.

Figure 8.36 shows the parallel version of the network, and Figure 8.37 the pipeline equivalent. Figure 8.36 has four columns of 'wiring posts' interspersed with three columns of processors. Locality can be visualised as the vertical distance of connections from posts to processors in Figure 8.36. Note that the vertical distances from processors to posts have been distorted by a factor of R for diagrammatical convenience, resulting in the vertical gaps between subsequent processor groups. The vertical distances (which are proportional to the stage spans) decrease by a factor of R as we move from left to right through the parallel processor.

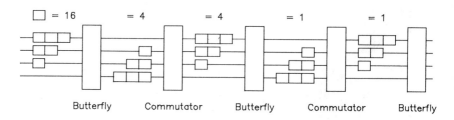

Fig. 8.37   Pipeline equivalent of radix-4 FFT machine, showing unit delays at each stage.

Pipe lengths
The decrease in span is accompanied by a factor of R increase in topological repetition. The quantity of span in the parallel machine has been traded for time delay in the pipeline machine. The time delays are implemented by wedges of delay which re-align samples spaced N/R words apart. The length of these wedge components corresponds to the spans of Figure 8.36, bearing in mind the distortion mentioned earlier. Accordingly, the pipe lengths decrease by a factor of R as we move through the pipeline processor (Figure 8.37).

The commutator
The pipeline FFT machine performs exactly the same transform as the parallel machine, but processes data in contiguous parallel sub-blocks of length R, where R is the transform radix (4 here). Although, as we saw in the previous example, the topology of FFT algorithms can be arranged to be constant across the array, it cannot be made constant in a downward direction, the direction in which we multiplex in the pipeline machine.[†]

[†] Note that the constant-geometry network is inappropriate for pipelining – locality is constantly poor.

The network topology, which was hardwired in the parallel and column machines, is implemented here using a dynamic routing device, or commutator (Rabiner and Gold, 1975), along with the antisymmetric wedges of memory on either side. Notice in Figure 8.36 that the first column topology repeats once, the middle column four times and the last column sixteen times. This property has an analogy in Figure 8.37 – the number of times the commutator runs through its switching pattern in a transform period.

The switching pattern itself relates to the algorithm topology, at the input to each processor group. Just as we replace the columns of processors in the parallel machine by a single processor in the pipeline machine, we replace the column of wiring posts with a wedge-commutator-wedge arrangement, which acts as a 'topological interface' between processors, performing the perfect shuffle which was hardwired in the previous machines. This arrangement will transpose an R $\times$ R matrix of signal sub-blocks. The length of these sub-blocks is the span at that stage in the transform, and forms the 'unit pipe length' for the particular transform stage. Figure 8.38 shows the action of the commutator in shuffling a 4 $\times$ 4 signal block.

Transform types and input buffering
The initial column of posts is replaced by the right-hand wedge only, as a commutator is unnecessary unless maximum block transfer rate is required. Simply tying the R input lines together allows execution of 'overlapped' transforms, useful in fast convolution (Rabiner and Gold, 1975), where the overlap ratio is (R–1)/R. We shall implement a machine of this type.

Full speed block transform capability requires fast input buffering. This usually takes the form of a 'swinging buffer' memory – a dual delay line of length N, with R equally spaced tap-out points. While one memory is filling at the input word-rate, the other is emptying on the R lines, at the word-rate supported by the bit-serial hardware it feeds. The input word-rate is thus R times the processing word-rate. Like the corner-turning memory of the parallel machine, we have not explicitly studied this memory.

Output data shuffling
The overlapped transform is frequently used in fast convolution, where the input signal undergoes an FFT, is term-by-term multiplied with a reference signal (the frequency domain equivalent of convolution), and then inverse FFT'd. This allows an order(N/log N) speed-up over conventional sum of lagged-products structures (Stockham, 1966). The inverse FFT (IFFT) is exactly equivalent to the FFT (save for a scaling factor and the use of conjugate twiddles (Rabiner and Gold, 1975). Thus the topology is identical, and a double dose of digit reversal results in the correct ordering of the output. The reference sequence must be input in digit-reversed order.

We shall shuffle the outputs, however, to simplify their interpretation. To this end, we must implement a digit-reversing network. Digit-reversal can be embedded in the transform itself (Parker, 1980), but this leads to poor locality.

If the wedge-commutator-wedge arrangement which performs the perfect shuffle of order 2 after column 1 is replicated at the pipeline output, it will

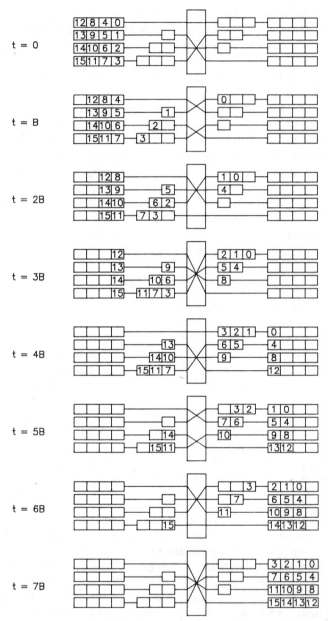

Fig. 8.38 Block shuffling action of the commutator. B is the unit delay in words, and switch pattern is shown before data transfer takes place.

perform a digit reversing shuffle. This is only possible because the relationship between processor output and effective network topology differs between stage 1 and stage 3 outputs.

A digit-reversing shuffle can be implemented as a cascade of decreasing-order perfect shuffles (or unshuffles). The order 1 shuffle is a null operation.

The order 2 perfect shuffle of the additional network, being a simple digit-swap, is identical to an order 2 unshuffle. The stage 3 topology is derived from that of stage 1 by a perfect unshuffle of order 3, as can be seen by inspection of the network in Figure 8.36. Thus we have a cascade of decreasing order unshuffles, which as stated earlier effects the digit-reversing shuffle.

Final design issues
We are already familiar with most of the elements which constitute the pipeline FFT – for instance the OPERATORS Xmult and Dft4. Although a dedicated primitive would be more elegant, OPERATOR 'Commutator' can be implemented as 2 instantiations of OPERATOR 'FourPole', which consists of 8 MULTIPLEX primitives controlled by a 2-bit code. The third control signal (cdel) is a delayed version of cnplus1.

OPERATOR FourPole [s] (cnplus1, cdel, cn) in1 THROUGH 4 -> –
                 out1 THROUGH 4
! latency is s

    SIGNAL s1 THROUGH 4

    MULTIPLEX [s/2,0,0] (cnplus1) in3, in1 -> s1
    MULTIPLEX [s/2,0,0] (cdel) in4, in2 -> s2
    MULTIPLEX [s/2,0,0] (cnplus1) in1, in3 -> s3
    MULTIPLEX [s/2,0,0] (cdel) in2, in4 -> s4
    MULTIPLEX [s–(s/2),0,0] (cn) s2, s1 -> out1
    MULTIPLEX [s–(s/2),0,0] (cn) s1, s2 -> out2
    MULTIPLEX [s–(s/2),0,0] (cn) s4, s3 -> out3
    MULTIPLEX [s–(s/2),0,0] (cn) s3, s4 -> out4

END

The overall control problem reduces to one of generating a succession of binary counted word frames, and implementing the 2-bit control codes at each stage. The latency of processing elements in the pipeline should be taken into consideration when connecting up control.

It should be borne in mind that (neglecting processor latency) the first block of transform output appears in synchronism with the last block of transform input (see the horizontal lines in Figure 8.36, corresponding to zero pipe delay). Thus the control code for the final shuffle commutator should be presented one word early with respect to any reference point used for the rest of the machine.

8.8 The linear array DFT

So far we have described only FFT machines. Although these machines improve on the DFT in terms of arithmetic hardware usage (order$(N \log N)$ for the FFT, order(N^2) for the DFT), hardware savings are not dramatic when N is low. Kung (1980) described a linear 'systolic' array of length N which evaluates the DFT by Horner's method, using the input sequence x(n) as polynomial coefficients. Equation (8.1) may be rewritten:

$$X(k) = ((. . .((x(N–1))W_N^k + x(N–2))W_N^k + . . . + x(1))W_N^k + x(0))   \qquad 8.9$$

Although this method is prone to rounding errors from repeated multiplication of the partial results by W^k, this again is not so important when N is low. The advantage of the approach is the high degree of processor modularity, and the locality of communication afforded.

Allen (1984) modified Kung's array for continuous operation on real data, and implemented it in FIRST, producing a CHIP for each stage of the linear array. He also demonstrated the ease with which the array elements can be multiplexed for bandwidth matching, and produced a further floorplan using the Golub complex multiplier described earlier.

The processing module
The DFT values are computed sequentially by passing partial results, together with the appropriate value of W (these are input in ascending rotational order), down the array. At each point in the array, they meet up with the polynomial coefficients x(n), which travel down the array at half the speed, and are latched in each processor for the transform duration. This ploy is used to reverse the input sequence while maintaining local communication. In cell n, the partial result p(k) is multiplied by W^k, and added to the input sequence element x(N–1–n) resident in the cell. At the end of the array, p(k) = X(k), and the

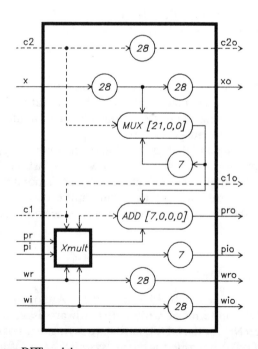

Fig. 8.39   Linear array DFT module.

Fig. 8.40   Floorplan of linear array DFT CHIP.

transform latency is 2N words.

There is a strong parallel between the word-level operation of this array, and the bit-level operation of a serial multiplier (Lyon, 1976). Figure 8.39 shows the basic processor cell (with system wordlength of 28 bits), and Figure 8.40 the CHIP floorplan.

Control

Allen ensured that his design was c1-synchronous at CHIP level, save for the PAD delays incurred in communication between CHIPs. This allows c1 to be passed down the array with the other signals, maintaining local communication. Control is needed at c2 level, to mark 'start of block'. The c2 control signal, of cycle length N, is passed down the array at the same speed as p(k) and W^k. At each processor, c2 'catches up' with a member of the input sequence x(n), and the MULTIPLEX primitive controlled by c2 steers this element into the word-long loop where it recirculates for N word times while being added into p(k).

8.9   Conclusions

We have implemented several types of Fourier transform machine, using only a small subset of the FIRST primitive set. The use of structure in design has demonstrated that previous projects can provide much of the material for a new system. Complexity can be hidden at the appropriate level in the hierarchy employed. The availability of a parameterised, high-level language compiler plus simulator allows not only design verification, but architectural exploration as well. The time saved by automating the low-level tasks of IC design can be fruitfully spent working at the system level, where the designer uses his talents most productively.

The FFT is a prime case for the development of further application-specific primitives. In this case custom complex multipliers and adders, or even full butterfly stages, may be merited. Some more sophisticated data switching elements would be advantageous here.

References

Allen, G. H., Denyer, P. B., and Renshaw, D. 'A Bit-Serial Linear Array DFT', *Proc. IEEE ICASSP'84*, pp 41A.1–4, San Diego, 1984.

Bergland, G. D., 'A Guided Tour of the Fast Fourier Transform', *IEEE Spectrum*, vol. 6, no 7, pp 41–52, 1969.

Cooley, J. W. and Tukey, J. W., 'An Algorithm for the Machine Calculation of Complex Fourier Series', *Math. Comp.*, vol. 19, pp 297–301, 1965.

Despain, A. M., 'Fourier Transform Computers using CORDIC Iterations', *IEEE Trans. Computers*, vol. C-23, pp 993–1001, 1974.

Filip, A. E., 'A Baker's Dozen Magnitude Approximation and Their Detection Statistics', *IEEE Trans. AES*, vol. AES-12, pp 87–89, 1976.

Garverick, S. L. and Pierce, E. A., 'A Single Wafer 16-Point 16-MHz FFT Processor', *Proc. 1983 CICC*, Rochester, New York, 1983.

Gentleman, W. M. and Sande, G., 'Fast Fourier Transforms – For Fun and Profit', *1966 Joint Fall Comput. Conf., AFIPS Proc.*, vol. 29, pp 563–578, Washington DC, 1966.

Gold, B. and Bially, T., 'Parallelism in Fast Fourier Transform Hardware', *IEEE Trans. Audio Electroacoust.*, vol. AU-21, pp 5–16, 1973.

Harris, F. J., 'On the Use of Windows for Harmonic Analysis with the Discrete Fourier Transform', *Proc. IEEE*, vol. 66, pp 51–83, 1978.

Ja'Ja', J., 'High-Speed Networks for Computing the Discrete Fourier Transform', *Proc. M.I.T. Conference on Advanced Research in VLSI*, pp 11–20, Cambridge, MA, 1984.

Kung, H. T., 'Special-Purpose Devices for Signal and Image Processing: an Opportunity in Very Large Scale Integration (VLSI)', *Proc. SPIE*, vol. 241, Real-Time Signal Processing III, pp 76–84, San Diego, 1980.

Linderman, R. W. *et al.*, 'Digital Signal Processing Capabilities of CUSP, a High Performance Bit-Serial VLSI Processor', *Proc. IEEE ICASSP'84*, pp 16.1.1–4, San Diego, 1984.

Lyon, R. F., 'Two's Complement Pipeline Multipliers', *IEEE Trans. Communications*, vol. COM-24, pp 418–425, 1976.

McClellan, J. H. and Purdy, R. J., 'Applications of Digital Signal Processing to Radar', pp 239–329 in A. V. Oppenheim (ed.), *Applications of Digital Signal Processing*, Prentice-Hall, 1978.

McClellan, J. H. and Rader, C. M., (eds.) *Number Theory in Digital Signal Processing*, Prentice-Hall, 1979.

Mead C. A. and Conway, L., *Introduction to VLSI Systems*, Addison-Wesley, 1980.

Murray, A. F., Denyer, P. B. and Donaldson, W., 'A CMOS Cell Library for Bit-Serial Signal Processing', *Proc. ESSCIRC'84*, pp 205–209, Edinburgh, 1984.

Nuttall, A. H., 'A Two-Parameter Class of Bessel Weightings for Spectral Analysis or Array Processing – The Ideal Weighting-Window Pairs', *IEEE Trans. ASSP*, vol. ASSP-31, pp 1309–1312, 1983.

Oppenheim, A. V. and Weinstein, C. J., 'Effects of Finite Register Length in Digital Filtering and the Fast Fourier Transform', *Proc. IEEE*, vol. 60, pp 957–976, 1972.

Parker, D. S., 'Notes on Shuffle/Exchange-Type Switching Networks', *IEEE Trans. Computers*, vol. C-29, pp 213–222, 1980.

Rabiner, L. R. and Gold, B., *Theory and Application of Digital Signal Processing*, Prentice-Hall, 1975.

Rader, C. M., 'Discrete Fourier Transform When the Number of Data Samples is Prime', *Proc. IEEE*, vol. 56, pp 1107–1108, 1968.

Reed, I. S., Yeh, C. -S. and Truong, T. K., 'A VLSI Architecture for Digital Filters Using Complex Number-Theoretic Transforms', *Proc. IEEE ICASSP'83*, pp 923–926, Boston, 1983.

Stockham, T. G. Jr., 'High Speed Convolution and Correlation', *1966 Spring Joint Conf., AFIPS Conf. Proc.*, vol. 28, pp 229–233, 1966.

Stone, H. S., 'Parallel Processing with the Perfect Shuffle', *IEEE Trans. Computers*, vol. C-20, pp 153–161, 1971.

Swartzlander, E. E. Jr. and Hallnor, G., 'Fast Transform Processor Implementation', *Proc. IEEE ICASSP'84*, pp 25A.5.1–4, San Diego, 1984.

Ting, C. -H., 'Fourier Transform Faster than Fast Fourier Transform (FFT)', *Proc. SPIE*, vol. 241, Real-Time Signal Processing III, pp 167–171, San Diego, 1980.

Volder, J. E., 'The CORDIC Trigonometric Computing Technique', *IRE Trans. Electron. Comput.*, vol. EC-8, pp 330–334, 1959.

Ward, J. S. *et al.*, 'Figures of Merit for VLSI Implementations of Digital Signal Processing Algorithms', *Proc. IEE Pt. F*, vol. 131, pp 64–70, 1984.

Winograd, S., 'On Computing the Discrete Fourier Transform', *Math. Comp.*, vol. 32, pp 175–199, 1978.

9

Transversal Filters

Stewart G. Smith

Department of Electrical Engineering
University of Edinburgh

9.1 Introduction

We continue with case studies of two types of transversal or finite impulse response (FIR) filter – a fixed-response filter, and an adaptive filter. The former, simpler system is presented as a completely parameterised design, demonstrating the use of the hardware description language to realise many differing systems from one source file. In contrast, the more complex adaptive filter, designed to a fixed specification, provides an insight into a more advanced architecture illustrating some of the concepts given in Chapters 5 and 6.

The transversal filter (correlator or convolver) is a fundamental signal processing structure (Rabiner and Gold, 1975). It relies on a single inner product step process that is amenable to many different forms of linear array implementation. This repetitive structure has been the subject of much architectural study, e.g. Kung (1982), and some implementations have been discussed in Chapter 5. The architecture of the FIR filter makes it a useful case study and so we first present some fixed-response FIR filters for sonar and speech applications.

The adaptive form of the transversal filter is a more challenging problem because the response vector of the filter is not fixed as in the earlier cases, but is internally computed as a function of the filter output. In the second part of this chapter we present a solution for an adaptive transversal filter with application as an automatic speech echo-canceller.

The complexity of these transversal structures is belied by their dependence upon filter length – impressively large transistor counts can always be obtained by cascading more stages. Nevertheless, the adaptive filter study is close to a commercial application, and at 350,000 transistors it is a good advocate of the methodology of this text. The design was undertaken by one system engineer over a few weeks.

9.2   The fixed-response filter

The FIR filter is characterised by an all-zero transfer function, which renders it unconditionally stable. It performs convolution (or correlation if one of the vectors is reversed in time) according to:

$$y(t) = \mathbf{S}^T\mathbf{H} \qquad\qquad 9.1$$

where $\mathbf{S}$ is the vector of N previous signal samples stored in the filter at time t, $\mathbf{H}$ is the vector of filter coefficients, and T denotes matrix transposition. The output of the filter is thus the weighted sum of the N most recent input signal samples.

Frequency selective filtering (Kaiser and Kuo, 1966) calls for the transformation of the desired frequency response into its equivalent time-domain sequence (impulse response), via the Inverse Discrete Fourier Transform (IDFT). This sequence, suitably truncated and weighted, may then be loaded into the filter as reference, allowing the required filtering function to be carried out. Matched filtering (North, 1963; Turin, 1976) on the other hand is an exercise in correlation, requiring reversal of either signal or, as chosen here, reference sequence. We shall simulate the FIR filter in the latter mode.

9.2.1   Target architecture

Convolution involves the calculation of the vector inner product of equation (9.1). We wish to implement the general structure of Figure 9.1, while minimising the number of device types employed, and the number of interconnects. To this end, we have chosen a pipelined, multiplexed forward-flow architecture, which eases the communication problem at the cost of increased system latency. We shall parameterise the degree of multiplexing.

A deltic processor (Baggeroer, 1978) uses one physical processor to realise several virtual processors by stepping through its associated vector state memory, pairwise multiplying components and accumulating the products. The amount of multiplexing allowed depends on the sample rate of the input signal. In this particular grouped architecture each deltic works on data relevant to the time sample preceding that of its previous neighbour. Thus the latency through the system in samples, relative to a fully parallel realisation, is increased by the number of cascading connections between deltic processors (see Chapter 5). However, the resulting architecture is highly repetitive and

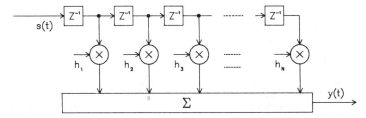

Fig. 9.1   Completely general FIR filtering structure

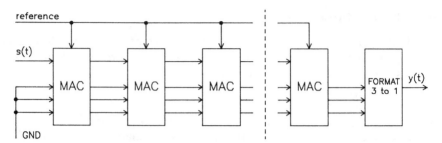

Fig. 9.2   Target architecture for FIR filter

modular, and processor utilisation is 100%.

Figure 9.2 shows the target architecture at system level. A cascade of identical multiply-and-accumulate chips carries out the convolution of the signal and reference (coefficient) vectors, and feeds a final output reformatting chip which contains the system CONTROL GENERATOR (CG).

Reference vector loading
Reference loading is a discrete event, controlled by e3 (an event pulse of width m words). This should occur automatically on switch-on, and thereafter in response to an external request. Note that the reference vector is presented to the filter on a word-by-word basis, while the input signal vector is input on a sample-by-sample basis (one sample time = m word times).

We shall see later that this choice of loading scheme will restrict our multiplexing options.

Word ranges and precisions
Our first concern here is to fix the system wordlength. To maintain the best possible sample rate, we intend to accommodate word growth in this application by multiple-precision (multiple-wire) techniques. Under this condition the longest word in the system is fixed by the input signal wordlength d. As this has to feed a multiplier data input, we allow for the required two guard bits and set the system wordlength s at d+2 bits.

One of the actions of the transversal filter is to strengthen signal components which correlate with the reference vector. This is carried out through the process of accumulation, where combinations of many small components can be important.[†] It is thus imperative to preserve all low-order bits from the convolution product, so the double-precision form of multiplier, DPMULTIPLY, is used. This product is enhanced to triple-precision prior to accumulation, in order to accommodate growth of the accumulated data.

Should the filter be longer than 2^{2s-r+2} points (where s is system wordlength and r is coefficient wordlength), quadruple-precision accumulation would be required to accommodate worst-case word growth. Thus, as stated earlier, our selection of accumulation precision places an upper limit on filter length.

[†]   It is for these reasons of dynamic range that FIR filters are often more suited to matched filtering tasks than FFT-based frequency-domain techniques, where multiplication can take place *after* accumulation. While multi-precision words may be easily accumulated, they are not so easily multiplied. Therefore frequency domain matched filters must employ either very long fixed-point wordlengths, or go floating-point.

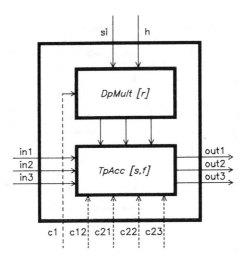

Fig. 9.3 Triple-Precision Multiply-Accumulate OPERATOR 'TpMac'

We shall re-format the filter output to single precision using a parameterisable FFORMAT3TO1 primitive

9.2.2 Implementation

With these preliminary considerations over, and with a target computing architecture in mind, we are able to commence implementation. In the following discussion, LS means least significant, and MS most significant.

The processing engine
We first specify, as basic processing engine, the operator TpMac (triple-precision multiply-accumulate). TpMac, shown 'top-down' in Figure 9.3, consists of lower-order operators DpMult and TpAcc (Figures 9.4 and 9.5). DpMult multiplies in double-precision, and also contains a FORMAT1TO2 primitive on the MS product wire, to convert the product to triple-precision. TpAcc, consisting of three cascaded-carry instantiations of the accumulating

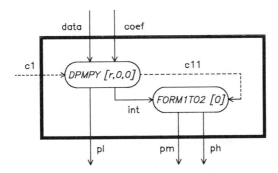

Fig. 9.4 Double-Precision Multiply and Formatting OPERATOR 'DpMult'

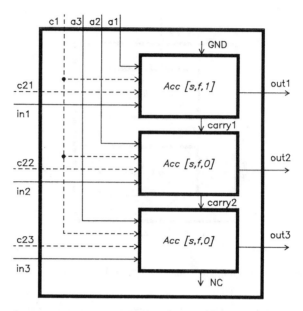

Fig. 9.5   Triple-Precision Accumulate OPERATOR 'TpAcc'

OPERATOR Acc (Figure 9.6), accumulates these products in triple-precision, while absorbing the multiplier latency.

Thus DpMult has a latency of $r + 2$ bits on the LS wire, and $r + 3$ bits on the other two wires. The input leg of the LS accumulator in TpAcc, fed from DpMult, has a compensating one bit predelay to line up the accumulation inputs. This is passed from TpAcc to Acc via parameter z, which is 1 in the LS accumulator, else 0 (see Figure 9.5).

The multiplexed processor

We now add state memory to the processing engine to form the repeatable physical processor. We have already commissioned the arithmetic engine, TpMac, which will reside in the operator Deltic. Deltic will consist of the

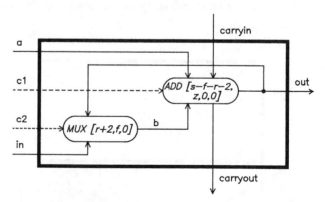

Fig. 9.6   Accumulate OPERATOR 'Acc'

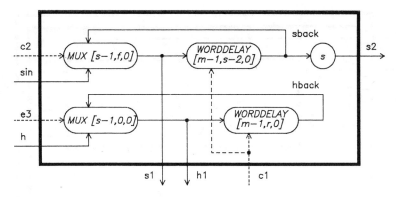

Fig. 9.7 Vector state memory OPERATOR 'StateMem'

operator TpMac along with its multiplexing state memory StateMem (Figure 9.7).

Unless we wish to reverse (in a blockwise manner) the reference sequence prior to loading (which would preclude independence of reference sequence from parameters such as number of physical processors p), we are constrained to a forward multiplexing scheme (see Chapter 5). The advantages of using a simple and generalisable loading scheme outweigh any potential gains from alternative multiplexing schemes.

The coefficient loop is simple to implement – its length must be m words. The signal loop has length m+1 words, following the template of Figure 5.7(b).

A boundary processor
It is likely that the final system will be partitioned into several chips, the most convenient partitioning point being between processors, i.e. we expect to include one or more whole processors on a chip. The last Deltic operator on a chip must have its latency reduced by one bit, to compensate for the pad delay

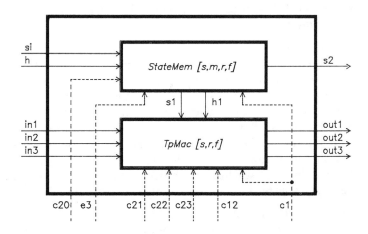

Fig. 9.8 Deltic processing OPERATOR 'Deltic'

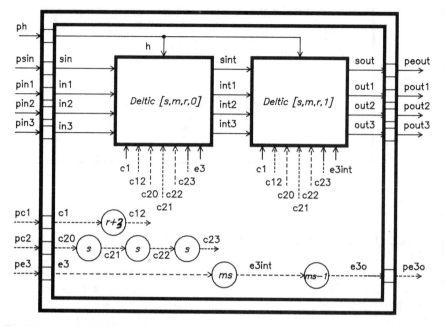

Fig. 9.9   Cascaded deltic processing CHIP 'CDelt'

incurred on the chip boundary. We circumvent this problem by introducing the parameter f, which we set to 1 on the last Deltic operator, and 0 elsewhere. Thus the same hardware description suffices for both implementations. Figure 9.8 shows the Deltic operator.

Note the use of the parameterised predelay on the signal input multiplexers in StateMem, to maintain correctness of loop length whilst through-latency varies with f. Figure 9.6 reveals that the same technique is used in the accumulator Acc, whose loop length must be constant (at one word). The optional predelay in FIRST primitives is frequently used to compensate for pad delays in this manner.

The convolution CHIP
The chip CDelt contains p cascaded Deltic operators, as shown (for the case p = 2) in Figure 9.9. Some control generation is done locally, and the e3 line cascades through the CDelt chip (whereas it feeds the internal Deltic operators from a tapped delay line). Local control generation saves considerably on pin count at the cost of a small increase in hardware. We have chosen to restrict control input to three pins per chip – had we generated all controls externally, this figure would have risen to nine. The penalty for this pin saving is that control signals, which are synchronous throughout the system, are generated locally on every CDelt chip instead of once only, on a separate chip.

The convolution SUBSYSTEM
The subsystem FirSub (Figure 9.10) consists of q CDelt chips in cascade. The cascading structure is identical to that of CDelt – after all, we have merely

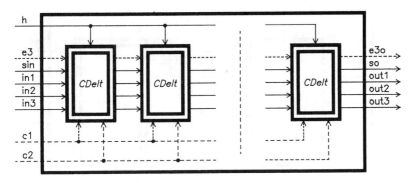

Fig. 9.10   Cascaded deltic processing SUBSYSTEM 'FirSub'

inserted chip boundaries in a cascade of Deltic processors. Each chip produces mp double-precision products, accumulated to triple-precision, which it passes forward down the linear array of chips which make up the subsystem.

The output function CHIP
It now only remains to construct a final chip to re-format the triple-precision accumulated subsystem output into single-precision. CForm (Figure 9.11) contains the primitive FFORMAT3TO1, whose parameters are chosen to represent the maximum possible accumulation by full-scale single-precision output. We leave the evaluation of these parameters until simulation.

The SYSTEM
We have arranged the system as a configuration of subsystem FirSub and chip CForm connected in cascade. Figure 9.12 shows the system, including control lines.

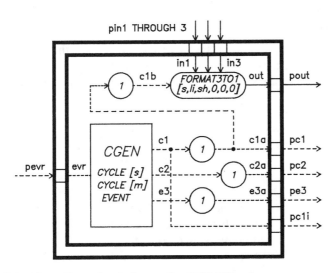

Fig. 9.11   Output formatting and control generation CHIP 'CForm'

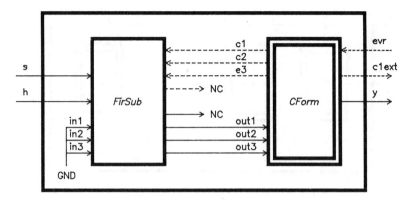

Fig. 9.12   Matched filter SYSTEM

Control

CForm also contains the system CONTROLGENERATOR, with two
CYCLEs and one EVENT. The two CYCLE parameters represent system
wordlength s and multiplexing level m respectively. The EVENT pulse is used
to load the reference vector, as described earlier.

Control at c1 level is simple to implement, as all processors work in
synchronism. We merely have to supply each primitive in each Deltic operator
with a c1 pulse in synchronism with incoming signals. Each CDelt chip contains
a small delay chain for this purpose. External to chips, c1 is global.

The c2 pulses are also globally distributed, as we arranged the latency of the
Deltic operator for this purpose. The e3 pulses, on the other hand, are fed to
each Deltic operator from a long tapped delay line which cascades through the
entire subsystem.

9.2.3   Example system

We now create an example system to demonstrate the function of the
transversal filter structure. We choose the following parameters – appropriate
to a 5 μm nMOS process and a sonar matched filtering application:

> process clocking rate ~ 8 MHz
> sample rate = 18 kHz

> $r = 8$ reference signal wordlength
> $s = 14 (d = 12)$ system wordlength (from 12-bit input signal)
> $m = 32$ multiplexing level
> $p = 2$ Deltic operators per CDelt chip
> $q = 8$ CDelt chips per FirSub subsystem
> $N = 512$ filter length (= mpq)

Initial checks
A useful initial check for correct function is to correlate two squarewaves, producing a triangular result. To this end, we enter squarewaves of half full scale amplitude at both signal and reference inputs. The output should then be a triangular wave of quarter full scale amplitude; as the root-mean-square (rms) value of a squarewave is equal to its amplitude, the mean-square (correlation peak amplitude) is simply the product of the input amplitudes.

In general terms, the scalar output of a matched filter is given by:

$$y(t) = K \sum_{n=0}^{N-1} s(t,n)h(n) \qquad 9.2$$

N being filter length and K being a scaling factor (decided in our case by FORMAT parameters).

It is important to monitor the system output at the correct time in the multiplexing frame. This time may be calculated by tracing the latency of the path from signal input to filter output, which turns out to be 5 words and 3 bits over and above the 16 sample delays inherent in the cascaded architecture (Figure 9.13). The illustrated process of time tagging (cumulative latency accounting) is a useful bit-serial design technique, as discussed in Chapter 6.

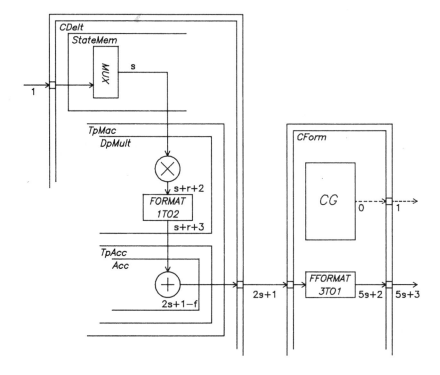

Fig. 9.13 Critical Path in matched filter SYSTEM (sample delays due to stages not shown)

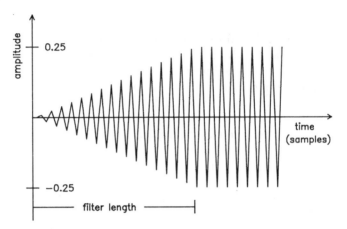

Fig. 9.14 Squarewave correlation experiment

Figure 9.14 (backed up by inspection of numerical simulator output) provides the expected result, verifying the multiplexing and cascading schemes chosen.

Matched filter simulations
The behaviour of the specified system is observed under the following conditions. The reference vector is a peak amplitude chirp signal scanning the frequency range from nyquist to dc. The input signal is a dc to nyquist chirp followed by a string of zero-values, this chirp amplitude being 6 bits down from full scale. The chirp signal may be expressed as:

$$c(n) = \sin(\frac{bn^2}{N})$$

where b is the chirp bandwidth (π here) and N is the duration of the chirp in samples.

The chirp, or linearly frequency modulated (LFM) signal (Klauder, 1960) has excellent properties for pulse compression.[†] At one point (sample no. N), a signal which is statistically nearly white over the filter length (i.e. has equal energy at all frequencies), and yet is intrinsically sinusoidal (has an rms value of 0.707), correlates perfectly with itself. This causes a spike of half maximum amplitude to appear at the filter output (mean-square = 0.5), with little surrounding energy (due to the near whiteness of the chirp). From equation (9.2), spike amplitude is:

$$y = K \sum_{n=0}^{N-1} 2^{-6}\sin^2 (\frac{\pi n^2}{N}) = 2^{-7}NK \qquad 9.3$$

The factor 2^{-6} inside the summation is the product of signal and reference vector amplitudes.

[†] Pulse compression (Cook and Bernfeld, 1967) is the process through which the echo return from a finite-length, finite-power transmitted signal burst (the pulse) is compressed in time by correlation in the matched filter. The relative timing and spread of the compressed sequence yields information on target range, velocity, etc.

We simulate the chirp input conditions of equation (9.3), and then repeat the experiment with the input signal buried in zero-mean Gaussian noise g(t) of standard deviation $\sigma_g = 2^{-4}$. The correlation spike is then subject to additive noise, which, if filter gain is inadequate, may render detection impossible. The effect of this noise could be reduced by ensemble averaging, but in a real-time situation we are constrained to one correlation per sample period. We can, however, estimate bounds on the output noise x(t), given statistical knowledge of input noise g(t), and ensure that our filter has sufficient gain to guarantee detection. Output noise is given by

$$x(t) = K \sum_{n=0}^{N-1} g(t)\sin\left(\frac{\pi n^2}{N}\right) \qquad 9.4$$

Since powers of uncorrelated signals are additive (Cook and Bernfeld, 1967), squaring and taking expectations gives:

$$E[x^2(t)] = NK^2 E[g^2(t)] E\left[\sin^2\left(\frac{\pi n^2}{N}\right)\right]$$

$$= NK^2 \sigma_g^2 2^{-1}$$

$$= NK^2 2^{-9} \qquad 9.5$$

This gives an expected noise amplitude:

$$\hat{x} = K 2^{-4.5} \sqrt{N} \qquad 9.6$$

Note that signal (or coherent) gain is proportional to N, whereas noise (or incoherent) gain is proportional to $\sqrt{N}$.

We may choose a gain factor K to maximise output resolution. As the filter input must contain two guard bits (for correct multiplier operation), and as the tap weight vector has an rms value of 0.5, then worst-case filter gain (when input and reference sequences correlate) is N/8, from equation (9.3). Choosing K = 8/N will then maximise output resolution.

In the case where N = 512, giving $K = 2^{-6}$, equations (9.3) and (9.6) predict:

$$y = 2^{-4}, \qquad \hat{x} = 2^{-6}$$

Figure 9.15 shows the result with the chirp input alone, and Figure 9.16 in the presence of Gaussian noise. The spike is still visible in the latter case, as worst-case noise interference cannot reduce the spike height to that of the noise floor. However when N = 32, giving $K = 2^{-2}$, equations (9.3) and (9.6) predict:

$$y = 2^{-4}, \qquad \hat{x} = 2^{-4}$$

and the spike is indistinguishable from output noise (Figures 9.17 and 9.18).

9.2.4   Comment on FIR case study

The matched filter design demonstrates the descriptive power of a language which supports parameterisation and arithmetic. The same source file may be easily adapted to a variety of applications. Two common uses of input predelay for design optimisation have been demonstrated.

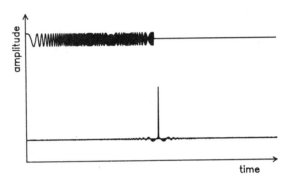

Fig. 9.15   Pulse compression, 512-point filter

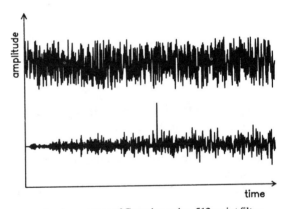

Fig. 9.16   Pulse compression in presence of Gaussian noise, 512-point filter

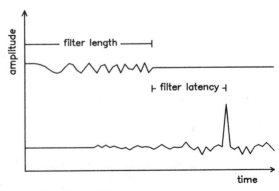

Fig. 9.17   Pulse compression, 32-point filter

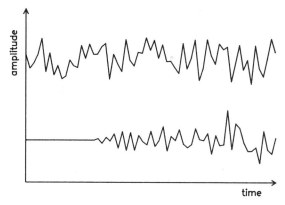

Fig. 9.18   Pulse compression in presence of Gaussian noise, 32-point filter

As we have seen, there are many ways of implementing the transversal filter structure. The reader may know of better ways than the one presented here – however the simple control and communication schemes employed allowed rapid, easy implementation. Control and multiplexing schemes were deliberately maintained at a low level of complexity. The next case study provides some tougher design issues.

9.3   LMS adaptive filter

We continue our study of transversal filters with the design of an echo-canceller based on an adaptive filter (Cowan and Grant, 1985). The main difference between adaptive and fixed-response filters is that the adaptive filter uses its previous output sample to alter its tap-weight vector before commencing computation of the next output sample. Thus the system latency, which the designer may trade against other issues in the fixed-response filter, must be minimised in the adaptive case.

9.3.1   Introduction

A great proportion of digital adaptive filter designs use variations of the Widrow LMS algorithm (Widrow *et al.*, 1975). The functional block diagram for such a filter is shown in Figure 9.19.

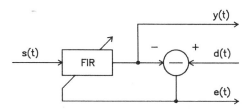

Fig. 9.19   Functional block diagram of Widrow LMS adaptive filter

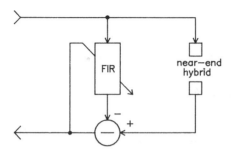

Fig. 9.20   Usual configuration for echo-canceller

A particular application area for adaptive filters is echo cancellation in telephone networks. Due to various reasons, detailed by Sondhi and Berkley (1980), the received signal is corrupted by delayed versions of the transmitted signal. One solution is to model the echo path, and subtract the received signal, filtered by the model, from the transmitted signal. If this process is carried out at both ends of the line, echo-free communication may be enjoyed. Figure 9.20 shows the usual configuration for a telephone line echo canceller.

9.3.2   Theoretical background

The filtering hardware within an adaptive filter consists of essentially the same FIR structure discussed in the first part of this chapter. The FIR filter produces its output sample by convolving its signal and tap weight vectors, i.e.

$$y(t) = \mathbf{S}^T\mathbf{H} \qquad\qquad 9.7$$

However, the tap weights are not fixed in the adaptive case – they are updated according to the Widrow LMS algorithm, which operates as follows. Firstly each output sample $y(t)$ is subtracted from a training signal $d(t)$ to produce the error sample $e(t)$, i.e.

$$e(t) = d(t) - y(t) \qquad\qquad 9.8$$

The algorithm forms an estimate of the correlation between the error sample and the signal sample at each tap in the filter, and updates each tap weight in such a direction as to reduce this correlation. The filter is said to have converged when the error signal and the signal vector are orthogonal.

A useful cost function, describing the distance of the tap weight vector from the optimal solution or Wiener vector (Wiener, 1949), is mean-square error (MSE). The object of the algorithm is then to minimise the MSE. The Widrow LMS algorithm estimates the MSE by squaring a single error sample, and minimises this by gradient methods. Substituting equation (9.7) in equation (9.8) and squaring gives

$$e^2(t) = d^2(t) - 2d(t)\mathbf{S}^T\mathbf{H} + \mathbf{H}^T\mathbf{S}\mathbf{S}^T\mathbf{H} \qquad\qquad 9.9$$

and differentiating w.r.t. the tap weight vector **H** gives

$$\frac{\partial e^2(t)}{\partial \mathbf{H}} = -2d(t)\mathbf{S} + 2\mathbf{S}\mathbf{S}^T\mathbf{H} \qquad 9.10$$

Equations (9.7) and (9.8) give

$$\frac{\partial e^2(t)}{\partial \mathbf{H}} = -2\mathbf{S}e(t) \qquad 9.11$$

The updates to the tap weights are performed by subtracting these correlation estimates (multiplied by a convergence factor μ) from each tap weight. The size of μ determines the accuracy and stability of the final solution, and the speed of convergence to that solution. The maximum bound on μ is governed by input signal statistics (Ungerboeck, 1972). The updating process may be expressed as

$$\mathbf{H}' = \mathbf{H} - \mu \frac{\partial e^2(t)}{\partial \mathbf{H}} \qquad 9.12$$

i.e.

$$\mathbf{H}' = \mathbf{H} + 2\mu\mathbf{S}e(t) \qquad 9.13$$

Equations (9.7), (9.8) and (9.13) represent the recursive algorithm to be implemented in the echo-canceller under design, i.e. a vector inner product, a discrete error computation, and a pointwise vector update.

9.3.3 System specification and initial system plan

The heart of the echo canceller is a straightforward adaptive filter. However, due to the nature of the echo path in long-distance telephone networks, the canceller may need to exhibit a long impulse response, requiring perhaps two thousand or more filter points to achieve accurate modelling. This involves the designer in problems of word growth over the filter accumulation, and necessitates partitioning of the system into identical cascadable blocks.

The Widrow LMS adaptive filter differs from the straightforward FIR filter in one important respect – it cannot proceed with computation of one output sample until the preceding output sample is complete, i.e. it cannot be pipelined. Thus processor latency must be minimised, and the architecture chosen in the matched filter study is not suitable in this case. We adopt a backward multiplexed architecture with parallel summation as described in Figures 5.9 and 5.11.

The adaptive filter then consists of several multiplexed LMS processors, working in a word and sample-synchronous manner. Their outputs are fed to a binary adder tree, which in turn feeds an error-update processor which returns the update sample to the LMS processors, thus completing the loop.

The echo-canceller chip set of this case study was specified as follows:

1. Filter bandwidth = 4 kHz (sample rate = 8 kHz)
2. Filter length = 512 in basic form, up to 2048 in full form

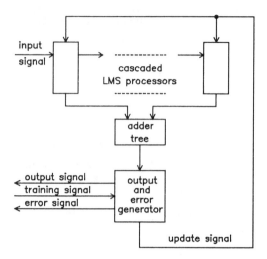

Fig. 9.21 Initial chip plan

    3. Converter resolution = 12 bits
    4. Tap weight resolution = 16 bits
    5. Maximum process clock rate = 8 MHz

It was assumed that a single LMS processor plus the multiplexing memory would fit on to a single chip. The level of multiplexing attainable was then a function of tolerable chip dimensions, processor latency, system clock rate and signal bandwidth. Figure 9.21 is the initial chip plan of the system.

9.3.4   System description

Starting from equations (9.7), (9.8) and (9.13) block diagrams may be produced, detailing the construction of a single LMS processor block, and the error-update block. Figures 9.22 and 9.23 show these blocks. Initially it would appear that the multiplier used in the filter output convolution should be double-precision. However, the nature of echo-cancellation is such that the filter produces a noisy estimate of the echo path, so a single-precision rounding multiplier, accumulated to double-precision where necessary, will suffice. For similar reasons the tap weights are designated as single-precision entities, although this precludes use of a convergence factor low enough to suppress tap weight perturbations due to near-end speech.

The next step is to determine the significance and format of words at each point in the system. The highest desired resolution in the system is the 16-bit tap weight. As we are using multi-wire accumulation, no further restrictions on wordlength occur, and the system wordlength may be set at 2 guard bits above 16, i.e. swl = 18. These guard bits guarantee correct operation of the bit-serial multipliers in the system. Thus the potential word-rate for the echo canceller engines is 8 MHz divided by 18 bits, i.e. 444.4 kHz.

Figures 9.22 and 9.23 display the significance (single arrows) and format

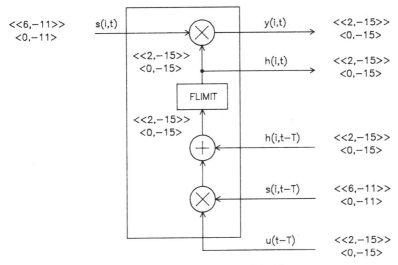

Fig. 9.22   LMS processor plan, showing number format and significance

(double arrows) of words at important points of the system (cf. Chapter 6). Format and significance in the adder tree is not treated, as the double precision nature of this structure precludes overflow. We design for worst-case word growth, and employ limiting at two points in the system to protect the guard-bits of the associated multipliers.

The system can be said to work in three distinct, cycling modes:

1.   Operation, i.e. performing convolution to produce an output sample (equation 9.7)
2.   Error-update generation, i.e. subtraction of the formatted output sample from the training signal (equation 9.8) then multiplying by 2μ, and
3.   Adaptation, i.e. multiplication of $2\mu e$ by each signal sample and accumulation in the tap weight registers (equation 9.13).

Due to the pipelining inherent in bit-serial systems, mode 3 may be executed in parallel with mode 1. Mode 2, however, cannot proceed until mode 1 produces the final accumulated output word, and mode 3 must await the appearance of the result of mode 2 before commencing. Thus mode 2, whilst computationally trivial in comparison to the other modes, provides a system bottleneck during which the other modes must idle.

The level of multiplexing in the LMS blocks may be decided at this stage. The full multiplexing potential of the system, ignoring idles and latencies for the present, is simply the ratio of system word-rate to system sample rate. In this case, the full potential is 444.4 / 8, i.e. 55.55. To obtain the actual potential, we must subtract the idles from this figure. The idles are given by the critical path length of the algorithm recursion loop, i.e. the number of word delays between the appearance at the convolution multiplier of the final multiplexed signal sample, and the first updated tap weight.

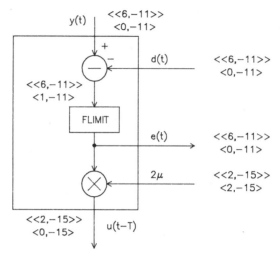

Fig. 9.23   Error-update processor plan, showing number format and significance

The critical path length must be accommodated at the end of each filter output cycle, since the next cycle may not commence until the error has been computed and returned to the LMS blocks. As each primitive, operator, etc., in the path has an intrinsic latency, this figure may be easily calculated. Figure 9.24 shows the critical path of the LMS system, with time tags marking the cumulative latency throughout.

The critical path length is estimated at around 7 words, giving a multiplexing potential of 48. However, in order to reduce the multiplexing memory requirement (and hence chip size), and also relax the 8 MHz bit rate, the multiplexing level was chosen to be 32. This leads to a revised system clock rate of $(32 + 7) \times 8$ kHz $\times$ 18 = 5.62 MHz.

As the critical path length is not an integer number of system wordlengths, a block of compensating delay must be introduced into the critical path, to give it an integer length. This may be accomplished by simply inserting a bit-delay block (the delay being parameterised for the present), or by entering arbitrary delay after such primitives as ADD and SUBTRACT, thereby possibly saving on chip floorspace. However, decisions about fine-tuning chip sizes should not be taken until the system design is near to completion.

The importance of ensuring that all loops have latency equal to an integer wordlength cannot be over-stressed. Our experience indicates that failure to comply with this constraint has been the most common cause of initial timing errors in system designs.

On completion of the system description, and estimation of partitioning into chips, the next step is to create source files for FIRST.

9.3.5   System implementation using FIRST

Having designed the system from the top down, it can now be implemented from the bottom up. The first step is to create the arithmetic operators. These

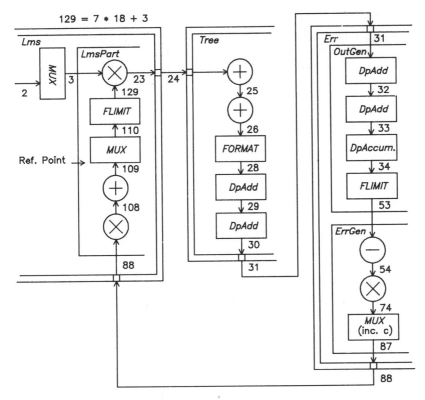

Fig. 9.24   Critical path in LMS system

are identified as follows:

1. LmsPart – an LMS processor block
2. DpAdd – a double-precision adder
3. DpAccumulate – a double-precision accumulator
4. OutGen – a block which produces and formats y(t) by accumulating the outputs of all LMSPART blocks, and
5. ErrGen – a block which produces $2\mu e$ using $y(t)$, $d(t)$ and 2μ.

Figures 9.25–9.28 depict these operators as computation engines constructed from FIRST primitives. All operators are stripped, i.e. hardware-minimal, although DpAdd (not shown) is trivial. Here time alignment has been sacrificed for hardware efficiency.

The next step is to construct the following three higher-level operators:

1. LmsOp – an LmsPart operator multiplexed to produce 32 filter points, with associated signal and tap weight state memory
2. TreeOp – an adder tree capable of summing the outputs of 16 LmsOp operators, i.e. 512 filter points, (whilst accommodating worst-case word growth), and

3. ErrOp – a block in which OutGen sums and formats the outputs of up to four TreeOp operators (i.e. 2048 filter points), accumulates in double-precision, and limits to single precision. The output is passed to ErrGen, which performs subtraction to produce the error sample, multiplies by 2μ, and recirculates the valid update to feed the LmsOp blocks.

By no coincidence, the system is now partitioned into feasible chips, and the three chip designs (Figures 9.29–9.31), corresponding to encapsulations of the three operators listed above, take the names Lms, Tree and Err. The compensating delay c, and the control timing accommodate the bit-delays introduced across chip boundaries. The CONTROLGENERATOR is placed on CHIP Err.

The SUBSYSTEM LmsSub (Figure 9.32) can be defined as 16 Lms chips with their outputs connected to a Tree chip, forming a 512-point LMS filter section. Thus the short filter (Figure 9.33) merely consists of LmsSub and Err, whilst the long (2048-point) filter has 4 LmsSubs instead of just one.

Two major design issues require detailed explanation – the multiplexing and the control regimes. Although we present their design as separate processes, they are closely related in reality.

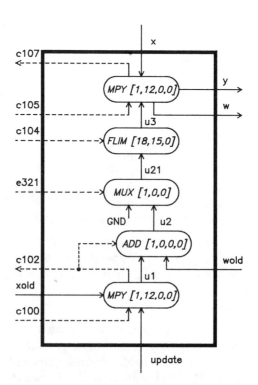

Fig. 9.25   Convolution and LMS update OPERATOR 'LmsPart'

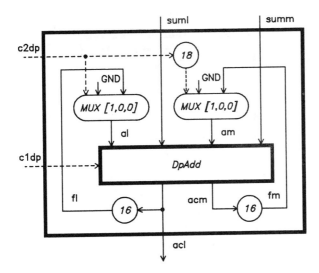

Fig. 9.26   Double-precision accumulate OPERATOR 'DpAccumulate'

9.3.6   The Lms multiplexing regime

As stated before, Lms contains the operator LmsPart, and the state memory to enable its time-division multiplexing.

We have already outlined the principle of the state memory loops for this application in Chapters 5 and 6. We use backward multiplexing to evaluate m

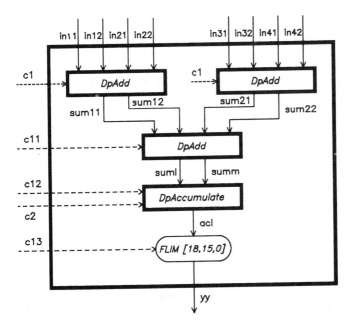

Fig. 9.27   Filter output generation OPERATOR 'OutGen'

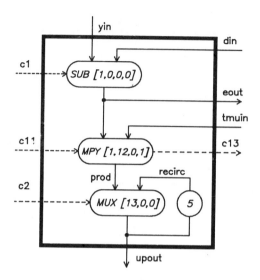

Fig. 9.28   Filter error and update generation OPERATOR 'ErrGen'

= 32 iterations per stage, with i = 7 idle cycles. The signal state loop was developed in Figures 5.11 and 6.4. It is implemented in this application within OPERATOR StateMemory, shown in Figure 9.34. The total signal loop delay is m + i – 1 = 38 words. The current sample input (x in Figure 9.34) to LmsPart is generated at the output of the multiplex element, whilst the cascade point is 32 words into the loop (less one bit to allow for the pad delay across chip boundaries). The old signal sample (xold in Figure 9.34) is taken from the same state loop, but appears at a different position to that suggested in Figure 6.4. The new tap position reflects the fact that LmsPart in this practical system

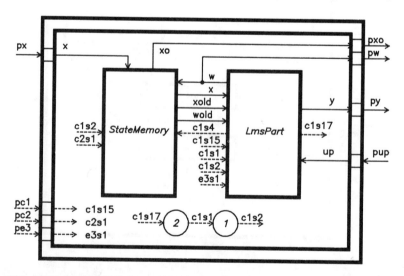

Fig. 9.29   Multiplexed convolution and LMS update CHIP 'Lms'

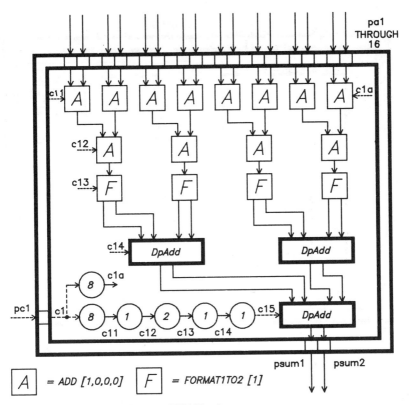

Fig. 9.30   Double-precision summing tree CHIP 'Tree'

is not time-aligned, and xold is required 40 bit-times earlier than x. We compensate for this by moving the xold tap 40 bits back in the state loop, in this case through the multiplex element, to effect the correct timing for this signal.

The majority of the coefficient loop (total length m + i = 39 words) is implemented in StateMemory, but some use is made of the implicit delay provided in LmsPart, which also contains a multiplex point to clear the coefficient loop and thus reset the system under event control.

9.3.7   The control regime on Err

The control network of the fixed filter study was trivial – here it is not so. We approach the synthesis of the control network in four main steps:

1. Identification and time tagging of objects in the signal paths,
2. Creation of an e3 (system cycle-level) control regime,
3. Creation of a c2 (word-level) control regime, and
4. Creation of a c1 (bit-level) control regime.

A working and near-optimally reduced control network follows from these simple steps.

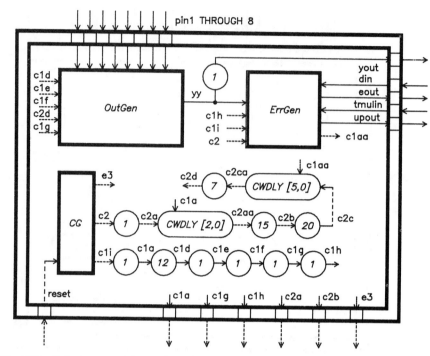

Fig. 9.31   Output, error, update and control generation CHIP 'Err'

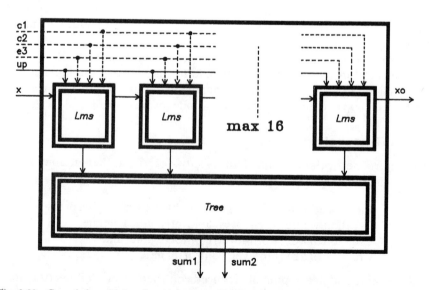

Fig. 9.32   Cascaded, multiplexed convolution and LMS update SUBSYSTEM 'LmsSub'

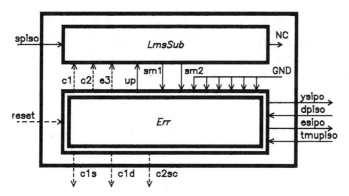

Fig. 9.33   LMS adaptive filter SYSTEM

Synchronising the signal paths

In the LMS adaptive system, there exists one primary signal path (other than memory loops for multiplexing, which are controlled locally). Referring to the system diagram, the signal path can be seen to leave the subsystem LmsSub, pass through chip Err, and return to LmsSub. LmsSub (containing Lms and Tree in cascade) may be regarded by Err as an object with fixed latency. However, as Err contains the CG, the signal path internal to Err must be further reduced to the components of stripped operators OutGen and ErrGen. This is because the CG must supply these primitives directly.

Care must be taken to include a pad delay p in the path as signals leave the chip. Other chips in the system should contain p in their latency figure. (For the purposes of this exercise, it is assumed that signals enter chips with zero delay, and leave with one bit delay. Whilst this assumption produces correct delay times, it should be borne in mind that in actual fact a half-bit delay is incurred both on entering and on leaving.)

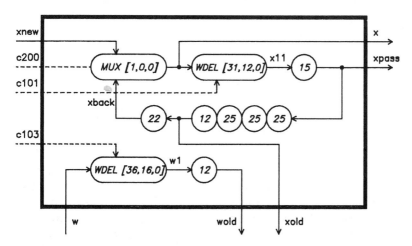

Fig. 9.34   Vector state memory OPERATOR 'StateMemory'

Thus an expression in latencies may be formed for the signal path:

$$SP = LmsSub + Err$$
$$Lms + Tree + Err$$
$$Lms + Tree + OutGen + ErrGen \text{ (including c)} + p$$
$$62 + 6 + 23 + 22 + c + 1$$
$$114 + c$$

The next highest multiple of swl ($= 18$) to 114 is 126, thus the compensating delay $c = 126 - 114 = 12$ bits, and $SP = 126 / 18 = 7$ words. Figure 9.24 shows the critical path, with compensating delay included in the latency of the MULTIPLEX primitive on Err.

The e3 (system cycle-level) control regime
The purpose of e3 is to realise an event in a system. In the LMS system, e3 is used to clear the tap weight memory loop, thereby initialising or resetting the system. The CG supplies a pulse on the e3 line of length equal to the system cycle length, usually as a result of an external, asynchronous request.

The e3 pulse leaves the CONTROLGENERATOR at time-tag zero – it is the designer's task to ensure its correct arrival at the chosen point by choice of reference point (RP) and path delay. If we connect the e3 output of the CG directly to Lms, we have an initial definition of the RP, the tap-weight clearing multiplexer on Lms.

The c2 (word-level) control regime
Control signals above the c1 level may have more than one function. The usual job of c2 is to mark either the start or the end of an active cycle. Note that in systems such as this, which idle for part of the cycle, start and end do not coincide.

In general, c2 is used much less frequently in a system than c1. Inspection of the LMS system reveals that, apart from supplying an external 'start convert' (SC) signal, c2 is used only 4 times:

1. to allow the new input sample to enter Lms,
2. to clear the accumulator,
3. to load the output SIPO register (ySIPO) and the error SIPO (eSIPO), and
4. to pass the new error sample out of ErrGen.

Whilst 2 is a start of cycle operation, 1,3 and 4 are end of cycle operations. (Use 1 can be either a start or an end of cycle operation, depending on choice of multiplexing scheme.) In an architecture which contains idles, start and end of cycle do not coincide.

If our RP marks a start of cycle, end of cycle operations carry a 'compound' time-tag consisting of the sum of the latency of the path back to the RP, and m–1 word delays, where m is the level of multiplexing chosen (32 in this case). Similarly, if our RP marks an end of cycle, start of cycle operations carry a compound time-tag consisting of the sum of the latency of the path back to the RP, and i+1 word delays, where i is the number of idle stages (7 in this case).

As m–1 is much greater than i+1, and we have freedom to commence clearing the tap weight loop anywhere within the idle segment, the latter choice would appear to be the better, as it involves minimal delay in the c2 path.

Now c2 is required on Lms 17 bit delays before e3, if e3 is truly an end of cycle pulse. If we take advantage of the fact that tap weight clearance may begin and end anywhere within the idle segment, we may bring e3 one word (i.e. 18 bits) forward, and thus c2 is required 1 bit after e3. Thus c2 on Lms carries the time-tag 1, and our choice of RP is beginning to look a good one.

Note that the c2 pulse which marks system outputs is also used as the SC signal to the a/d converters. This pulse does not need to be synchronous – it must merely allow the converters enough time to settle. In systems where this settling time is critical, a separate, optimal SC signal should be provided.

The following table shows the c2 tags:

object	time-tag	cycle-tag	pad-tag	compound-tag
Lms	2	0	–1	1
DpAccumulate	32	8 x 18	0	176
ySIPO	55	0	–1	54
ErrGen MUX	74	0	0	74

The compound-tag consists of the time-tag (the latency of the path from the object back to the RP), the cycle-tag (a multiple of the system wordlength, depending on the function of both the object and the RP at cycle level), and the pad-tag (1, 0 or –1 depending on siting of object, RP and CG).

Control supplied to operators on-chip with the CG does not incur a pad delay. As the RP is off-chip, a one-bit compensating delay (pad-tag) must be subtracted from the compound-tag of objects off-chip (see table entries for Lms and ySIPO). Were the RP on-chip, then 1 bit would be added to the tags of on-chip objects.

We now sort this list to produce an efficient tapped delay line to implement the c2 network.

object	compound-tag	delay
Lms	1	1
ySIPO	54	53
ErrGen MUX	74	20
DpAccumulate	176	102

The 53- and 120-bit delays are implemented by cascading CWORDDELAY and CBITDELAY primitives.

The c1 (bit-level) control regime

The purpose of c1 is simple – it marks the lsb of words entering any primitive, etc. Before describing the process of generating the c1 structure, it should be noted that, as well as supplying all the objects listed in the SPs, c1 must also load the PISO registers which supply the inputs to the system (sPISO, dPISO and tmuPISO). It must also control the CWORDDELAY blocks in the c2 path. As we saw, two of the c2 delays consist of a CWORDDELAY and a

CBITDELAY in series. As the order of these two blocks is unimportant, they may be ordered in such a manner as to minimise c1 delays.

The following table shows the c1 regime:

object	time-tag	pad-tag	tag mod SWL
LmsSub	88	−1	15
sPISO	2	−1	1
OutGen	31	0	13
OutGen(1)	32	0	14
OutGen(2)	33	0	15
OutGen(3)	34	0	16
tmu & dPISOs	53	−1	15
ErrGen	53	0	17
ErrGen(1)	54	0	0 -> 2
c2 @ 1	1/16	0	1/16
c2 @ 74	74/81	0	2/9

As shown, time-tags can be reduced modulo the system wordlength, due to the periodic nature of c1. If two tags are equal mod SWL, they may share the same control line. As ErrGen(1) is a multiplier, it is a c1 source as well as a sink, and provides an extra c1 line.

The bottom of the table deals with the control to the c2 worddelays. As the word delay and bit delay blocks may be arbitrarily ordered, a choice of time-tags exists for the c2 worddelays (indicated by the '/' in the table). The designer chooses a reduced tag which already exists in the first part of the table. If both or neither already exist, then either order suffices (although fan-out must be considered in large networks). If the first tag choice already exists, the word delay comes first, and if the second exists, the bit-delay comes first.

The final table for c1 is shown below.

object	tag mod SWL	parameter
ErrGen(1)	0 -> 2	
sPISO	1	[1]
c2 @ 1	1	
c2 @ 74	2	
OutGen	13	[12]
OutGen(1)	14	[1]
OutGen(2)	15	[1]
LmsSub	15	
OutGen(3)	16	[1]
tmu & dPISOs	16	
ErrGen	17	[1]

The objects which share the same tag (mod SWL) have been connected, and the table sorted to produce the chain of control delays shown in the parameter column. Note also that the process of reducing and sorting mod SWL may also be applied to c1 internal to chips, operators etc. anywhere in the system. It has been done to a certain extent on Lms, where it is important to minimise the c1 network.

The choice of whether control for any object in the path is generated on chip beside the CG, or simply passed from the previous object (delayed appropriately) is at the discretion of the designer. This decision usually compromises pinout or chip area. For instance, Tree contains some CBITDELAY which allows it to share the c1 line to Lms. Thus LmsSub has only one c1 line, thereby saving one pin and some valuable waterfront on Err.

In summary, the steps in constructing the control path were as follows:

1. Identify the signal paths of the system, and time-tag all objects in the path.
2. Select an initial cycle RP which ensures that e3 appears where required at the start of the active cycle segment, or during the idle cycle segment. If e3 is used more than once, fix RP to minimise e3 control delay.
3. Identify all objects requiring c2 control, and calculate their compound tags. Sort and mark the c2 path from the RP to the last object in the SPs requiring c2 input. Insert time-aligning delays in the c2 path. Move the RP (i.e. rotate c2 path mod cycle length) until c2 control delays are minimised. Under unusual circumstances a compromise between e3 and c2 delays may have to be reached.
4. Mark the c1 path from the RP to the last object in the SPs requiring c1 input. Insert time-aligning delays in the c1 path. Reduce, select c2 word delay order, and sort the c1 path until c1 control delays are minimised.

A control network has now been synthesised using structured techniques. While not guaranteed optimal in terms of silicon area, it will work. Slight further reduction might be possible by distributing the compensating delay throughout the critical path. Considering that each primitive has the optional predelay facility, and some have arbitrary postdelay, the possibilities explode. Optimisation of this nature, and control path synthesis, could fairly easily be automated.

9.3.8 Chip synthesis

The system flow diagram is now complete, and may be entered to the silicon compiler for chip composition. Dimensions of the completed chips are as follows:

CHIP	width (λ)	height (λ)	aspect ratio
Lms	2125	1874	1.13
Tree	2139	1212	1.76
Err	2349	1575	1.27

Chip floorplans are given in Figures 9.35–9.37. A version of CHIP Lms from earlier in this design study is featured in Plate 4.

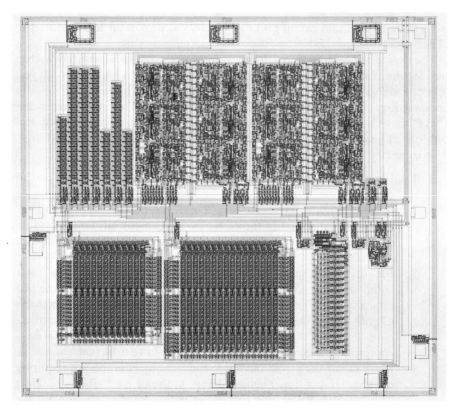

Fig. 9.35   Floorplan of CHIP 'Lms'

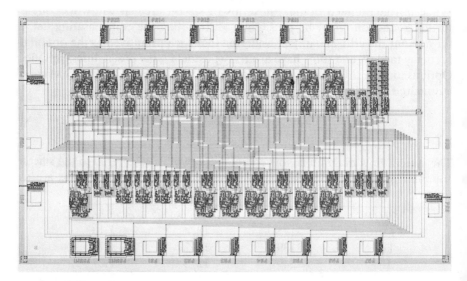

Fig. 9.36   Floorplan of CHIP 'Tree'

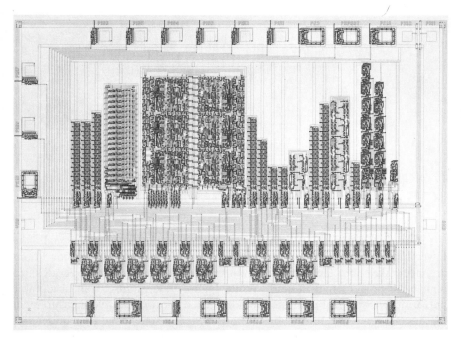

Fig. 9.37   Floorplan of CHIP 'Err'

9.3.9   System simulation

First of all a 32-point (1 Lms chip) system is tested with grounded inputs, to check for synchronisation at c1 level. Then a 64-point system (2 cascaded Lms CHIPs) is tested with sinusoidal inputs – a two-tone signal, and a single-tone signal. The two tones are at frequencies of 331.25 and 831.25 Hz, both at amplitudes of 0.25 relative to a full scale of unity. The lower frequency is common to both signals.

Firstly the input signal is the two-tone (at 12-bit significance), and the training signal the single-tone (at 16-bit). These significances maximise dynamic range of the system. A convergence rate μ of 1/32 is chosen. The filter easily cancels the higher tone (Figure 9.38), and the steady-state impulse response after convergence (error signal is zero) is shown in Figure 9.39. As there are countless solution vectors to this problem, the filter converges on a solution whose power is distributed unevenly – the taps at the front of the filter were already forming a solution as the filter flushed out.

Next the 64-point system is given the single-tone signal as input signal (at 12 bits), training on the two tone input (at 16 bits). The convergence factor is chosen to be 1/32. In this case the filter does not reproduce the training signal – being a linear system, it cannot synthesise the tone which is not present in the filter input. The residual error signal contains this tone.

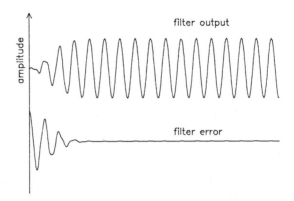

Fig. 9.38   Simulation of LMS adaptive filter showing convergence

Figure 9.40 shows the splitting of the two tones in the training signal – the lower appears in the filter output, and the higher in the error. These conditions are more like those faced by an echo-canceller, where the filter operates in a high error-power environment. While Figure 9.40 points to an acceptable performance, spectral analysis should be used for quantitative measurement of cancellation. The filter quickly finds a steady-state condition under this relatively large μ. However, the deficiency of the 16-bit tap resolution is exposed – perturbations of tap weights affect the filter output and limit the cancellation performance. Ideally, only the lower bits of the tap weight should be affected, with the stable higher bits forming the convolution multiplier coefficient. The impulse response after convergence is similar to that noted previously, but contains a distorting component at the higher frequency caused by perturbation (Figure 9.39).

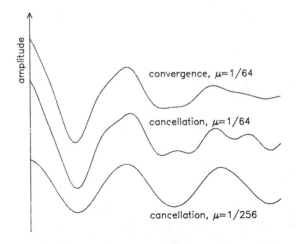

Fig. 9.39   Cancellation of unwanted tone, high convergence factor

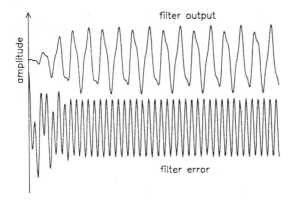

Fig. 9.40 Cancellation of unwanted tone, low convergence factor

We repeat the experiment with a convergence factor of 1/256 (Figure 9.41). The impulse response is much purer spectrally than that shown in the previous experiment, and does not decay so quickly. Both phenomena are due to the lower convergence factor used. Figure 9.39 shows the comparison of solution vectors.

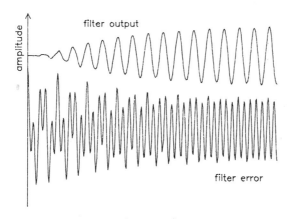

Fig. 9.41 Impulse responses from previous three experiments

9.3.10 Comments on the adaptive filter case study

A system has been synthesised which implements a long LMS adaptive filter. Some practical echo cancellers employ a greater degree of architectural sophistication (e.g. double-talk detection, input signal normalisation, etc.). The graduation from simple adaptive filter to echo canceller remains an area of work outstanding.

The system should be much more rigorously simulated, at full length and on real-world speech data corrupted by echoing channels of a non-stationary nature. It may transpire that the 16 bit coefficient resolution fails to produce the required amount of cancellation and S/N ratio. However, the conservative nature of the design as it stands should allow an increase of system wordlength without pushing the process clocking limit or increasing chip sizes beyond acceptable limits.

In retrospect, a 12-bit multiplier for convergence factor seems excessive – 8 bits would suffice and allow shortening of the critical path length. No assumptions were made about parameters of the solution vector sought (e.g. coherent and incoherent gain, maximum tap value) – we designed for worst case. In a real application bounds on these parameters can be quite accurately estimated, resulting in greatly improved performance over a 'general' system. In this case the double precision adders in the convolution summing tree might be unnecessary – indeed some re-formatting of the sum to increase significance might be desirable.

The direct implementation of the Widrow LMS algorithm requires an architecture which idles whilst the error sample is being computed. The simple expedient of updating with the second previous error sample and signal vector removes this bottleneck, allowing pipelining of the adaptive filter. Simulations have shown this to be an acceptable degradation of the Widrow LMS algorithm at low convergence factors, as employed in echo cancellers. However, the direct implementation brought some interesting design issues to light.

9.4   Conclusions

We have presented two FIR filter case studies, the first demonstrating the usefulness of parameterisation for architectural exploration, and the second the fairly optimal realisation of a more complex design. These systems represented, respectively, the second and first attempts of a silicon-naive systems designer to produce chip sets for signal processing applications, and each took less than one month of design time. Another few days of simulation verified the correctness of the designs.

References

Baggeroer, A. B., 'Sonar Signal Processing', in: *Applications of Digital Signal Processing*, A. V. Oppenheim (ed.), Prentice-Hall, pp 331–437, 1978.

Cook, C. E., and Bernfeld, M., *Radar Signals*, Academic Press, 1967.

Cowan, C. F. N., and Grant, P. M., (eds.), *Adaptive Filters*, Prentice-Hall, 1985.

Kaiser, J. F., and Kuo,, F. F., *System Analysis by Digital Computer*, Wiley, 1966.

Klauder, J. R., 'The Design of Radar Signals Having Both High Range Resolution and High Velocity Resolution', *Bell Syst. Tech. J.*, vol. 39, pp 809–820, 1960.

Kung, H. T., 'Why Systolic Architectures?', *IEEE Computer Magazine*, vol. 15, pp 37–46, 1982.

North, D. O., 'An Analysis of the Factors Which Determine Signal/Noise Discrimination in Pulsed Carrier Systems', *Proc. IEEE*, vol. 51, no 7, pp 1016–1027, 1963.

Rabiner, L. R., and Gold, B., *Theory and Application of Digital Signal Processing*, Prentice-Hall, 1975

Sondhi, M. M., and Berkley, D. A., 'Silencing Echoes on the Telephone Network', *Proc. IEEE*, vol. 68, no 8, pp 948–963, 1980.

Turin, G. L., 'An Introduction to Digital Matched Filters', *Proc. IEEE*, vol. 64, no. 7, pp 1092–1112, 1976.

Ungerboeck, G., 'Theory on the Speed of Convergence of Adaptive Equalisers for Digital Communication', *IBM J. Res. Dev.*, vol. 16, pp 546–555, 1972.

Widrow, B. *et al.*, 'Adaptive Noise Cancelling: Principles and Applications', *Proc. IEEE*, vol. 63, no 12, pp 1692–1716, 1975.

Wiener, N., *Extrapolation, Interpolation and Smoothing of Stationary Time Series, with Engineering Applications*, Wiley, 1949

10

An Adaptive Lattice Filter

Malcolm J. Rutter
Department of Electrical Engineering
University of Edinburgh

10.1 Introduction

The lattice structure is a form of prediction-error (PE) filter. It has application in data communications equalisation, spectral analysis and spectral shaping. The latter two categories cover such applications as RADAR moving target indication (MTI) and bandwidth compression by the linear predictive coding of speech (LPC).

10.1.1 The prediction-error filter

The problem of linear prediction is to predict optimally the next signal sample s(t), given the previous N samples (Haykin and Kesler, 1979). This may be done using a finite impulse response (FIR) filter in the form:

$$y(t) = - \sum_{i=1}^{N} s(t-i)a(i) \qquad\qquad 10.1$$

The filter weights, a(i) are chosen to give the best prediction function by transforming the autocovariance function of the input signal. This may be illustrated by noting that a sinusoidal signal has a sinusoidal autocovariance function and is totally predictable; a white signal, on the other hand, has a delta-function as an autocovariance function and is totally unpredictable.

To make a prediction-error (PE) filter we subtract the estimated output y(t) from the actual value of s(t) to give an error of estimation, e(t). Thus

$$e(t) = s(t) - y(t) \qquad\qquad 10.2$$

$$e(t) = s(t) - \sum_{i=1}^{N} s(t-i).a(i) \qquad\qquad 10.3$$

$$e(t) = \sum_{i=0}^{N} s(t-i).a(i) \qquad\qquad 10.4$$

where a(0) is unity.

Figure 10.1 is a virtual machine interpretation of the PE filter defined by equation (10.1). It is called a forward PE filter because it attempts to predict the next signal sample to arrive. Just as it is possible to estimate the signal sample in advance of the time-frame of the filter, it is also possible to estimate

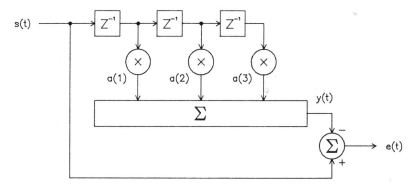

Fig. 10.1   A third-order forward prediction-error filter.

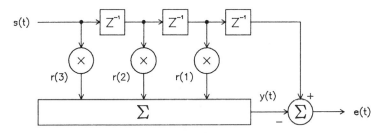

Fig. 10.2   Third-order backward prediction-error filter.

the sample one before the remembered time-frame. A backward PE filter is illustrated in Figure 10.2.

The filter coefficients are optimised to minimise the prediction error, e(t), in a least-mean-squares sense. Under this condition the output signal has the properties of orthogonality and whiteness. The property of orthogonality implies that the error signal is orthogonal to any of the signal elements within the predicting filter. Thus:

$$E[s(t-i).e(t)] = 0 \qquad\qquad 1 \leqslant i \leqslant N \qquad\qquad 10.5$$

Where E[ ] is the expectation operator.

The second property is that of whiteness; the spectral density of the output signal should be maximally flat. This is best understood by modelling the process generating the input signal as autoregressive (AR) type excited by white noise. Figure 10.3 shows such an AR filter. The filter which will exactly cancel the AR transfer function and make the signal precisely white is a forward PE filter. The coefficients of the forward PE filter will then have the same values as those of the AR filter.

10.1.2   The lattice structure

The lattice structure shown in Figure 10.4 is one which simultaneously provides backward and forward prediction-error outputs. On entry to the filter, the

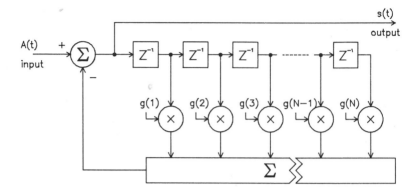

Fig. 10.3 The autoregressive filter model.

input signal is divided into two distinct signal paths, one providing the forward errors and the other, containing unit delay elements, providing the backward errors. As signals pass through successive stages they are modified to form prediction-error signals of successively higher orders. Thus a lattice structure of order N generates all forward and backward prediction errors of orders up to N.

While the transversal PE filter uses prediction-error coefficients, the lattice coefficients are K(1...N), the so-called PARCOR coefficients. These too may be transformed mathematically into or from the aperiodic autocovariance function of the input signal. The unusual structure of the lattice allows PARCOR coefficients to be calculated adaptively in individual recursive algorithms, allowing faster convergence and tracking.

The values of the coefficients may be calculated using open-loop (Makhoul, 1977) or closed-loop (Griffiths, 1977) techniques. Open-loop methods involve measuring correlations at various points in the circuit and using the results to

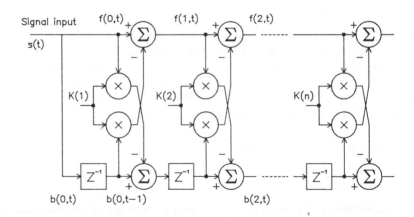

Fig. 10.4 The lattice structure.

set the coefficient values. For example, the optimum value of a PARCOR coefficient is equal to the cross-correlation between the two input signals for its stage. Closed-loop (feedback) techniques make use of the orthogonality properties of the lattice; an incorrect coefficient value will cause a non-zero mean product, which is used to steer the coefficient back towards the orthogonality condition.

10.1.3 Applications

Three main fields of application exist in equalisation, spectral analysis and spectral coloration for signal-to-noise ratio improvement. In adaptive equalisation, and adaptive filtering in general, the output usually comprises a number of input signals optimally summed in a linear combiner structure as shown in Figure 10.5. Where there is strong correlation between tap input signals, Widrow (1971) showed that convergence is slowed when using the combiner algorithm. This is especially so of the transversal filter (Chapter 9) in which the combiner signals are taken from the stages of a shift register. The backward PE signals from a converged lattice are mutually orthogonal, so the lattice is a useful decorrelating transform to apply to an input signal. The result is the reliably converging structure shown in Figure 10.6.

A second major application field is in spectral analysis. Since the lattice is a whitening filter, the PARCOR coefficients may be used to obtain the autocovariance function of the input signal. Applying a Fourier transform will produce a periodogram of the input signal. Alternatively, the PE coefficients may be calculated and transformed to give the cross-power spectral density of the whitening filter. The latter is then inverted to give a maximum-entropy or autoregressive spectrum. This spectral analysis technique finds an application in the linear predictive encoding (LPC) of speech, in which the spectrum of the speech is transmitted instead of the signal itself (Makhoul, 1975).

The final major applications area is in altering the spectral coloration of signals using the lattice structure. The whitening filter's ability to notch out spectral features may be used in a RADAR moving target indicator (MTI). This separates target from background clutter by notching out constant spectral features, leaving only the changing ones (Gibson and Haykin, 1983). The technique of line enhancement, described by Treichler (1977) involves replacing the signal with a predicted estimate of itself. The estimation process

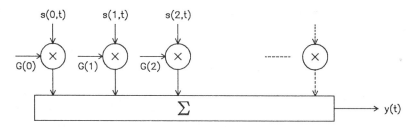

Fig. 10.5 A linear combiner.

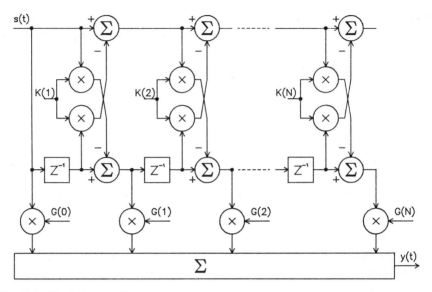

Fig. 10.6   The lattice equaliser.

is described by equation (10.1). Since the estimate is a weighted average of many signal samples, the noise is reduced, leaving only the stationary spectral information.

10.2   The algorithm

We follow the algorithm given by Satorius and Alexander (1979). This algorithm is divided into the signal path (lattice), a recursion to evaluate the PARCOR coefficients, and a further recursion to evaluate a step-size for the PARCOR coefficient recursion. All signal values and PARCOR coefficients are initialised to zero. The signal values are then calculated

$$f(0,t) = b(0,t) = s(t) \qquad\qquad 10.6$$

$$b(n,t) = b(n{-}1,t{-}1) - k(n,t).f(n{-}1,t) \qquad\qquad 10.7$$

$$f(n,t) = f(n{-}1,t) - k(n,t).b(n{-}1,t{-}1) \qquad\qquad 10.8$$

Where f and b represent the forward and backward signals respectively.

The PARCOR recursion is of closed-loop gradient type (see Figure 10.7 and Griffiths, 1977):

$$k(n,t) = k(n,t{-}1) + \mu(n,t).[f(n,t).b(n{-}1,t{-}1) + f(n{-}1,t).b(n,t)] \qquad 10.9$$

Where μ is a step-size used in the recursion.

The noise added to the signal by the stochastic adaptive process is proportional to the step-size, as discussed by Ungerboeck (1972). Unfortunately the rate of convergence (ROC) is inversely proportional to the step-size, so its value is critical to correct system operation.

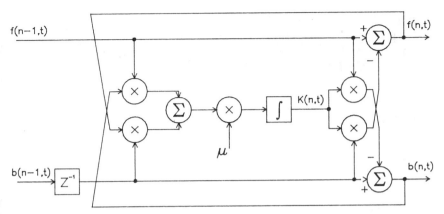

Fig. 10.7 Flow chart of the Mead lattice algorithm.

Since the ROC of a gradient algorithm is heavily dependent upon input power (Widrow, 1971), a useful step-size estimate is the inverse of the input power. The power input to a stage may be recursively estimated:

$$Q(n,t) = (1-\alpha).Q(n,t-1) + \tfrac{1}{2}\alpha(f^2(n,t)+b^2(n,t)) \qquad 10.10$$

$$\mu(n,t) = \frac{\beta}{Q(n,t)} \qquad 10.11$$

Where Q is the power estimate, $1/\mu$ is the approximate length of the exponential averaging process and β is some constant of proportionality.

Simulations show that a PARCOR recursion step-size of 1/40 relative to unity input power is a reasonable value. In some cases the step-size is started at a high value to give a rapid initial convergence. The step-size value then returns to normal levels as its own recursion (equation (10.10)) progresses. After coefficients of the structure have converged to values close to their optimal ones, the step-size is reduced even further. With this low step-size, typically 1/100 relative to unity input power, the filter can track gradual changes in its input signal statistics.

In the absence of a bit-serial divide primitive equations (10.10) and (10.11) are not suitable, so an alternative formulation must be found. We note that the final recursion merely estimates a second-order coefficient that controls the convergence of an adaptive process. As such its precise value has little effect on the final converged result. We can thus attempt an approximation to equations (10.10) and (10.11) by taking a first-order Taylor expansion:

$$\mu(n,t) = (1+\alpha).\mu(n,t-1) - \beta.(1+\alpha)^2.\mu^2(n,t-1).(f^2(n,t)+b^2(n,t)) \quad 10.12$$

This is equivalent to increasing the step-size by a small percentage, and then reducing it by an amount proportional to the power estimate. Clearly the $(1+\alpha)$ term in the first term on the RHS of equation (10.12) is essential to the recursion. The $(1+\alpha)$ term in the second term, however, may be dropped, causing only a slight reduction in accuracy. This gives the recursion:

$$\mu(n,t) = \mu(n,t-1).(1+\alpha-\beta.\mu(n,t-1).(f^2(n,t)+b^2(n,t))) \qquad 10.13$$

Simulation showed that this Taylor step-size recursion was slightly less stable than that of equation (10.10). For given values of α and β, the step-size has a slightly higher variance for a given data sequence. Nevertheless, we may simplify the calculation further by setting β equal to unity and dropping it from the calculation. This merely makes the exponential memory of the step-size recursion dependent upon the selected steady-state value of the step-size, an acceptable restriction.

Two further problems arise: with a zero signal input, the value of μ will ramp upwards indefinitely. Furthermore, if a noise impulse on the signal input raises the power estimate term above unity, the step-size will go negative. It would not normally recover from this abnormal condition. The problems are both solved by using limiters. One is placed within the step-size recursion to limit the value of the step-size to a maximum of 0.25. The other is used at the output of the power estimate subcalculation, to ensure that it never rises above unity. Figure 10.8 is a flow chart of the step-size recursion used.

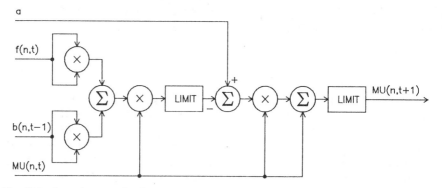

Fig. 10.8   Step-size recursion flow chart.

10.3 System specification

The specification for the system is modelled on applications in modem equalisation and LPC vocoding.

Sampling frequency:	20 kHz
Stages:	16
Input/Output Precision:	12 bits (including sign)

Further system constants governing rate of convergence, step-size, etc., are taken directly from the work of Satorius and Alexander (1979). It is expected that some applications will require a slow, accurate step-size factor. Provision is therefore made for reducing the step-size to 1/200 with respect to a signal of unit power. Simulations by Grant and Rutter (1984) show that the lattice structure is very susceptible to algorithm noise, but that such a low step-size gives an adequately accurate performance. Another requirement is that the step-size be initialised to a value of 0.25, falling during operation to its steady-state value. This ensures a rapid initial convergence followed by slower, more accurate adjustments as the filter settles.

10.4   Serial implementation

10.4.1   Target architecture

The main constraint on the algorithm is the forward signal channel in the filter section. This signal has to pass through each stage consecutively. The number of processing engines is nevertheless open to consideration, for the signal could be run through sixteen separate consecutive processors or one processor multiplexed sixteen ways. Intermediate configurations are also possible, such as two processors handling alternate input samples.

A rough calculation on the filter flow-graph shows that at the required precision, the delay through the forward channel would be approximately 26 bits. This is therefore taken as the delay between successive stages of the filter. Multiplying this by 16 stages and a 20 kHz clock frequency gives a bit rate of 8.320 MHz. This is approximately the maximum clocking rate for the 5 micron nMOS library. Thus the most economical solution appears to be to multiplex one processing engine sixteen ways to construct the sixteen-stage filter.

Having decided on the array architecture, the algorithm is partitioned into its natural arithmetic components: filter, PARCOR recursion and step-size recursion. These major operators are then augmented with memory and multiplexing elements. Figure 10.9 shows the system composition as a 5-chip set. Chips CL, CK, CMU1 and CMU2 will contain the primary lattice, PARCOR and stepsize engines respectively. Control generation and the majority of the state memory requirement will be housed on Chip COS.

10.4.2   The processing engines

The arithmetic engines are developed in Figures 10.10 through 10.13. These are direct implementations of the lattice section (Figure 10.4, implemented as Figure 10.10) the PARCOR recursion (Figure 10.7, implemented as Figure 10.11) and the stepsize recursion (Figure 10.8, implemented as Figures 10.12 and 10.13).

In each case the functional flow-graph has been developed to a flow-graph of FIRST primitive operators, including equalising delays where appropriate. The use of double or single precision multipliers and the provision of FORMAT and LIMIT operators is decided by the dynamic range requirements at each point in the system. Some of these issues are discussed in the following section.

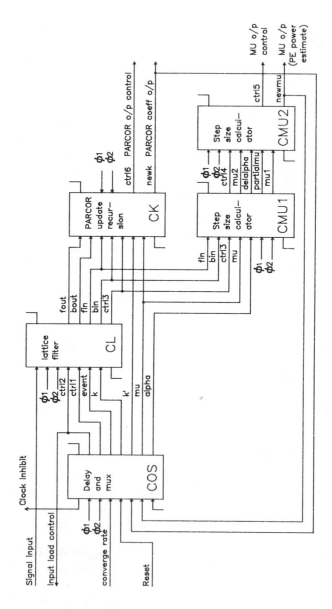

Fig. 10.9 Top view of five-chip adaptive lattice system. Unconnected nodes in the upper right and lower left of all devices are for V_{DD} and V_{SS} supplies respectively. All packages contain 16 pins.

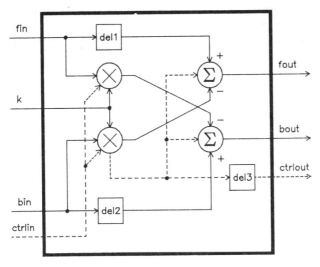

Fig. 10.10   Lattice operator flow chart.

10.4.3   Word formats and ranges

A previous design using TTL components (Rutter, 1983) used fractional two's complement arithmetic to precisions of 12 or 24 bits. There are several reasons why this simple scheme of range definitions does not work here.

In the FIRST chip set, each arithmetic element is separate. It is not practical to follow each additional element with its own limiter, as one may do with a central processor. This implies a less rigorous control over word-growth, which must be allowed for in later stages. The area covered by a multiplier is dependent upon the precision of its coefficient. It is therefore desirable to minimise wordlength while retaining accuracy of calculation.

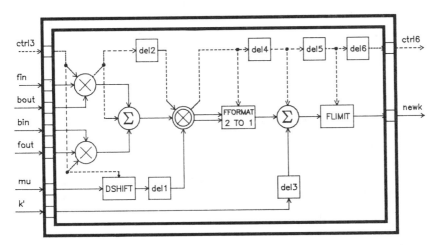

Fig. 10.11   PARCOR operator and chip (CK).

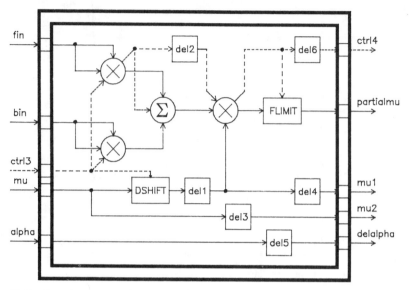

Fig. 10.12   Step-size operator (part 1, MU1) and chip (CMU1).

The reciprocal relationship between input power and step-size renders fractional two's complement arithmetic impracticable. When the input power to any stage is low, the step-size must grow to a value sometimes exceeding unity. Word-growth in the lattice occasionally causes numerical significance to exceed unity. Although a high precision is not required of the step-size recursion, it is nevertheless given a high dynamic range (19 bits). This is to accommodate both the high initial value and also the low steady-state value, when changes would be by even smaller increments.

The lattice signals are limited by the ADC to a nominal range of ±1. Word-growth down the lattice could take the signal outside this range; a range of ±4 is allowed. The twelve-bit accuracy of the ADC is preserved throughout the signal path.

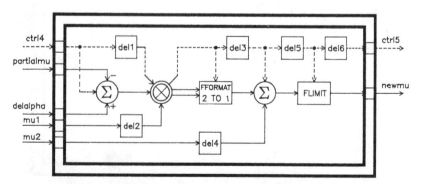

Fig. 10.13   Step-size operator (part 2, MU2) and chip (CMU2).

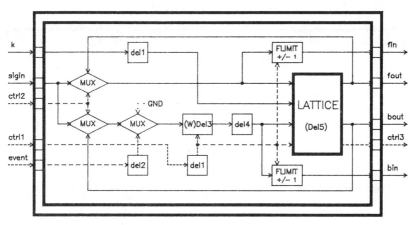

Fig. 10.14 Lattice chip (CL).

Having established the range of the signal, the ranges of the other variables may be calculated. First the variance of each variable is estimated for all operating conditions. The precision of the variable is then set three bits below this value. For example, the signal power-step-size product determines the level of the algorithm noise on the PARCOR coefficient. For the PARCOR recursion to work properly, the precision of the coefficient must be better than the rms value of this stochastic process. This sets the precision of the PARCOR coefficients to an accuracy of 2^{-17}. The PARCOR coefficients are also used in truncated form in the signal filter section, where accuracy can be traded for a reduced chip size.

The maximum possible values of variables are also calculated in order to establish the wordlength of the signal. The wordlength is taken as the range between the maximum value and the precision of the variable.

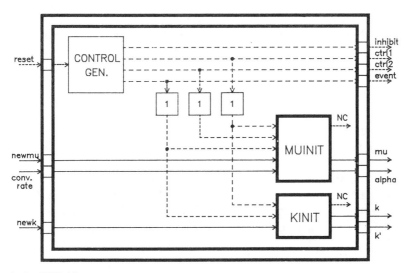

Fig. 10.15 COS chip.

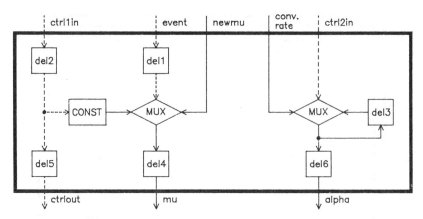

Fig. 10.16   MUINIT operator.

When calculating multiplier coefficient precisions, the wordlength of the variable is used. In some cases this results in an excessively high coefficient precision and the wordlength must be reduced. In some cases the maximum theoretical value is statistically unlikely and a maximum equal to eight times the maximum rms value is taken. If Gaussian statistical behaviour is assumed, this arbitrary threshold will be crossed only once every 10^{15} calculations.

Single-precision multipliers truncate or round an output to minimise word-growth. At certain points in the step-size and PARCOR recursion, this would leave the minimum rms value of the output below the multiplier output precision. The problem is solved using the double-precision multiplier form and subsequently reformatting its two output streams into one word.

The system wordlength is the maximum precision to which a number may be maintained within the system, without using multiple bit-streams. The system wordlength is determined by the delay around the f-channel of the lattice filter, where the signal must double back around one stage to become the input to the next. This delay establishes the system wordlength as 26 bits. This easily accommodates the maximum precision required for variable values, which is estimated at 19 bits.

10.4.4   Multiplexing and chip construction

The system may now be completed by adding state memory in the form of delay loops and multiplexers. We use a simple forward-multiplexed scheme to effect the direct f-channel cascade between stages.

The implementation of the f and b loops around the lattice operator is shown in Figure 10.14, which constitutes the Chip CL in Figure 10.9. The PARCOR and step-size engines occupy three chips already. The state memory associated with these functions is implemented on Chip COS (Figure 10.15) as operators

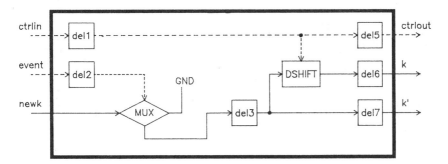

Fig. 10.17 KINIT operator.

MUINIT and KINIT, which are expanded in Figures 10.16 and 10.17.

The relationship and interconnection of these chips to form the complete system was previously defined in Figure 10.9. FIRST-generated floorplans for this five-chip set are shown in Figure 10.18. These are generated directly from the preceding flow-graphs. It is worth while to note that this function might well be integrated as a single component in (say) a 3-micron technology, without altering the FIRST-level system design. In either case the FIRST implementation replaces an equivalent system containing 120 TTL chips.

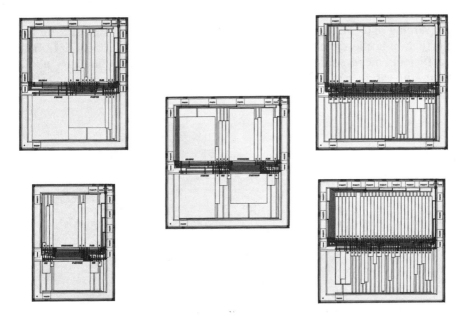

Fig. 10.18 Compiled chip floorplans for the five chip lattice system.

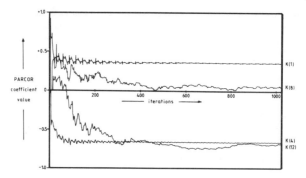

Fig. 10.19 Convergence of the coefficients of a lattice structure onto a stationary signal (reducing step-size).

10.5 System simulation

The first system test involves a composite signal, comprising 5 sinusoids and some noise. The object here is to determine the accuracy of convergence and not to test the rate at which the system could converge. Accordingly the step-size is started at a high value and gradually reduced over many iterations. The system was run for 1000 iterations, to be sure that steady-state values are attained. The final steady-state step-size is set to $1/(166.Q(0))$, where $Q(0)$ is the mean input signal power.

Figure 10.19 shows the PARCOR coefficients of the simulator model converging onto the test signal. The effect of the reducing step-size on the fluctuation in the signal is clearly visible in coefficients $K(1)$ and $K(4)$. The coefficients move straight to their steady-state values and fluctuate about them, the variance of the fluctuations reducing gradually with time and step-

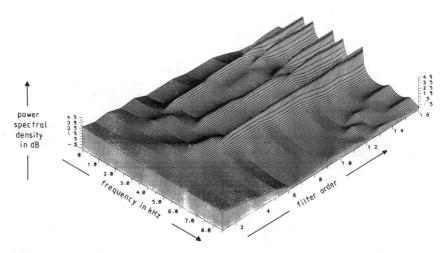

Fig. 10.20 AR spectral estimate of five sinusoid signal based on PARCOR coefficient values from FIRST simulation.

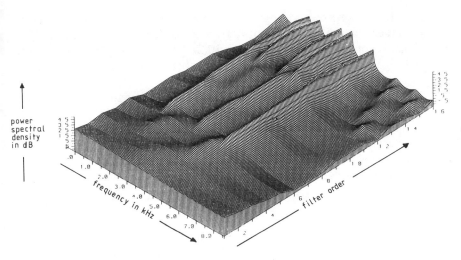

Fig. 10.21   Ideal simulation of AR spectral estimate.

size. The greater fluctuation in coefficients K(8) and K(12) are as a result of the build-up of noise down the lattice, caused by the stochastic adaptive process. The latter do not move directly towards their steady-state values, but are deflected by the initially incorrect PARCOR values of earlier stages. This phenomenon is described in greater depth by Gibson and Haykin (1980).

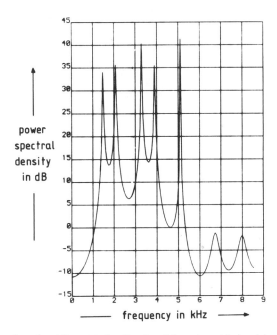

Fig. 10.22   Sixteenth order AR spectral estimate of five sinusoid signal based on PARCOR values from FIRST simulation.

Figure 10.20 shows the autoregressive estimate of the input signal spectrum, based on the values of the simulator-derived PARCOR coefficients after 1000 iterations. It appears identical to Figure 10.21, which was calculated from the original algorithm. Figure 10.22 is a graph of the sixteenth-order spectrum only.

The frequencies of the spectral peaks show a mean deviation from nominal of –12.6 Hz, with a maximum deviation from nominal of 23.6 Hz.

When the amplitudes of the five spectral peaks are measured in decibels and the mean is taken as a reference point, the maximum deviation from the mean of a spectral peak is +3.9 dB. The noise floor is estimated at approximately –47 dB, 3 dB below its nominal value.

References

Gibson, C.J. and Haykin, S. 'Learning Characteristics of Adaptive Lattice Filtering Algorithms', *IEEE Trans. ASSP*, vol. ASSP-28, no 6, pp 681–691, 1980.

Gibson, C.J. and Haykin, S. 'Radar Performance Studies of Adaptive Lattice Clutter-Suppression Filters', *IEE Proc.*, vol. 130, pt F, no 5, pp 357–367, 1983.

Grant, P.M. and Rutter, M.J. 'The Application of Gradient Adaptive Lattice Filters in Channel Equalisation', *Proc. IEE*, vol. 131, pt F, no 5, pp 473–479, 1984.

Griffiths, L.J. 'A Continuously Adaptive Filter Implemented as a Lattice Structure', *IEEE Trans. ICASSP*, Hartford, pp 683–686, 1977.

Haykin, S., and Kesler, S. 'Prediction-Error Filtering and Maximum-Entropy Spectral Estimation', in: *Non-Linear Methods of Spectral Analysis, Topics in Applied Physics*, S. Haykin (ed.) vol. 34, Springer-Verlag, Berlin, 1979.

Makhoul, J. 'Linear Prediction, a Tutorial Review', *Proc. IEEE*, vol. 63, no 4, pp 561–580, 1975.

Makhoul, J. 'Stable and Efficient Lattice Methods for Linear Prediction', *IEEE Trans. ASSP*, vol. ASSP-25, no 5, pp 423–428, 1977.

Mead, K.O. and Ryder, W.H. 'Improvements in or Relating to Self-Adaptive Linear-Prediction Filters', UK Patent GB 2 026 289 B, 1982.

Rutter, M. J., 'Theory, Design and Application of Gradient Adaptive Lattice Filters', Ph.D. Thesis, University of Edinburgh, Edinburgh, Scotland, 1983.

Satorius, E.H. and Alexander, S.T. 'Channel Equalisation Using Adaptive Lattice Algorithms', *IEEE Trans. COMM*, vol. COM-27, no 6, pp 899–905, 1979.

Treichler, J. 'The Spectral Line Enhancer – the Concept, an Implementation and an Application', Ph.D. dissertation, University of Stanford, Stanford CA, 1977.

Ungerboeck, G. 'Theory on the Speed of Convergence in Adaptive Equalisers for Digital Communication', *IBM J. Res. Dev.*, vol. 16, no 6, pp 546–555, 1972.

Widrow, B. 'Adaptive Filters', in: *Aspects of Network and System Theory*, R.E. Kalman and N. de Claris (eds.), Holt Rinehart and Winston, N.Y., 1971.

11

Filters:
An Integrated Digital Filter Subsystem

Richard F. Lyon

Laboratory for Artificial Intelligence Research
Schlumberger Palo Alto Research

11.1 Introduction

In order to satisfy various needs in audio-band filtering, and particularly for speech recognition system front-end filterbanks, an integrated digital filter subsystem has been designed using a bit-serial methodology. The chip, dubbed 'Filters', is a 4 mm by 6 mm nMOS chip with 4 μm features. It can implement 32 second-order filter sections (i.e. IIR, biquadratic, or complex pole-zero stages) at 16 kHz sample rate, or proportionately fewer filter sections at higher sample rates. The architecture includes features to support cascade, cascade/ parallel, and conventional parallel filterbanks of various orders, including optional half-wave and full-wave detection nonlinearities and envelope smoothing.

The development of the Filters chip proceeded in parallel with the development of an architectural methodology for VLSI digital signal processing (Lyon, 1981). The methodology included simplified layout styles and functional abstractions that made it possible to make this chip work using only manual layout tools and no simulation. Several other chips were also designed with the same methodology and components, for related functions.

11.2 Structural and functional description

The Filters chip is very nearly identical in structure and function to the example second-order section design of Jackson, *et al.* (JK&M) (1968). The implementation approach that they suggested, with an eye towards the coming technology of LSI, involves connecting hardware modules (adders, multipliers, and shift register memories) in exactly the configuration of the signal flow diagram of the intended function. They showed that by adding larger amounts of shift register delay memory where the flow diagram has delay elements, the hardware configuration can be effectively time-shared (multiplexed) over several independent applications of its function to different signals.

The basic second-order section flow diagram uses four multipliers, four adders and two delays, in a familiar arrangement. The coefficients used by the four multipliers are the four degrees of freedom that allow placement of a complex conjugate pair of poles and a complex conjugate pair of zeros at the desired locations in the Z plane. It is often useful, however, to have a fifth degree of freedom: the gain of the filter at a particular frequency. A fifth multiplier is sometimes included as another term in the feed-forward (numerator) polynomial, which makes it easier to put zeros far outside the unit circle in the Z plane, or sometimes as an overall gain, which leaves zero placement and the associated coefficient quanitisation requirements independent of the gain control. As will be discussed later, the latter approach was selected for the Filters chip.

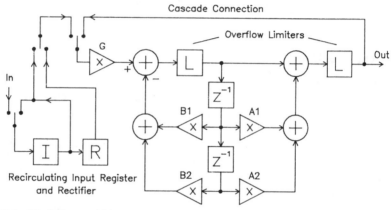

Fig. 11.1   Block diagram of the Filters chip.

Figure 11.1 shows the block diagram of the Filters chip, which represents both its functional flow diagram and its logical and physical structure. The realisation of the circuit from this level of description only requires a few operator module designs implementing the desired functions, with mutually compatible interfaces and a technique to make the timing work out correctly. The chip differs from JK&M's second-order section example in the logic design of the multipliers, in the circuit implementation technology, and in the following six minor functional modifications:

1.   A fifth multiplier has been included to control the gain of each section, as mentioned above.
2.   An input holding register has been added to allow an input sample to be repeated several times, as input to several parallel filters.
3.   A controllable rectifier has been added to the input register, so that either the half-wave or the full-wave rectified version of the input signal, or the input signal itself, can be filtered.
4.   Two overflow detector and corrector circuits have been incorporated into the design to prevent overflow oscillations within a filter section and to reduce the effect of transient overflows at filter section outputs.

5. The accumulator that JK&M included for adding together the outputs of parallel filter channels has been omitted from Filters, as it was not needed in filterbank applications.

6. The shift register memory has been changed to a variable serial delay memory, so that the multiplex factor and sample rate can be traded off after the hardware is built.

The application of this filtering subsystem to the implementation of a novel cascade/parallel filter structure for speech recognition is discussed in Section 11.5.

11.3   Specifications

The Filters chip operates on 24-bit data words, with four 16-bit coefficients and an 8-bit gain coefficient. All data and coefficients are in an identical 24-bit fixed-point-fraction two's complement format, regarded as values between -2 and $+2$. Overflow detector/corrector circuits limit their output values to be between $-\frac{1}{2}$ and $+\frac{1}{2}$, which guarantees suppression of overflow oscillations; after overflow correction, the two highest bits may be regarded as 'guard bits'.

Neglecting diagnostic pins, the chip pins are the following: Data-In, Data-Out, Gain-In, A1-In, A2-In, B1-In, B2-In, LSB-Time-In, Clock-In, VDD, Ground, the four control bits Input-Hold/Load, Rectify-Enable, Full/Half-Wave and Input/Feedback, and a 5-bit parallel code for the number of filter sections desired (binary numbers from 2 through 30 specify the memory delay, corresponding to 4 through 32 filter channels). The prototype chips are packaged in standard 40-pin ceramic dual-inline packages.

The maximum clock frequency and bit rate for the Filters chip is 12 MHz. The word time is 24 bit times, for a word rate of 500 kHz, and a total multiply rate of 2.5 M/second. The Data-In to Data-Out latency is 48 clock cycles (two words). The signal sample rate is up to 500 kHz divided by a multiplex factor from 4 to 32.

11.4   The Filters chip design

The design of the Filters chip involved designing the few kinds of bit-serial operators that appear in Figure 11.1. A central timing generator or controller is not needed in this methodology, as each operator takes one LSB-Time timing signal input along with its data input, and delivers to the following operator an LSB-Time output signal along with its data output signal. The overall filtering subsystem that results is another such component and can easily be composed with other operators at any level to make higher-level systems. Coefficient generation can be done locally to each subsystem, so no central control section is ever needed in a system, or it can be done centrally if that is more convenient.

Plate 5 shows a photomicrograph of the Filters chip, which occupies the upper half of a multi-project device. The floorplan of this device is shown in

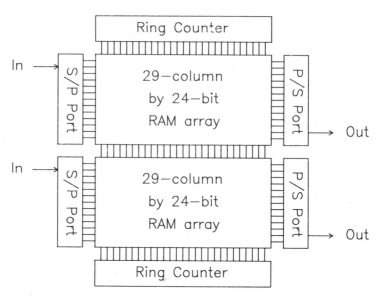

Fig. 11.2 Floorplan of the Filters chip, with computational modules on the left and memory on the right.

Figure 11.2 with the computational modules on the left, and the delay memory and its control on the right. Two very different layout styles were chosen for the computational and memory operators, due to the different types of circuits that they required. The computational burden of digital filtering is dominated by multiplication, as is well known, but also includes the requirements of addition, overflow detection and correction, timing and control, etc. To accommodate all of these diverse functions and more, it was decided to base the layout structure on a flexible generalisation of the modular structure of the multiplier.

The multiplier used is a modular serial pipelined design with identical two's complement fix-point-fraction data format for both inputs (Lyon, 1976), and using modified Booth's algorithm (5-level) coefficient recoding. A multiplier consists of a coefficient recoder module followed by N/2 multiplier modules for N bits of coefficient accuracy. The layout style was chosen to match the regular repetition of modules horizontally, and to allow stacking of irregular-size modules vertically (i.e. in the Y direction in the chip plane). Details of the multiplier design and related cells are available in a published design library (Newkirk and Mathews, 1983).

The modules are laid out on a regular grid of vertical metal lines, with a power, ground, and clock triple repeating at intervals of 100 λ (200 μm). Two of these triples, for two clock phases, make up a module width. Inverter and logic gate cells overlay power and ground lines, with corresponding input pass transistors adjacent to the clock lines. The channel between input cells and output cells is used for pass-transistor logic and for wiring within a module, whilst the channel between one module's output stage and the next module's input stage is used for inter-module wiring. In both the logic channel and the wiring channel, horizontal wires are usually poly-silicon (so they can cross the power, ground and clock lines), and vertical wires are usually metal, or diffusion for pass transistors. Most horizontal connections and many vertical connections (including all power, ground, and clock distribution within the grid area) are made by abutting related or unrelated modules or submodules. Other non-local horizontal connections are made by poly wires crossing small dummy wiring submodules. A few long-distance connections are routed on metal wires outside the grid area, so that they don't become the critical timing paths.

Multiplier modules themselves are made of vertical stacks of irregular submodules such as adders, timing shift registers, data shift registers, and coefficient register/gating elements. These submodules are designed to be shared when possible, so that, for example, two multipliers can share a data shift register if they are multiplying the same data value by two different coefficients, as occurs twice in the second-order section (this double multiplier trick was first applied to serial pipelined designs by Cheng and Mead, 1976). The timing shift registers are also shared over both double multipliers. Vertical wires distribute data and timing signals from the shared register stages through the other submodules. This sharing saves over 240 inverters and pass transistors, thereby remedying some of the apparent cost penalty of distributed and duplicated timing and control (relative to a central timing generator scheme); this technique is still logically distributed, and generates timing signals very near to where they are used, avoiding global wiring.

The general scheme of semi-regular cells, with fixed geometry in one dimension and variable in the other dimension, is often referred to as 'poly-cells' when used at the rather fine grain of gates and flip-flops. The use of this geometric style at the medium grain of two-phase clocked modules, with random logic and local wiring within modules, allows the regularity of the system-level architecture to show through in the final layout. By contrast, the traditional polycell approach results in a random wiring-dominated layout. Computerised automatic layout techniques are applicable at any grain size, but since the computer aids of 1978 supported only hierarchical manual layout, the larger grain and macro-scale regularity were tremendously helpful.

The delay memory section of the chip uses a dense custom array layout style, based on the need for 1440 RAM cells and specialised memory read/write, selection, and timing logic, as shown in Figure 11.3. It was determined that the most appropriate combination of memory density, speed, addressability, and power consumption would be achieved by an array of 3-transistor dynamic RAM cells, organised with a pair of words per column, with sequential addressing of columns, and having serial-parallel conversion registers integrated with the read/write logic. This dual serial-parallel-serial organisation allows a nearly square aspect ratio, and leaves data in one place till it is needed at the output, thus saving power and area relative to shift-register approaches.

The sequential addressing logic is simply a shift-register that can be short-cycled so it addresses M words repeatedly. The logic is shared across the two

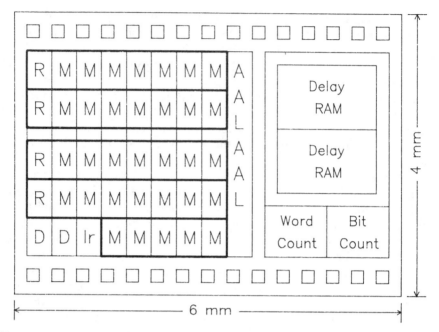

Fig. 11.3   The serial/parallel/serial dual delay memory operator of the Filters chip.

delay blocks, with modified shift register cells of one phase on the top edge of the memory driving write enable lines, and the cells of the other phase on the bottom edge driving read enable lines. Two PLAs are used to count bits and words, to provide all the timing signals required for memory bus precharge, write enable, address shift clocks, conversion strobes, etc. No provision is made for refreshing the dynamic cells, since in normal operation a word is only remembered for one sample period before it is read and overwritten.

The logical design of a subsystem such as Filters requires that the timing of two inputs to an operator be adjusted, by delaying whichever input is available earlier such that both inputs arrive at the same time. But if the later input depends functionally on the previous output of the operator, and arrives too late to be used as input to the next execution of the operator, then the subsystem cannot be realised by adding delays; instead, delays have to be removed from somewhere in the loop. This problem comes up in feeding back the output of the filter section to be used as input in the next time slot (i.e. in cascading stages). To relieve the problem, the main delay contributor, the gain multiplier, was shortened to only eight coefficient bits instead of 16 bits like the others. Since this multiplier supplies only an overall gain, its accuracy has no effect on pole and zero placement, and is therefore not a problem.

There are also two overflow detector/corrector circuits in the loop critical path, and these are designed to have a delay of only 4 bits, which is the smallest possible such that the output is guaranteed to be limited to one-quarter of the overall range and of the same sign as the input, without a combinatorial logic path from input to output. The resulting nonlinear function is not an ideal limiter, but is a sawtooth-like overflow detector/corrector.

The operator and chip layouts were created using Icarus (Fairbairn and Rowson, 1980), an interactive hierarchical layout drawing system that was being developed at Xerox concurrently with the Filters subsystem. The design was converted to CIF 2.0 format (Sproull and Lyon, 1980), for fabrication and checking. Unfortunately, by 1980 the Filters design was still more complex than any of the MIT, Berkeley, CMU, or Xerox CIF-checking software tools could handle, due primarily to the large number of RAM cells with non-manhattan geometry. Therefore, portions of the design were simulated separately, but not before their first prototypes were fabricated and never in their final interconnected configuration.

Chips were fabricated through the Xerox multiproject chip implementation system, and were tested using a simple desktop tester driven from a Xerox Alto computer, using a test facility written in the Smalltalk programming language. Using these facilities, the memory was prototyped twice, the multiplier was prototyped three times, and the Filters chip itself was prototyped twice, resulting in working parts.

11.5   A cascade/parallel filterbank for speech analysis

The particular application at which the Filters chip was targeted was a 32-channel cascade/parallel filterbank with half-wave detection and smoothing, to simulate the frequency analysing function of the cochlea, or inner ear (Lyon, 1982). Each of 32 places along the basilar membrane in the cochlea is treated as a filter channel, responding primarily to a relatively narrow band of frequencies corresponding to that place.

The action of the cochlea is modelled by a cascade of notch filters representing the propagation of pressure waves in the cochlear fluids. Under sinusoidal stimulation, waves propagate from the end of the cochlear chamber driven by the middle ear up to the place where the notch filter limits further propagation. At each sampled place, a resonator models the conversion of the pressure wave to a displacement of the basilar membrane; the energy in the wave is diverted to the motion detectors as the pressure wave is being notched out. The outputs of the parallel resonators, representing displacement, are half-wave rectified to model the action of the hair cells, the biological motion detectors that sense tiny motions and stimulate auditory nerve cells. The rectified signals are then smoothed with an over-damped lowpass filter to account for the limited ability of hair cells to follow the details of waveforms above a few kilohertz. Figure 11.4 illustrates the filtering structure of this cochlear model.

Such a compound operator can be constructed by cascading three copies of the Filters chip; the first chip does cascaded notch filtering, the second does parallel resonator filters, and the third does rectification and parallel smoothing filters. Figure 11.5 shows the overall block diagram of the hardware that implements the cochlear filterbank model, including coefficient sources

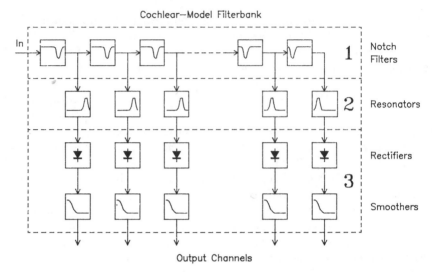

Fig. 11.4   A filterbank structure to model the cochlea, or inner ear, and its partitioning onto three Filters chips.

(zero-input operators) implemented as counters and read-only memories. Several chips could also be used at each of the three levels, to implement either more channels or a higher sample rate or both.

The operation of the cochlear-model operator depends on the values of many pre-determined fixed coefficients, which are stored in ROMs connected to the Filters coefficient input pins. The cochlear-model operator also has a level of timing called 'frames', which occur at the original audio sample rate. During each frame, each of the 32 multiplexed filter sections in each Filters chip is updated. The Filters chip does not, however, have a frame-time timing signal input, as its detailed function during each word-time is determined by the coefficient streams. The overall cochlear-model operator does require a frame-time timing input along with the audio input data stream (the audio sample is available on only one of the 32 word time-slots of the incoming bit-

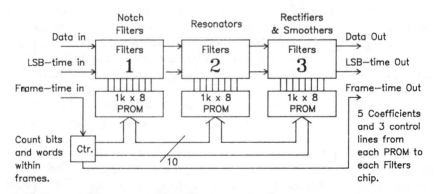

Fig. 11.5   The system block diagram of a cochlear model filterbank implemented with Filters chips and read-only coefficient memories.

stream). This timing signal also synchronises the counters that address the ROMs to provide the coefficient streams.

11.6   Conclusions

The intention of the speech recognition project within the VLSI Systems group at Xerox was to continue to implement further stages of speech processing in special-purpose VLSI subsystems, both to stress the VLSI design environment and to arrive at a low-cost speech recognition system. Whilst this approach still looks attractive as a way of finally implementing a well-developed system for low-cost production, it was not sufficiently flexible as an approach to speech research. Since that time, two new approaches have arisen to offer encouraging new possibilities. The first, the use of silicon compilers to generate quickly special-function subsystems within a standardised technology and architectural methodology, will allow experimenters to generate quickly prototype integrated systems at a moderate cost (Denyer and Renshaw, 1983). The second, the use of flexible programmable architectures that are reasonably well matched to a problem area in the amount and type of available parallelism, will allow a larger community of researchers, who know nothing of VLSI, to share in the use of a single machine design for a wider variety of applications (Lyon, 1984).

The Filters chip and variations on it still represent an extremely efficient approach to implementing filtering-intensive systems in a wide variety of applications, due to the inherent area-time efficiency of bit-serial arithmetic and the ease of bit-serial interconnect. But the lack of a family of bit-serial support and interface chips remains somewhat of an obstacle to the widespread acceptance of this technique.

11.7   Acknowledgements

The Filters chip and the methodologies that it gave rise to would not have been possible without the support and technical advice of Lynn Conway, Carver Mead, Carlo Séquin, and Bert Sutherland. The assistance of Jim Cherry, Rich Pasco, Bob Hon, and Doug Fairbairn was also greatly appreciated.

References

Cheng, E.K. and Mead, C.A., 'A Two's Complement Pepeline Multiplier', *IEEE Int. Conf. on Acoustics, Speech and Signal Accessing*, pp 647–650, 1976.

Denyer, P.B. and Renshaw, D., 'Case Studies in VLSI Signal Processing using a Silicon Compiler', *Proc. IEEE Int. Conf. on Acoustics, Speech, and Signal Processing, Boston*, 1983.

Fairbairn, D. and Rowson, J., 'An Interactive Layout System', in: *Introduction to VLSI Systems*, Mead and Conway, Addison-Wesley, 1980.

Jackson, L.B., Kaiser, J.F. and McDonald, H.S., 'An Approach to the Implementation of Digital Filters', *IEEE Trans. Audio and Electroacoustics AU-16*, 1968. (Also reprinted in Rabiner and Rader, *Digital Signal Processing*, IEEE Press, 1972.)

Lyon, R.F., 'Two's Complement Pipeline Multipliers', *IEEE Trans. on Communications COM-24*, 1976. (Also reprinted in Salazar, *Digital Signal Computers and Processors*, IEEE Press, 1977.)

Lyon, R.F., 'A Bit-Serial VLSI Architectural Methodology for Signal Processing', *VLSI 81 Very Large Scale Integration*, (Conf. Proc., Edinburgh, Scotland, John P. Gray, editor), Academic Press, 1981.

Lyon, R.F., 'A Computational Model of Filtering, Detection, and Compression in the Cochlea', *Proc. IEEE Int. Conf. on Acoustics, Speech, and Signal Processing*, Paris, 1982.

Lyon, R.F., 'MSSP: A Bit-Serial Multiprocessor for Signal Processing', in: *VLSI Signal Processing*, eds. Cappello *et al.*, IEEE Press, 1984.

Newkirk, J. and Mathews, R., *The VLSI Designer's Library*, Addison-Wesley, 1983.

Sproull, R.F. and Lyon, R.F., 'The Caltech Intermediate Form for LSI Layout Description', in: *Introduction to VLSI Systems*, Mead and Conway, Addison-Wesley, 1980.

12

MSSP: A Bit-Serial Multiprocessor for Signal Processing

Richard F. Lyon

Laboratory for Artificial Intelligence Research
Schlumberger Palo Alto Research

12.1 Introduction

The Multi-Serial Signal Processor (MSSP) is a single-instruction-stream multiple-data-stream (SIMD) multiprocessor for signal processing. Its replicated processor and memory element, the Serial Signal Processor (SSP), is a custom nMOS VLSI chip using bit-serial data paths, pipelined bit-serial arithmetic units, and a bit-serial multi-port memory.

The architecture of the MSSP machine and the design of the SSP chip combine novel features to mesh the implementation technology, the application domain, and the compilation software requirements. The resulting system is highly parallel and pipelined and achieves a computation rate of about 250 million 32-bit arithmetic operations per second at a cost several orders of magnitude lower than other approaches. Even better performing next-generation versions of the MSSP are being designed.

The MSSP architecture was originally proposed in April 1982, partly as a vehicle for VLSI tool development and VLSI instruction, and partly because our speech recognition project needed improved computing capabilities in order to speed up experiments with models of hearing (Lyon, 1982). In keeping with modern VLSI techniques and capabilities, the primary design goals for the MSSP architecture were simplicity and efficiency, with preference for simplicity due to a relative shortage of design resources. In particular, only one custom chip type was to be used. The resulting machine will provide low-cost numerical super-computing on a reasonable but restricted class of problems, which will allow it to satisfy the needs of many modern research and application areas.

12.2 MSSP structural description

This section describes the components from which the MSSP system is constructed, as an introduction to its architecture. At the top level, the MSSP consists of a controller and an array of processors (each with its own memory).

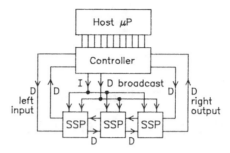

Fig. 12.1   Top-level block diagram of the MSSP machine.

The controller broadcasts an instruction stream and a data stream to the processors, and the processors communicate with a few directly-connected neighbours. The initial configuration, shown in Figure 12.1, is a one-dimensional nearest-neighbour-connected array of 100 processors, with the end processors also communicating with an I/O section in the controller. The one-board controller communicates with a general-purpose host computer via a MultiBus interface.

The replicated processor is the Serial Signal Processor (SSP), a single 5 mm square nMOS chip with 4-micron features. The SSP consists of a multi-port memory and a small collection of arithmetic function units connected to the memory ports. The current SSP configuration, shown in Figure 12.2, has a pair of multiply/add/limit units and a general two-input arithmetic-logic unit (ALU). The memory has sixty-four 32-bit words, eight input ports, and eight output ports.

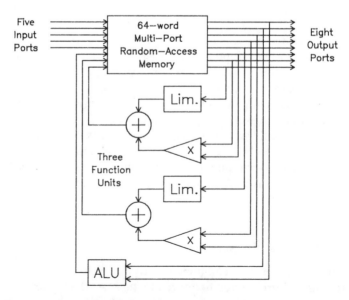

Fig. 12.2   Processor element (SSP chip) block diagram.

All data interconnections, within and between SSP chips, are made through memory ports, on single-wire paths. The eight memory output ports connect directly to the eight inputs of the function units and also go off-chip for sending data to neighbour chips. Three memory input ports take results from the three function units, and the other five memory input ports take data from chip input pins, which may be connected to the outputs of other chips. With the five available uncommitted input ports, several array interconnection schemes are possible, including grids of one or two dimensions.

The microcode broadcast serially on five wires from the controller to the processors consists mainly of the read and write addresses for all the memory ports, but also includes a few bits for ALU control, etc. Addresses determine which data items are to be sent to each function unit, and where the results from the function units are to be written back into memory. Other than memory addressing, no data path steering is provided.

The MSSP is designed to operate with a 16 MHz clock, and has a major cycle (word time) of 32 clock cycles, or 2 μs. In that time, each SSP chip executes eight memory reads, eight memory writes, two multiplications, up to three adds or subtracts, and some input and output transfers. Output to a specific off-chip port may conflict with the use of a function unit connected to the same memory port.

12.3 MSSP architectural oddities

The name Multi-Serial Signal Processor (MSSP) is meant to convey the primary unusual aspects of the MSSP architecture: it is a bit-serial machine, uses multiple processors, and is specialised for regular numeric applications such as signal processing.

The project goals and prejudices led to several features of the VLSI chip architecture and the system architecture that are atypical for a bit-serial machine, or for a single-instruction-stream/multiple-data-stream (SIMD) multiprocessor, or for a machine specialised for signal processing.

Unlike most bit-serial signal processors, the SSP element is programmable in a fairly conventional way, not hard-wired for a particular class of operations. The MSSP is an experiment on the suitability of the bit-serial approach to programmable numerical computing, with the potential payoff of excellent cost/performance.

In contrast to massively parallel SIMD array machines such as the CLIP4 (Duff, 1978) that use huge two-dimensional arrays of slow one-bit processors, MSSP is designed to use a modest number of relatively powerful processors with a large fixed data word size. Many applications can effectively use a one-dimensional array of such processors, while two-dimensional systems are usually not good for much beyond image processing.

In multiprocessors, it is particularly unusual for the individual processor elements to have multiple concurrently operating function units, like the SSP's two multipliers and three adders. In dedicated bit-serial systems, multiple levels of functional parallelism are more common (Powell, 1981), and can more than make up for the missing parallelism at the bit level.

Unlike some SIMD machines, MSSP provides no shared memory and no switching network (but has only a few hard-wired data paths between elements), and provides only a bare minimum of control logic and no specialised registers in the replicated elements. Thus each processor-memory element, while computationally powerful, is little more than a numeric data-path. This simplicity is not viewed as a defect, but is important in that it leads to good overall system efficiency.

Unlike many architectures specialised for digital signal processing (DSP) applications, MSSP is not a fixed-throughput machine with arbitrary limitations on resources, but rather a modular expandable architecture that can be matched to the application. And rather than embodying stringent restrictions such as coefficient/data segregation as is found in many DSP architectures, MSSP allows flexible programmable use of arbitrary numeric quantities.

Importantly, MSSP has not followed the familiar one-chip solution paradigm common to many other signal processing efforts, and so has not needed to push the chip technology or circuit design art to get a high-performance low-cost system. Better chip technology will of course lead immediately to better MSSP systems.

The most novel structural component of the SSP is the multi-port serial memory, which acts as both the bus and the main memory. As in TRW's unusual *polycyclic* architecture (Rau *et al.*, 1982), it allows full function unit interconnectivity with programmable delays and no contention, but it does so with lower cost and more generality than the polycyclic interconnect scheme.

These and other unusual aspects of the architecture have a certain harmony with each other and with the speech processing applications that MSSP is intended to serve. It remains to be seen how easy it is to map problems from new application areas efficiently onto this architecture. The biggest constraint on suitable application areas is the single instruction stream – controlling all the processors in lock-step on different data, without specific support for conditional execution.

12.4   The programmer's view of MSSP

The MSSP is a vector processing machine, with no support for scalar operations or for control structures other than fixed-count loops. The programmer is expected to design and code parallel algorithms accordingly. But an important goal of this project is to hide low-level architectural features, such as details of the pipelining and the parallel resources and the bit-serial nature of the machine, from the programmer. The processing element, and thus the vector machine, has a simple and familiar programmer's model, while maintaining efficient use of pipelined and functionally parallel resources.

The SSP chip is a very simple processor-memory element that can execute only one type of operation: assignment with a primitive expression. That is, the assignment $A: = f(B,C,...)$ is the only statement type, where A, B, and

C are variable names referring to locations in the processor's small memory space, and $f(\cdot)$ is a primitive function. Composing useful functions from the primitives requires that variables be allocated for the intermediate results (there is no accumulator, stack, or other temporary register space). Thus the entire state of any computation is in main memory.

The most often used primitive function is a multiply-add: $A := B * C + D$. Other options, such as negation of either term, are provided, as are a reasonable collection of ALU functions for logical, nonlinear, or conditional operations. The programmer's view is that instructions of this form execute sequentially, in the order written, with each one finishing its assignment before the next one starts. At a higher level, depending on the support software, the programmer can also deal with looping constructs, multiple independent or synchronised tasks, and so on. Since the overall architecture is SIMD, these issues are dealt with by the compiler, the controller, or the host uniprocessor, rather than by individual processor-memory elements.

The only data type handled by the SSP is a 32-bit fixed-point two's-complement number, normally regarded as a fraction with 28 bits to the right of the point. The ALU also allows ways of using numbers as flags and masks.

The initial implementation of the SSP chip has only 64 memory locations, but due to dynamic assignment of locations to variables, more than 64 variables might appear in a program; locally-scoped intermediate result variables with different names will automatically share memory locations when appropriate. So, while the programmer does not need to limit himself to a known total number of variables, he does need to know that he can run out of space.

The programmer will need to be aware, to some extent, of the interconnection topology of the multiple SSP chips. The plan is to have only a one-dimensional two-way nearest neighbour interconnection initially, with an overlaid tree interconnection pattern added later to take advantage of the planned memory expansion. Assignment statements like $A := left(B)$ would be written to coordinate I/O transfers between SSP chips; A is assigned the value of B from its left neighbour. The function *left* is not really a functional operation on the value of variable B, but rather a macro that commands the element to read the value of variable B and send it out towards the right, and take what comes in from the left and assign it to variable A. Thus all SSP chips in the linear array simultaneously transfer data from left to right.

The only way to move data in memory is to do an assignment through a function unit; for example, $A := B$ will compile to move the value of B through a multiplier/adder or the ALU, depending on which is available. There is no way to index memory by data values either, so to implement a delay line in memory it is necessary to move the data explicitly or to unroll a program loop to use different locations in a ring fashion.

A useful primitive function that has been provided in the ALU hardware is $A := select(B, C)$, which selects B if B is non-negative, and C otherwise. This operation can be used for half-wave and full-wave rectification, limiters, break-point nonlinearities, conditional assignment, etc. A value used for B might be the result of a data operation, or it might be a preloaded constant dependent only on the location of the processor in the array, for example to control edge conditions.

12.5   The SSP chip design

The area of the SSP chip is dominated by two large blocks, the memory and the pair of multipliers, as shown in Figure 12.3 and Plate 6. Both of these evolved from previous memory and multiplier blocks that were designed for the *Filters* chip at Xerox PARC, and for a subsequent family of dedicated special-function signal processing chips (Lyon, 1981a). Similar multiplier and memory components have been adapted by Denyer and Renshaw (1983) to a silicon compiler for automatic generation of special-function signal processing chips. In attempting to generalise the functionality of such chips to a wider class of problems, it was finally realised that the most reasonable alternative to single-function dedicated designs was a completely programmable design with flexible interconnection capabilities unrelated to any particular algorithms. The SSP chip is the result of selecting a multi-port memory as the flexible communication mechanism.

The starting memory design was a serial-parallel-serial organisation of 3-transistor RAM cells, which in the Filters chip was addressed strictly

Fig. 12.3   The SSP chip layout, with memory on top, function units below (also see Plate 6).

sequentially. Multi-porting it involved splitting the data bus into separate read and write buses, and extending each through an array of port registers. The selection logic was replaced by separate read and write address decoders to make it random-access with independent read and write capability. Thus, on each memory cycle, a read and a write can occur concurrently. Eight memory cycles need to fit in thirty-two clock cycles (one major cycle), so each memory cycle can take up to four clock cycles – two to precharge the bus and two to drive and latch data. This 4:1 timing ratio seems to be about the right relationship between the speed of fast serial logic and the speed of long parallel buses without sense amplifiers. The resulting memory has a total read/write bandwidth of 16 ports * 16 Mbps = 256 Mbps, with fixed latency and no contention.

The multipliers are based on the 5-level recoded (modified Booth's algorithm) version of the two's complement serial pipelined multiplier (Lyon, 1976). The layout was redone using a pair of small optimised PLAs per stage; one recoder stage, fifteen identical multiplier stages, and a final scaling stage make up the complete multiplier. The resulting structure computes truncated 32-by-32-bit products as fast as operands can be pumped into it, with a pipeline latency of about a word and a half. The scaling is adjusted so that operands have a value range of -8 to $+8$ (i.e. inputs are regarded as fractions with 4 bits to the left of the point, including the sign). No other scaling mechanisms, such as shifters, are provided.

The multiplier stage cells are laid out on a pitch of only 100λ, with a height of 408λ – about one third smaller than the original (Newkirk and Mathews, 1983) and somewhat faster, too. The smaller functional subunits, such as limiters, sign switchers, adders, various ALU blocks, and a control-bit latch, were designed on the same grid of power, ground, and clock distribution as the multipliers. A modest number of random wires (the hard part of the design) interconnect the pieces.

A ring of bonding pads for inputs, outputs, power, and clocks was laid out and routed algorithmically using new parameterised pad designs and other custom DPL functions (Batali *et al.*, 1981).

The layout was converted to CIF2.0 (Sproull and Lyon, 1980), design rule checked, circuit extracted, and thoroughly simulated before fabrication. Chips were fabricated by VTI's foundry service in the process they call HMOS, which is compatible with Mead-Conway nMOS with $\lambda = 2$ μm. Both buried and butting contacts were used, with no problems, using conservative simplified design rules (Lyon, 1981b). The chips are just over 5 mm on each side, and have good yield.

12.6   Controller design for MSSP

The controller for the MSSP machine must generate an 80 Mbps instruction stream (160 bits per major cycle), and interface three data streams from the host to the processors (to the left and right ends and a broadcast to all processors) and two data streams from the processors to the host (from the end processors). Many levels of capability can be imagined for the design of such a controller. For example, the controller could do runtime resource assignment, subroutine calling, loop counting, code rearrangement, multi-tasking, etc.; it could do tests on data from the processors, and alter the control flow accordingly. Instead of such a complex controller, however, the level-zero controller that has been built provides no control features beyond straight-line code execution. Control structures such as simple loops are handled at compile time, and other control features can be provided by the host processor, a SUN workstation accessible through a MultiBus interface.

To compile loops with known repeat counts, the compiler simply unrolls the loop using source-level macros, and generates straight-line code. Multiple looping tasks that run synchronously but at different rates, such as a sample-rate task and a frame-rate task in a speech analyser, are jointly unrolled into one long program segment whose repetition rate is a common divisor of the repetition rates of the individual tasks. Indices can also be computed at compile time, so each copy of the loop body may be slightly different.

Since loop unrolling produces long sequences of mostly repeated code, the controller uses a two-level memory scheme so that repeated instructions need only be stored once (in the *code memory*), and only indices into the code memory are repeated, (in the *program memory*). To accommodate long loops, the program memory has 16K locations. Each location provides a 9-bit index into a table of only 512 distinct instructions, each 160 bits wide.

Each program memory location also contains an enable bit for each of the five I/O streams, and a stop bit. Straight-line program segment executions are initiated by the host (by loading the program counter and issuing a run command), and are terminated when a stop bit is encountered. The host must execute runtime support code that coordinates segment execution and I/O buffer service. The controller provides hardware FIFOs on the I/O streams to reduce the timing demands on the host.

A key feature of the architecture that allows multiple tasks to be jointly unrolled is the lack of special registers, such as accumulators or flag registers, that would otherwise cause conflicts between concurrently executing tasks. A smarter controller would take advantage of this feature by determining at runtime, for multiple asynchronous tasks, which task could run on each major cycle, based on pipeline constraints between program steps. There is no overhead in switching between tasks in this way. An even smarter controller might mix primitive operations from several tasks into a single instruction cycle, with dynamic assignment of actual function units to primitive operations. The sequencer in such a controller would have time for several steps per major cycle, and could implement other features, such as subroutines, scalar data operations, and conditional branches as well.

12.7 MSSP support software system

A Lisp-based compilation system has been developed to translate high-level code for signal processing algorithms into microcode for the MSSP. Presently, the compiler accepts an intermediate-level of code that is a direct analogue of the sequential assignment programming model described above. Generating that level from other source languages is straightforward, as long as the source-level constructs used are restricted to fit the numerical domain closely enough. Application-dependent Lisp-embedded languages are a natural approach.

The compilation scheme is inspired by the MIPS (Microprocessor without Interlocked Pipe Stages) project at Stanford University (Hennessy *et al.*, 1981), in which it was shown that moving the complexity of a pipelined machine from the hardware to the software could result in significant net performance gains. The compiler uses a *pipeline rearranger* with knowledge of the hardware constraints to convert sequential high-level programming constructs to legal and efficient overlapped machine operations.

Sequential program segments, or *basic blocks*, are independently compiled, then later loaded into the controller's memories. Each step of a sequential program is explicitly represented as a node in a timing dependency graph. Depending on what variables a step reads or writes, and depending on the pipeline latency of the primitive function used, one-sided timing constraints are calculated and entered as edges between the nodes. Each edge specifies how soon a step may be started relative to when a previous step was started. Based on this information, steps can be assigned to function units and code can be packed in time into an instruction stream segment, accommodating whatever parallelism is found.

A critical-path-finding algorithm and first-fit packing strategy yield nearly optimal code; more clever rearranging algorithms could yield a slight improvement in some cases. Typically, if only one task has been unrolled into a segment, many potential uses of function units will remain as effective no-ops, due to the long pipeline latencies. When multiple nearly-independent tasks are jointly unrolled, most no-ops can be converted to useful parallel operations.

The definition of the algorithm at the high or intermediate level can have a big impact on how much of the machine resources can be used concurrently. For example, a straightforward FIR filter implementation that uses a memory location as an accumulator will have to wait several cycles between multiply-adds, but one that uses a tree of adds will do as many parallel and overlapped multiply-adds as the hardware allows (with some cost in terms of more memory usage).

12.8   A sample MSSP program

A structure as simple as a cascade of second-order canonic filter sections makes a good filterbank model of wave propagation in the cochlea (Lyon, 1982), with each filter channel (the signal between cascaded stages) representing a sample location in the cochlea. Assuming for now a machine with at least as many processors as model channels, the simplest approach is to have each SSP chip run one second-order filter.

Each filter stage takes input from its left neighbour and sends the filter output to its right neighbour. Each output would also be used within the SSP, as input to further stages of the hearing models. The left-most SSP gets its *left-in* data stream from the controller, which is delivering a speech waveform to be analysed. Before the filtering can be run, coefficients must be loaded into the memory, following the same left-to-right path from controller to processors. This section presents the code for the filtering basic block only; the coefficient-loading block is even simpler. The basic block is written to compute two consecutive samples, rather than just one, in order to avoid moving data in the filter's state memory.

Figure 12.4 shows the signal flow-graph, the sequential assignment program, and the instruction constraint graph for the second-order filter section example. The graph is drawn with nodes placed on a time line in the locations where the compiler assigned them. The forward-backward critical path finding and assignment algorithm used puts every instruction as close to the end as possible; the ones with slack could equally well have been put as close to the beginning as possible, or anywhere in between.

The local variables $t1$ and $t3$ can both refer to the same memory location, as their regions of definition do not overlap in time. Similarly, Y, X, and $t2$

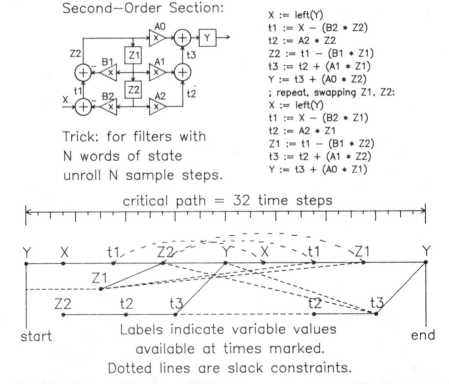

Fig. 12.4 Signal flow-graph, sequential assignment program, and instruction graph for the second-order filter section example.

can share a location. Thus the sample program uses 5 locations for coefficients, and 4 locations for data.

This program has been compiled and simulated on our software emulator, yielding exactly the correct numerical output. It is being used as one of several test cases on the actual MSSP hardware. The initial MSSP prototype is a reduced configuration, so for a complete cochlear filterbank the code is slightly modified to execute several channels per processor. The compiler has been enhanced to map automatically multiple channels of a task to each processor; for example, in the case of two stages per processor, occurrences of $X: = left(Y)$ are converted to $X1: = left(Y2)$ and $X2: =Y1$, and the rest of the code is simply duplicated with copies 1 and 2 of the variables. There is no time penalty for running up to five second-order filter channels per processor, since the stages are completely overlapped.

12.9   MSSP performance

The above example program executes one second-order section step (5 multiplies and 4 adds) per processor in a loop that repeats every 16 major cycles (32 μs); this is faster than real-time for signal sample rates below 31 kHz. The resulting computation rate, in terms of arithmetic operations on *fractions*, is $9/32 = 0.28$ mega-*frops* per processor. The maximum rate possible on one processor is 5 arithmetic operations in 2 μs, or 2.5 mega-frops (counting multiplies and adds as operations, but not counting sign changes or hard limiting, which can occur concurrently on the operands). Thus, this single task runs the machine at an efficiency of only $0.28/2.5 = 11\%$.

The efficiency of multiplier usage is $[(5 \text{ mults})/(32 \mu s)]/(1.0 \text{ mega-frops}) = 16\%$; in no case are both multipliers in use at once. The other 84% of the capability of the multipliers, and other unused resources, is still available for use by other stages of processing that are compiled to run concurrently with the filtering. For example, if five filter sections are run per processor, the repetition cycle is not lengthened, and the efficiency increases to $25/32 = 78\%$ of multiplier usage.

In the 100-processor machine, designed to match the number of channels in a high-quality cochlear model, the total machine performance can be up to 250 mega-frops. Even at 11% efficiency, the performance beats more expensive array processors by a reasonable factor (net 28 mega-frops, *vs* less than 12 mega-flops for an FPS AP-120B); when used efficiently, the MSSP is another order of magnitude better. As usual with array processors, the performance bottleneck will be I/O, and the small memory of the MSSP will exacerbate this problem.

12.10   MSSP extensions

To extend the usefulness of the MSSP machine, two stages of extensions are being considered. The first uses the existing processor chips, and augments each with an external 64K-by-1 fast static RAM. The RAM data-in and data-out pins can connect directly to serial input and output ports. Broadcast address and timing control from a modified controller can then allow either a single memory read or memory write on each major cycle. Although the bandwidth to this 2K words of secondary memory is less than the bandwidth to on-chip memory by a factor of sixteen, the extra storage space provides a great increase in capabilities.

The first extension plan also includes adding another pattern of interconnect between processors, to allow quick accumulation of values from all processors through a tree of adds. This makes the machine much more useful for spatial convolution, transforms, and pattern matching. The planned technique maps processors from left to right onto a tree by pre-order traversal (so that each node is adjacent to its left son if it has one), and requires only one new wire into each node to bring the input from the (non-local) right son node; the path from the left son uses the existing wire from the right neighbour. The resulting configuration is illustrated in Figure 12.5.

The addition of one wire from external memory and one tree connection wire brings the total number of inputs to a processor up to five (counting left, right and broadcast inputs), using up all available input ports.

The second stage of extension involves the design of a next-generation processor, which may be a high-performance CMOS chip connected on a hybrid substrate to four 8K-by-8 fast static RAMs. If the RAMs can be cycled in 30 ns, this processor can have 32 memory ports into an array of 8K 32-bit

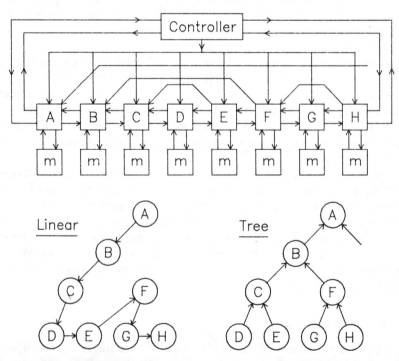

Fig. 12.5 Enhanced MSSP machine with added memory and tree interconnect, showing both linear and tree interpretations of the interconnect patterns.

words, with about 8 multipliers and 12 adders, at a bit rate of 32 Mbps and a total memory bandwidth of 1 Gbps.

An array of 100 of these will provide up to 2 gigafrops, and still fit on a few small boards. With the large memory, the tremendous parallelism of arithmetic resources will be easy to use efficiently in applications such as pattern matching, matrix multiplication, image processing, Fourier transforms, and channel-organised hearing models of the sort for which the architecture was originally designed.

12.11   Conclusions

The MSSP architecture promises to provide a family of high-performance numerical processing machines, for applications that can utilise the SIMD mode efficiently. Continued experimentation will determine whether the promise is actually realised in the case of speech analysis, and how it extends to other applications. If the machine turns out to be as useful and efficient as predicted, it will have demonstrated that the efficiency advantages of bit-serial arithmetic in VLSI extend beyond special-purpose machines to programmable machines.

12.12   Acknowledgements

The MSSP project has benefited from a number of eager migrant workers who have been willing to go along with the author's odd ideas and add good ideas of their own. Lynn Quam (now at SRI) and Wayne Burleson (MIT co-op student, now at VTI) did the detailed chip design, layout, checking, and simulation. Ian Robinson (Fairchild AI Architecture group) did the controller design, construction, and checkout. Niels Lauritzen (MIT co-op student) developed the support software system on the Lisp machine. Bruce Horn (consultant) wrote diagnostic and support code to run on the host Sun workstation. John Gordon (new hire) has done system integration, host software, and testing. Steve Rubin (Fairchild AI Architecture group) supported a variety of VLSI tools software locally, and helped us get chips fabricated.

References

Batali, J., Mayle, N., Shrobe, H., Sussman, G. and Weise, D., 'The DPL/Daedalus Design Environment', *VLSI 81 Very Large Scale Integration*, (Conf. Proc., Edinburgh, Scotland, John P. Gray, ed.), Academic Press, 1981.

Denyer, P.B. and Renshaw, D., 'Case Studies in VLSI Signal Processing using a Silicon Compiler', *Proc. IEEE Int. Conf. on Acoustics, Speech, and Signal Processing*, Boston, 1983.

Duff, M.J.B., 'Review of the CLIP4 Image Processing System', *Proc. AFIPS Natl. Comput. Conf.* vol. 47, 1978.

Hennessy, J., Jouppi, N., Baskett, F. and Gill, J., 'MIPS: A VLSI Processor Architecture', *VLSI Systems and Computations* (CMU Conf. Proc., H. T. Kung and Guy Steele, eds.), Computer Science Press, 1981.

Lyon, R.F., 'Two's Complement Pipeline Multipliers', *IEEE Trans. on Communications*, 1976.

Lyon, R.F., 'Simplified Design Rules for VLSI Layouts', *Lambda Magazine* (now *VLSI Design Magazine*), First quarter 1981(a).

Lyon, R.F., 'A Bit-Serial VLSI Architectural Methodology for Signal Processing', *VLSI 81 Very Large Scale Integration*, (Conf. Proc., Edinburgh, Scotland, John P. Gray, ed.), Academic Press, 1981(b).

Lyon, R.F., 'A Computational Model of Filtering, Detection, and Compression in the Cochlea', *Proc. IEEE Int. Conf. on Acoustics, Speech, and Signal Processing*, Paris, 1982.

Newkirk, J. and Mathews, R., *The VLSI Designer's Library*, Addison-Wesley, 1983.

Powell, N.R., 'Functional Parallelism in VLSI Systems and Computations', *VLSI Systems and Computations* (CMU Conf. Proc., H. T. Kung and Guy Steele, eds.), Computer Science Press, 1981.

Rau, B.R., Glaeser, C.C. and Picard, R.L., 'Efficient Code Generation for Horizontal Architectures: Compiler Techniques and Architectural Support', *Proc. 9th Annual IEEE Symp. on Computer Architecture*, 1982.

Sproull, R.F. and Lyon, R.F., 'The Caltech Intermediate Form for LSI Layout Description', in: *Introduction to VLSI Systems*, Mead and Conway, Addison-Wesley, 1980.

13

A VLSI Architecture for Sound Synthesis

John Wawrzynek and Carver Mead

Department of Computer Science
California Institute of Technology

13.1 Introduction

Sounds that come from physical sources are naturally represented by differential equations in time. Since there is a straightforward correspondence between differential equations in time and finite difference equations, we can model musical instruments as simultaneous finite difference equations. Musical sounds can be produced by solving the difference equations that model instruments in real time.

The computational bandwidth that is needed to compute musical sounds is enormous. For the sampled waveform representation of sound, we need to produce samples at a rate of about 50K samples/second. If we assume that there are about 100 computational operations per sample for each voice, that is 5 million operations per second per voice. An operation involves a multiplication and an addition. By a voice we mean one horn or one string of a string instrument. A mid-size computer of today is capable of about only 250,000 arithmetic operations per second which means, by our model, it is only capable of computing about 1/20 of a single voice. When the data-shuffling and housekeeping operations necessary to run a real instrument model are included, the factor increases another order of magnitude – so it is hopeless to compute the sounds in real time. Today's most powerful computers are capable of computing only a small number of voices.

Even the new concurrent machines do not hold much promise. These machines, sometimes called homogeneous machines, fail to support the generation of sound because they are built with a fixed interconnection between their processors. In order to map a problem like musical sound generation onto such a machine, the processors must be programmed to provide the communication between various parts of the model. This results in the machine spending much of its time shuffling data around.

In the past the enormous computation bandwidth of sound generation has been avoided by using musical shortcuts such as waveform table lookup and interpolation. While this approach and those built upon it can produce pleasing musical sounds, the attacks, dynamics, continuity, and other properties of real instruments simply cannot be captured. In addition, traditional methods suffer from the shortcoming that the player of the instrument is given parameters that don't necessarily have any direct physical interpretation and are just artifacts of the model. It would be nice, for example, to supply a musician or composer with a string instrument with string whose mass, stiffness and tension can be varied dynamically. This capability is possible if a representation of the instrument is based on its physics.

An even larger problem with the shortcut methods of the past is that they have produced models that require updates of internal parameters at a rate that is many times that which occurs in real musical instruments. The control, or update, of parameters has become an unmanageable problem.

A natural architecture for solving finite difference equations is one with an interconnection matrix between processors that can be reconfigured (or programmed), as illustrated in Figure 13.1. A realisation of a new instrument involves a reconfiguring of the connection matrix between the processing elements along with configuring connections to the outside world both for control and updates of parameters.

Processing elements are placed together to form an array and then joined by a reconfigurable interconnection matrix. A general purpose computer supplies updates of parameters to the processing elements and provides an interface to the player of the instrument. The external computer also supplies the bit patterns for the interconnection matrix. Synthesised signal outputs go to a digital to analogue converter.

In order to implement a reconfigurable connection matrix, a bit-serial representation of samples facilitates the use of single wire connections between computational units, drastically reducing the complexity of implementation. In fact, a bit-serial implementation makes the entire approach possible.

Bit-serial implementations also have the advantage that computational elements are very small and have inexpensive realisations. One potential drawback with bit-serial systems is that they must run at a clock rate that is higher then that of their parallel counterparts. In our implementations, even with 64 bit samples, the bit clock rate is only 3 MHz, which is far below the limits of current IC technology.

For our basic unit of computation we have chosen a unit we call a UPE (Universal Processing Element) (Wawrzynek and Tzu-Mu Lin, 1983) which computes the function:

$$A + B \times M + D \times (1-M) \qquad\qquad 13.1$$

It is very similar to the two's complement bit-serial multipliers proposed by R.F. Lyon (1981). In its simplest mode of computation, where $D = 0$, the function of a UPE is a multiplication and an addition. This simple element forms a digital integrator that is the basic building block for solving linear difference equations. If D is not set to 0, the output of the UPE is the linear interpolation between B and D where M is the constant of interpolation. Interpolation is important in sound synthesis in particular for mixing signals. All the inputs and outputs to the UPE are bit-serial. UPEs can be connected together with a single wire.

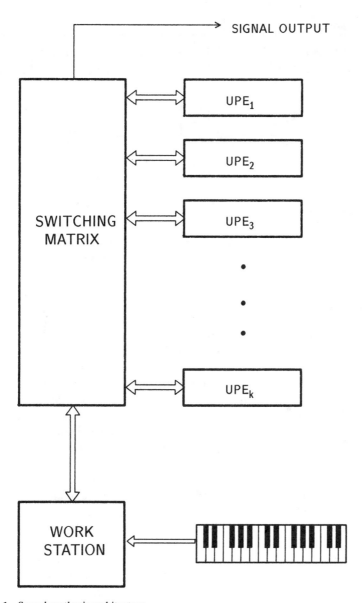

Fig. 13.1   Sound synthesis architecture

13.2   The processing element and connection network

Each UPE consists of 32 stages 0, 1, ... 31, as shown in Figure 13.2. There is one simple stage for each bit in the multiplier word, B, applied as an input to the UPE. The multiplier bits are stored in inverse order in flip-flops, such as the one shown in the detail of stage 0.

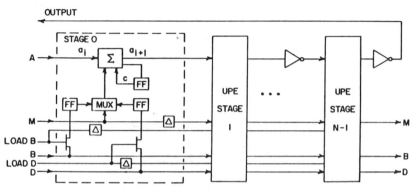

Fig. 13.2 UPE stages

Each simple stage contains an AND function for one bit of multiplication, a flip-flop for one bit of storage for the carry, and a three input adder to sum the output of the preceding stage (or the input A in the case of the first stage) with the one bit product and the carry from the last one bit multiply. At each bit time the output of each adder, a_{i+1}, contributes to one bit in the final result $A+(M \times B)$.

The AND function is implemented with a multiplexer that chooses the input to the adder between a bit of the stored word B and a bit of the stored word D. The multiplexer is controlled by the multiplicand M so that each stage computes $b.m + d.(1-m)$ and the entire array computes $A + [B \times M + D \times (1-M)]$. If the word D is zero, then each of the multiplexers effectively performs as an AND gate, with each stage computing $b.m$, and the entire array of UPE stages computing $A + [B \times M]$. If the word D is not zero, the final result is the linear interpolation between D and B, with M being the interpolation constant, i.e., the result equals $A + (B-D) \times M + D$.

The multiplier B is stored in the multiplier register in reverse order, that is with bit b_0 in stage 0, bit b_1 in stage 1, and so on, by placing the multiplier on the B input line one bit at a time, as a load control pulse is passed from state to stage. As each stage receives the load pulse, it loads its flip-flop with the current bit on the B input line. The D input is loaded into a separate register in the same manner when it is required. The multiplicand M is not stored in a register, but is delayed one bit cycle in each stage so that it can flow through and be operated by each bit of the multiplier B, one bit at a time. Thus, as the multiplier B is being loaded, it is possible to begin passing the multiplicand M into the array of stages and perform the first 32 bits of multiplication.

In the course of the mutiplication operation, each bit of the final result is formed by every stage adding its result to the result from the previous stage, and passing it on. Consequently, there is a propagation delay for each bit of the final result proportional to the number of stages. This delay can be avoided by using a conventional pipelining technique (Cheng and Mead, 1976) which consists of the addition of an extra bit-time delay element on the a_{i+1} line, and on every one of the lines which connects from one stage to the next. These extra delay elements are not shown in Figure 13.2 to simplify the diagram.

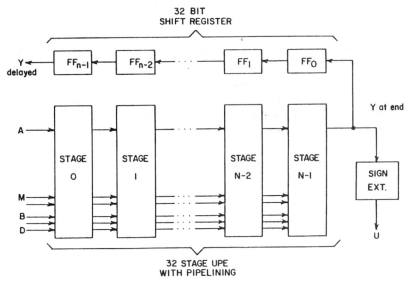

Fig. 13.3 UPE architecture

The advantage of pipelining is that propagation delay for the array is proportional only to the delay in one stage, and not to the number of stages, although it does cause an initial delay through the pipeline. However, if the data being processed is a continuous stream, as in sound synthesis, this delay, proportional to the total number of stages, contributes only to the latency of the system, but does not affect its throughput.

Figure 13.3 illustrates the architecture used in each UPE. It contains 32 pipelined stages (0 through 31), along with the same number of stages of a shift register, shown as flip-flops FF_0, FF_1 ... FF_{31}. The end result Y at the output of the 32 stages is fed into a sign extension circuit which generates a U output by passing only the most significant 32 bits of the Y output, and then extending its sign bit over the next 32 bit cycles. Because the Y output is the product of two 32-bit numbers, it consists of 64 bits. Consequently, the first 32 bits of that product not used for the U output are stored in the 32-bit shift register. Since the Y output is thus delayed by 32-bit cycles, both the Y output and the U output appear in synchronism. It should be noted that the entire system of Figure 1 is synchronised by word pulses (not shown). In our system the word pulses are those controlling the digital to analogue conversion. The B input and the D input (not shown), are 32-bit two's complement numbers, whereas M and A are 64-bit two's complement numbers. However, it should be understood that the bit-serial architecture implemented to perform multiplication and linear interpolation does not depend upon use of the two's complement. The two's complement representation is chosen only because it is more convenient.

A modification to the array of stages is necessary to accommodate two's complement numbers. Any n bit two's complement number with m bits of fraction may be written as:

$$\sum_{i=0}^{n-2} b_i.2^{i-m} - b_{n-1}.2^{n-1-m}$$

where b_0 represents the least significant bit (LSB). Since each stage of the multiplier holds one bit of the word B, with stage n –1 holding b_{n-1}, the last stage (most significant) must perform a subtraction of the incoming signal instead of an addition as in the other stages. The last stage is implemented with an inverter on the incoming partial product along with an inverter on its output as shown in Figure 13.2. A two's complement number at the M input must be sign extended to guarantee correct operation. For example, if M is a 32-bit number then after all 32 bits of M have been fed in, an additional 32 bits, each a copy of the sign bit, must follow.

Using a fractional representation for numbers facilitates the computation of linear interpolations with the same efficiency as multiplication. This capability is made possible by the fact that if the multiplicand M is a positive fraction and is represented by .xxxxx, then the one's complement $\overline{M} \approx 1 - M$. It is this fact that is employed in implementing the AND function required for the one bit multiplication in each stage by a multiplexer (MUX), as shown in Figure 13.2.

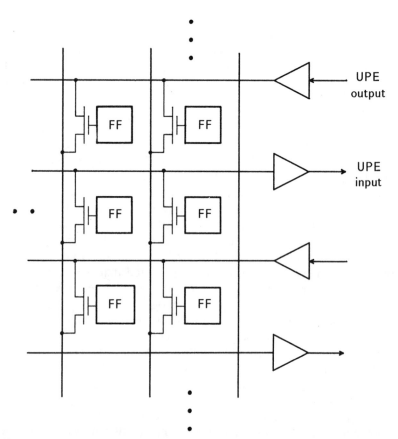

Fig. 13.4 Interconnection matrix

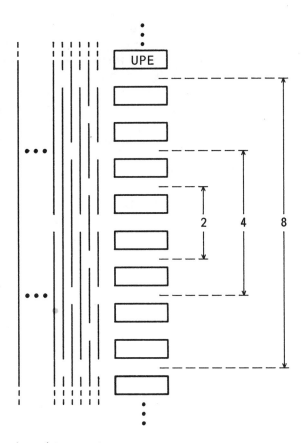

Fig. 13.5   Discretionary interconnect

It should be recalled that the MUX is controlled by the multiplicand M to choose between the two signals B and D.

The last point that should be noted about the basic architecture of the UPE is that each stage receives its input from the stage of lower order. The first stage (stage 0) has no stage of lower order and therefore takes its inputs from the switching matrix shown in Figure 13.1. The input A for stage 0 need not be 0 in which case a number A is added to the final result.

The interconnection matrix is shown in more detail in Figure 13.4. Each UPE output is programmed to connect to one line that is broadcast to a neighbourhood of other UPEs. Inputs to UPEs are programmed in a similar manner by connection to one of the broadcast outputs. Configuring the interconnect is achieved by placing bit patterns in the control flip-flops.

Inputs to UPEs that do not come from other UPEs, come from the controlling computer through an interface similar to the one connecting UPEs. Once a UPE receives an input it is held, so new values are sent only when the parameters of the model change.

For music synthesis, most interconnection patterns exhibit a high degree of locality. For this reason, the interconnection network need not provide full connectivity. Figure 13.5 shows a scheme where there are a large number of short local wires, and proportionally fewer wires of greater length. Many instrument models have been found to map well into this wiring scheme.

Before describing typical applications of the UPEs with various examples, we will introduce a symbol to be used for a UPE, with delays implemented as described above. It consists of a rectangle with the four inputs A, M, B and D, and the two outputs Y and U. The M, B and D inputs and the U output are 32-bit two's complement numbers between 2 and –2, which are sign extended to 64 bits in the case of M and U. The A input and the Y output are two's complement numbers between 8 and –8, as follows:

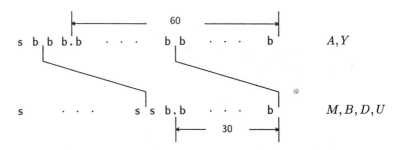

These two types of numbers restrict the way several UPEs may be interconnected. Except in special cases, the type of any output which feeds an input must match. For simplicity we adopt the convention that when D = 0, it is not shown.

13.2.1   UPE hardware

A photomicrograph of an experimental UPE chip is shown in Plate 7. This nMOS device contains 10 UPEs and no interconection matrix. The UPEs are stacked left to right with all of their signal inputs and outputs connected to bonding pads.

This device is in use in an experimental sound synthesis system with the interconnection matrix implemented at the circuit board level.

13.3   Basic elements for sound synthesis

13.3.1   General linear filter

An M-th order linear difference equation (Oppenheim and Schafer, 1975) may be written as:

$$y_n = \sum_{i=0}^{N} a_i x_{n-i} + \sum_{i=0}^{M} b_i y_{n-i} \qquad\qquad 13.2$$

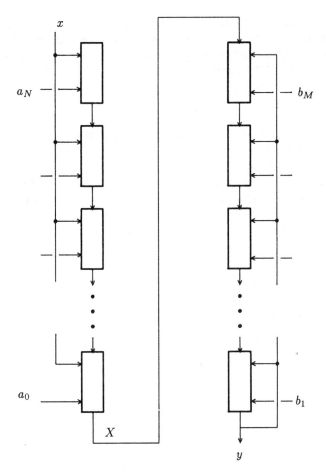

Fig. 13.6   UPE implementation of general filter

where x_n is the input at time sample n; y_n is the output at time sample n; and the coefficients a_0 ... a_N, b_1 ... b_M are chosen to fulfil a given filtering requirement. The function is evaluated by performing the iteration (13.2) for each sample time. This is the general form of a linear filter; any linear filter can be described as a special case of equation (13.2).

Figure 13.6 illustrates a UPE network which directly implements the general linear filter equation.

Each UPE (with $D = 0$) performs the function $(A + M \times B)z^{-1}$, i.e. a multiply, an addition and one unit of delay. Referring to Figure 13.6, the input values are processed by distributing the input signal x to each of $N + 1$ UPEs, each one multiplies the input by a filter coefficient a_i, sums the result of the last UPE, and passes the total on for further processing. Since each UPE provides one unit of delay, the signal at the output of the input processing section is:

$$X = a_0x_{n-1} + a_1x_{n-2} + a_2 x_{n-2} + ... + a_M x_{i-M+1}$$ 13.3

This result is summed with the result of the output processing section.

The output y_n is distributed back to each of M UPEs. Each UPE multiplies the output by a filter coefficient b_i, provides one unit of delay, sums its result with that of the last UPE, and passes the total on. The result at the end of the output processing section is:

$$y_n = b_1 y_{n-1} + b_2 y_{n-2} + \ldots + b_N y_{n-N} + X \qquad 13.4$$

The result of the input processing section is added to the output processing section by feeding it into the UPE holding the b_n coefficient, since its A (addend) input is not used. Adding the result from the input processing section to the UPE holding the b_n coefficient has the effect of adding a net delay through the system equal to the number of UPEs in the output processing section.

From Figure 13.6 it is clear that the number of UPEs needed to implement equation (13.2) is equal to *the number of coefficients in the input (non-recursive) processing section plus the number of coefficients in the output (recursive) processing section.*

13.3.2   Second-order section

As an example of a linear filter, consider the second-order linear difference equation:

$$y_n = \alpha y_{n-1} + \beta y_{n-2} + x_n \qquad 13.5$$

Applying the z-transform we form the system function:

$$H(z) = \frac{Y(z)}{X(z)} = \frac{1}{1 - \alpha z^{-1} - \beta z^{-2}} \qquad 13.6$$

Solving for the roots of the denominator leads to two cases. In the case where $\alpha^2 + 4\beta \leq 0$ the poles of H(z) are complex conjugates. They appear in the z-plane at $z = Re^{j\theta_c}$ and $z = Re^{-j\theta_c}$ as shown in Figure 13.7. Here $\theta = 2\pi \times$ freq/f_s $= \omega T$, where $f_s = 1/T$ is the sampling frequency. R is the radial distance of the

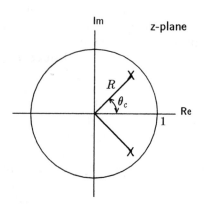

Fig. 13.7   Second-order resonator poles

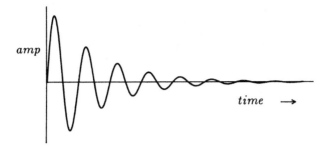

Fig. 13.8   Time domain impulse response

poles from the origin in the z-plane and θ_c is the angle off the real axis.
Now we can rewrite equation (13.6) as:

$$H(z) = \frac{1}{(1-Re^{-j\theta_c}z^{-1})(1-Re^{-j\theta_c}z^{-1})}$$ 13.7

Multiplying out the denominator we get:

$$H(z) = \frac{1}{1 - 2R\cos\theta_c z^{-1} + R^2 z^{-2}}$$ 13.8

Rewriting equation (13.5) yields:

$$y_n = 2R\cos\theta_c y_{n-1} - R^2 y_{n-2} + x_n$$ 13.9

It is easy to show that equation (13.9) leads to a sinusoidal time domain impulse
response of the form:

$$\gamma R^{n-1}\cos[(n-1)\theta_c + \phi], \qquad n \geqslant 1$$ 13.10

where γ and ϕ depend on the partial fraction expansion of equation (13.9). For
values of $R < 1$ the response is a damped sine wave (Figure 13.8) with R
controlling the rate of damping and θ_c controlling the frequency of oscillation.

With $R = 1$, the impulse response is a sine wave of constant amplitude, i.e.
the system is an oscillator.

The system frequency response is found by substituting $e^{j\theta}$ for z in H(z). At
$z = e^{j\theta}$, H(z) is identical to the discrete Fourier transform. The digital
resonator acts as a bandpass filter in this case, with a centre frequency of θ_c
and a bandwidth proportional to R, as shown in Figure 13.9.

The digital resonator is implemented directly using two UPEs. Referring to
Figure 13.10, the left UPE computes:

$$(-R^2 Y + X)z^{-1}$$

the right UPE computes:

$$[2R\cos\theta_c Y + (-R^2 Y+X)z^{-1}]z^{-1} = 2R\cos\theta_c Y z^{-1} - R^2 Y z^{-2} + X z^{-2}$$

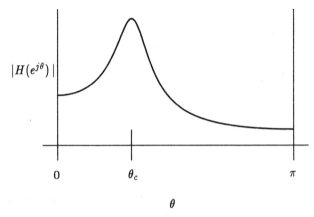

Fig. 13.9   Magnitude of frequency response of case 1

hence,

$$y_n = 2R\cos\theta_c y_{n-1} - R^2 y_{n-2} + x_{n-2}.$$

Using the UPE implementation described above, oscillations in audio range have been run for tens of hours with no detectable change in amplitude.

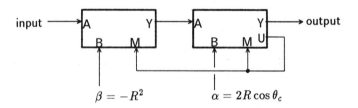

Fig. 13.10   UPE implementation of second-order section

13.3.3   Nonlinear element

The range of functions computable by UPEs is not restricted to linear ones. Certain phenomena in nature are best modelled as nonlinear functions. For example, consider the class of functions that relate pressure to velocity at the mouthpiece of a blown musical instrument. A function that is characteristic of flute-like instruments is shown in Figure 13.11(c). This function and its variations, shown in Figure 13.11(a) to 13.11(d), are computed using three UPEs, as is shown in Figure 13.12. The input signal x is sent to u_1 that multiplies x by itself creating a squared term. This same technique is used again to arrive at the function:

$$y = k_0 + k_2 k_3 + k_3 Gx + k_2 x^2 + Gx^3$$

which is a third-order polynomial. For $k_0 = 0$ and $k_3 = -1$ the coefficient G controls the nonlinear gain, as illustrated in Figure 13.11(c) and 13.11(d). The

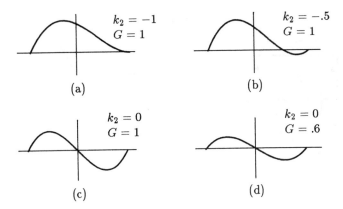

$k_2 = -1$
$G = 1$

(a)

$k_2 = -.5$
$G = 1$

(b)

$k_2 = 0$
$G = 1$

(c)

$k_2 = 0$
$G = .6$

(d)

Fig. 13.11   Non-linear function

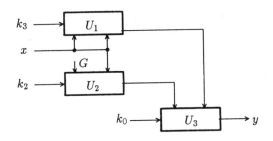

$k_3 \rightarrow \boxed{U_1}$

x

$\downarrow G$

$k_2 \rightarrow \boxed{U_2}$

$k_0 \rightarrow \boxed{U_3} \rightarrow y$

Fig. 13.12   Non-linear element implementation

coefficient k_2 controls the symmetry about the vertical axis, as shown in Figures 13.11(a) to 13.11(c).

This technique of generating polynomials can be extended to produce polynomials of arbitrarily high degree.

13.3.4   Integrator

A very simple configuration using one UPE forms a digital integrator. The Y output is fed back to the A input and the B and M inputs are controlled externally, as shown in Figure 13.13(a). The computation performed is:

$$y_n = B \times M + y_{n-1}.$$

At each step in the computation, the quantity $B \times M$ is summed with the result of the last step. This arrangement produces a ramp function whose slope is the product $B \times M$. As the computation proceeds, the output y_n eventually overflows the number representation and wraps around to a negative number, where the computation continues. The waveform for constant B and M is drawn in Figure 13.13(b).

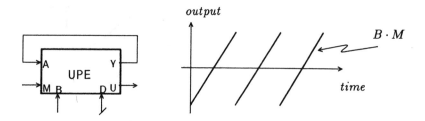

Fig. 13.13   Integrator

13.3.5   FM

Because of the discontinuity, the ramp signal is not bandlimited, and therefore cannot be used directly for sound synthesis, without aliasing components. However, in a scheme suggested by R. Lyon, the signal is remapped by passing it through a function, such as the one described in Section 3.1.3. In the case where the remapping function is equal at the extremes of the number representation, as in the third-order polynomial presented above, the resulting waveform is continuous. The resulting signal does not have the aliasing problems of the ramp function and can be used directly for musical sound application.

In this composite system, where the ramp output feeds the nonlinear section, as shown in Figure 13.14, the B × M input to the ramp may be thought of as controlling the phase of some periodic function y, and is either positive or negative. Since the B × M input may be a signal generated by another arrangement of UPEs, frequency modulation (FM) may be attained. The function generated by the nonlinear element is the carrier signal and the signal fed to the B × M input is the frequency modulation signal. This scheme is

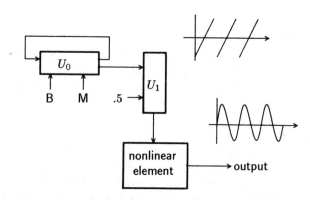

Fig. 13.14   Frequency modulation

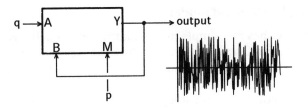

Fig. 13.15 Random number generator

therefore equivalent to the waveform-table lookup techniques commonly used in conventional computer music programs.

13.3.6 Noise

Random signals find frequent application in sound synthesis. A pseudorandom number generator can be constructed with one UPE as shown in Figure 13.15. This approach uses a linear congruence method (Knuth, 1968) implementing:

$$x_n = p.x_{n-1}\,mod_r + q$$

where

$$r = 2^{32}$$

The mod_r operation is achieved by feeding the 64 bit output Y into the 32 bit input, B. Only the low 32 bits of Y get loaded, which effectively generates $mod(2^{32})$.

13.3.7 Mixer

The linear interpolation feature of the UPEs can be used for mixing signals. Referring to Figure 13.16, one signal is fed into the B input and another into the D input. The M input controls the relative balance of the two signals in the output signal. This approach has the advantage over other schemes, that the output level is held constant as the relative mix of the two input signals is changed.

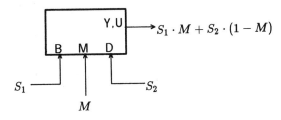

Fig. 13.16 Mixing signals

13.4   Musical instrument models

This section describes two simple musical intrument models based on UPEs. Both models are implemented and are being used to generate musical sounds. While these models produce pleasing sounds, they are rather simplistic models of the physics of the musical instruments that they emulate, and are meant as examples and a basis for future study. While these models have been used to produce extremely high quality timbres of certain instruments, they are certainly not capable of covering the entire range of timbres in the class. The development of a new timbre can be thought of as building an instrument, learning to play it, and then practising a particular performance on it. This activity requires a great deal of careful study, and may involve extensions or modifications to the model.

13.4.1   Struck instrument

Struck or plucked instruments are those that are played by displacing the resonant element of the instrument from its resting state and then allowing it to oscillate freely. Tone quality in such instruments is a function of how the system is excited, and of how it dissipates energy. Examples of plucked and struck instruments include: plucked and struck strings, struck bells, and marimbas, etc.

Figure 13.17 illustrates a struck instrument model implemented with UPEs. The model may be decomposed into two pieces; the *attack section* and the *resonator bank*. The attack section models the impact of the striking or plucking device on the actual instrument. An impulse is fed to a second-order section that is tuned with a Q value close to critical damping. A detailed version of the attack section is shown in Figure 13.18. In this figure, the output of the *attack resonator* is feed to the input of the *noise modulation section*. The noise modulation section generates the function:

$$y = NM.x.RNG + SG.x$$

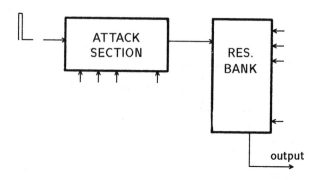

Fig. 13.17   Struck instrument

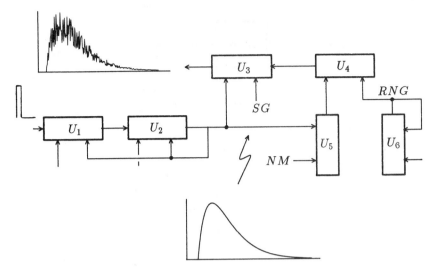

Fig. 13.18 Attack section

where RNG is the output of a random number generator. This computation adds to the signal input x an amount of noise proportional to the level of x. The balance of signal to noise is controlled by the ratio, SG:NM, and the overall gain is controlled by SG + NM.

The output of the noise modulation section is used to drive a parallel connection of second-order sections used as resonators. The resonators are tuned to the major resonances of the instrument being modelled. The parameters of the attack section: attack resonator frequency and Q value, signal to noise ratio, and attack level, are all adjusted to produce a variety of musical timbres.

Second-order sections are combined to form a resonator bank, as shown in Figure 13.19. Each resonator, labelled RES_1 to RES_n, is implemented as described in Section 13.3.2. The output of each resonator is connected to a single UPE that scales the output of the resonator and adds the signal to the signal from the other resonators. The final output emerges at the output of the UPE connected to RES_n.

The gain at resonance of a 2-pole second-order section varies drastically over the frequency range. This variation causes scaling problems when fixed point arithmetic is used. Either the input to or the output from each resonator must be adjusted to compensate for the implicit gain of the resonator. Several techniques exist for normalising resonator gain. One proposed by Smith and Angell (1982), uses the addition of two zeros to the second-order system function. By placing a zero at $\pm\sqrt{R}$ the dependence on θ in the system function may be eliminated. Resonator gain normalisation could pose a particularly severe problem in the case of resonators banks as shown in Figure 13.19. Scaling the input to each resonator increases the amount of UPEs by a factor

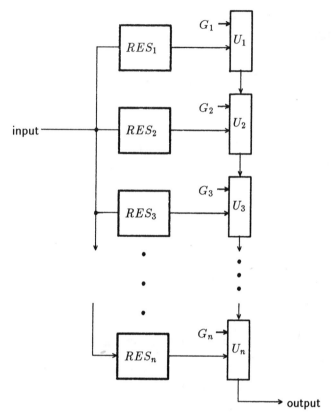

Fig. 13.19 Resonator bank

of one-third and increases the control bandwidth by the same amount. Alternatively, the input to the entire system can be scaled down, to avoid overflow in the section with the most gain, and then the output scaled up to the appropriate level. This approach is a problem in systems that use fixed point arithmetic because the amount of gain available at each multiplication is limited, and hence many multiplier stages at the output must be used.

In many sound generation applications the R values of each stage in the resonator bank are close in value. Therefore, it is possible to synthesise two zeros using an average value for R and then distributing the result to each resonator.

In a typical application, a piano-like keyboard is used to control the instrument. The pressing of a key triggers the following actions: (1) the key position determines the coefficients loaded into the resonator bank; (2) the key velocity controls the level of the coefficient NM in the attack section (higher key velocities correspond to more noise being introduced into the system and hence a higher attack level); and (3) the key press generates an impulse that is sent to the attack resonator.

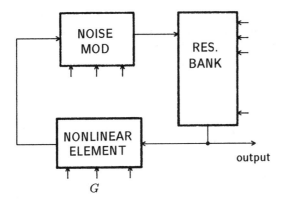

Fig. 13.20 Dynamic model

13.4.2 Dynamic model

Figure 13.20 shows a simple model for blown instruments, implemented using UPEs. This model has been motivated by the observation that a blown musical instrument may be viewed as a nonlinear forcing function at the mouthpiece exciting the modes of a linear tube.

The dynamic model is composed of three pieces described in earlier sections: (1) the nonlinear element that computes a third-order polynomial; (2) the noise modulation section that adds an amount of noise proportional to the size of the signal at its input; and (3) the resonator bank that has second-order resonators tuned to frequencies corresponding to the resonances of the musical instrument.

These elements are connected in a cascade arrangement forming a closed loop. In the case where the closed loop gain is sufficiently high, and the system is disturbed, it oscillates with modes governed by the tuning of the resonator bank. Typically, the loop gain is controlled by the gain of the nonlinear element G. For small values of G the feedback is too small and the system does not oscillate. If G is just large enough, the system will oscillate with a very pure tone as it operates in the nearly linear range of the nonlinear element. If the nonlinear gain G is set to an even higher value, the signal is increased in amplitude and is forced into the nonlinear region. The nonlinearity shifts some energy into higher frequencies, generating a harsher, louder tone.

In a typical application, the loop gain is set by controlling the nonlinear gain G according to the velocity of a key-press on a piano-like keyboard. A slowly pressed key corresponds to a small value for G, and thus a soft pure tone. A quickly pressed key corresponds to a larger value for G, and hence a louder, harsher tone. When the key is released G is returned to some small value, one that is just under the point where the loop gain is large enough to sustain oscillation. By not returning G to zero the signal dies out exponentially with time, with a time constant that is controlled by the value of G used.

A small amount of noise is injected constantly into the loop, using the noise modulation section, so that the system will oscillate without having to send an impulse to excite it.

This model has been used successfully for generating flute-like tones.

13.5   Conclusion

Our solution to the problem of sound synthesis is one that employs the flexibility provided by VLSI to build an architecture that is tailored to the computation involved in physical modelling of musical instruments. Our architecture is one that exploits the natural parallelism of the problem at every possible level. With current IC technology it is possible to place approximately 40 UPEs and an interconnection matrix on a single chip. This configuration allows the realisation of a single instrument voice of about the complexity of the instruments presented in this paper on a single IC. Such a chip computes more than 3 million operations/second.

Musical sound synthesis has many attributes common with other problems in science and engineering. These are problems where a fixed (or slowly varying) interconnection between processing elements is sufficient. Once the interconnection topology is defined, the computation proceeds for a relatively long time before another interconnection change is made. Conventional signal processing can be viewed in this manner. In general this class of problems are those that may be represented as systems of difference equations, where 'time' in the problem being modelled may be represented by time in the computation. Our belief is that the architecture presented here will find general application among this class of problems, as an efficient and sometimes necessary alternative to general purpose computers.

13.6   Acknowledgements

Many people have contributed in unique ways to the Music Project at Caltech. Tzu-Mu Lin (at the time, a Ph.D. candidate at Caltech) did much of the basic work on the UPE design. Lounette Dyer (graduate student) has built a high-level front end to the hardware and brings a musical sensitivity to the project. Hsui-Lin Liu (postdoctorate, now at Schlumberger Research) comes from a background in seismology and acoustics and did work on physical modelling of musical instruments. Dick Lyon (Schlumberger Research), on whose multipliers the UPE is based, has provided countless ideas and is always an inspiration. Greg Bala (undergraduate, now at IBM) has worked with the project from its beginning and has contributed application software. Ron Nelson (composer and Professor of Music at Brown University) has worked with the project to make our instrument models more realistic and usable. David Feinstein (graduate student) has done some exquisite mathematics which helped us develop instrument models. Vibeke Sorenson (instructor at Art Center College of Design) was the first user of the sound synthesis hardware.

Special thanks are due to Telle Whitney (graduate student) for her critiques and many discussions.

We would also like to thank Ron Ayres (USC/Information Sciences Institute) whose integrated circuit layout programs were used to generate the custom chips. The circuit boards that hold the custom chips were designed and built by Brian Horn. Jim Campbell and Alan Blanchard have contributed hardware support.

This work was supported by the System Development Foundation.

References

Cheng, E. K. and C. A. Mead, 'A Two's Complement Pipeline Multiplier', *Proc. of 1976 IEEE International Conf. on Acoustics, Speech and Signal Processing*, Philadelphia, PA., 1976.

Knuth, D. E., *The Art of Computer Programming*, vol. 2, Addison Wesley, Reading, 1968.

Lyon, R. F., 'A bit-Serial VLSI Architecture Methodology for Signal Processing', *VLSI 81 Very Large Scale Integration* (Conf. Proc., Edinburgh, Scotland, John P. Gray, ed.), Academic Press, 1981.

Oppenheim, A. V. and R. Schafer, *Digital Signal Processing*, Prentice-Hall, Englewood Cliffs, New Jersey, 1975.

Smith, J. O. and J. Angell, 'A Constant-Gain Digital Resonator Tuned by a Single Coefficient', *Computer Music Journal*, vol. 6, no. 4, 1982.

Wawrzynek, J. C. and Tzu-Mu Lin, 'A Bit Serial Architecture for Multiplication and Interpolation', California Institute of Technology, Computer Science Department Display File 5067, 1983.

APPENDIX

A.1 Introduction

Our design methodology attempts to bridge the signal processing and VLSI design communities. The keystone of this bridge lies in the realisation of the basic processing functions in the primitive library. These are implemented in the circuit and layout domain and used in the system domain as functional elements. As an illustration of this key relationship we detail below the development of the bit-serial multiplier primitive. We proceed from functional specification to validated silicon via the following sequence:

> Define the multiply algorithm
> Cast the algorithm for serialised execution
> Create the primitive floorplan, to guide leaf-cell design and composition
> Design leaf-cell logic, and verify (switch-level simulation)
> Convert logic design to circuit design and verify (timing simulation)
> Map the circuit design to layout topology (sticks)
> Flesh the topology to finished geometry and verify (circuit extraction and
>   circuit simulation)
> Write composition routines and verify interfaces
> Run test characterisations (see Chapter 7)
> Validate via fabrication, testing and characterisation.

A.2 The multiply algorithm

Let a, b be respectively n-bit and m-bit fractional two's complement numbers where, without loss of generality, $m \leqslant n$. The number b will be termed the coefficient (multiplier) and the number a will be referred to as the data (multiplicand). Then the coefficient can be written as:

$$b = -b_{m-1}2^0 + b_{m-2}2^{-1} + \ldots + b_0 2^{-m+1}$$

and the product can be expressed as:

$$ba = -b_{m-1}a2^0 + b_{m-2}a2^{-1} + \ldots + b_0 a2^{-m+1}$$

Thus the product is a sum of weighted partial products. The partial products are formed by multiplying successive bits of b by the word a. Successive partial

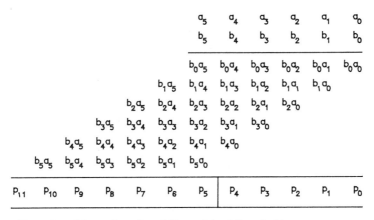

Fig. A.1 Formation of the product of two 6-bit words by shift-and-add.

products are scaled by a factor of 2^{-1}, corresponding to a simple shift operation. The partial products are summed with the exception of the most significant, which is subtracted.

Figure A.1 shows the formation and relationships between the set of partial products for a 6×6 bit multiplication to yield a 12 bit product.

There are many ways to execute the summation of partial products to form the result. We require an execution which will result in a modular hardware architecture. Thus we choose a regular form of summation based upon conventional full binary addition (two addends and carry inputs, sum and carry outputs). Figure A.2 is a numerical example of this process for the product 1.10111 by 1.01101, to give the result 00.0010101011.

The process is based on iterative formation of the partial product sums, which accumulate the contributions from each partial product. This admits the use of the full binary addition process, which is indicated symbolically in Figure A.2.

To accommodate bit growth in these sums it is necessary to extend the addend words by one bit (MSB extension). This is accommodated by extending the data (multiplicand) by one bit throughout the computation and locally extending the partial product sums.

Rows 3,7,11, etc., in Figure A.2 represent the successive partial product sums. Rows 4,8,12, etc., represent the partial products formed by ANDing combinations of bits from the data and coefficient words. Rows 5/6, 9/10, 13/14, etc., represent the full addition of the partial product and partial product sum, delivering the next iteration of the partial product sum (sum out) to rows 7, 11, 15, etc., and propagating carries horizontally in rows 6, 10, 14, etc. Note that rows 25/26 effect subtraction of the final partial product because of the negative weight of the coefficient MSB. The initial partial product sum in row 3 is set to zero, as are the initial carry-in nodes in each carry row. The final carry out in these rows is ignored.

The interpretation of scaling through the multiplier is such that a fractional coefficient results in the preservation of the scale of the data in the product,

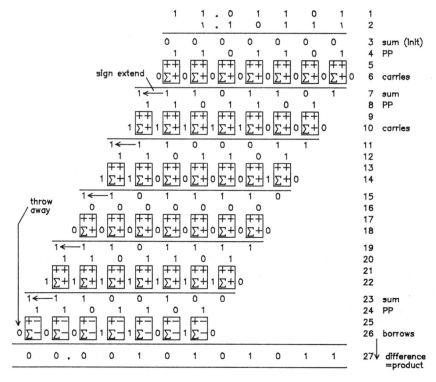

Fig. A.2 Organisation of partial product summation using binary full add operations.

relative to the MSB.

If we now take the sign extended data to be n bits and the coefficient to be m bits, then mn full add operations are required to form the product. Note that the first row of full add operations may be dispensed with, at the expense of modularity. The multiplication process defined in Figure A.2 may be mapped directly into hardware to form a bit-parallel multiplier, of order (mn). Alternatively, we seek a bit-serial mapping of area order (m) and time order (n).

A.3   Multiplexing for serial execution

Consider the sequential constraints on the execution of the computation shown in Figure A.2. The processes of full addition require the prior formation of all input bits including the earlier partial product sum, the partial product formed from the data and coefficient words and the carry from the next least significant bit of the same partial product sum. This imposes the sequential constraints illustrated in Figure A.3.

The diagonally connected processes indicated in Figure A.3 indicate the earliest position in the sequence of computation that each addition may occur. Note that the early product bits, which are formed from the rightmost cells,

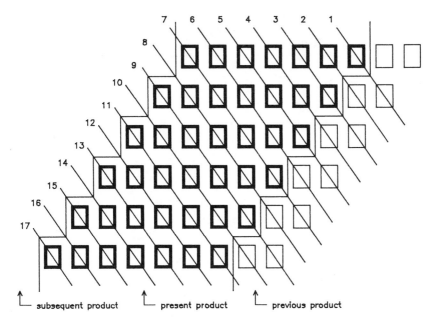

Fig. A.3   Sequential constraints on product formation.

appear two steps apart in this sequence.

Now we may pipeline this process by introducing a clock to synchronise the diagonals of execution. The greatest number of adders in any diagonal for any m and n will be less than or equal to m. This number reduces progressively at the beginning and end of the execution sequence and indeed may never reach its maximum value (this happens when n>2m–2) as is the case in Figure A.3.

To multiplex the computation, we plan to provide a linear array of m physical adders to execute the various processes across each diagonal. This is the basis of the bit-serial multiplier, which will also include provision to set data in the array to arrive at the adders in the correct sequence.

Figure A.4 shows the sequences of data movement and formation as a hodograph of processor position (horizontally) against time (vertically). Note that the coefficient bits b_i appear in fixed processor locations for the duration of the computation, suggesting a hardware latch requirement. The data bits are simply required in sequence through each cell, with a delay of two steps between adjacent processors. The implied progression of sum bits is diagonally forward indicating a rate of one processor per time step. The carry bits are passed forward in time within the same processor place.

Notice the formation pattern of the product bits. The first (m–1) of these appear at the outputs of the first (m–1) processors, staggered in time by two steps. The most significant n bits of the product appear consecutively at the output of the last processor. Without modification, we may ignore the internal product bits and use the output of the last processor to generate a truncated n-bit product. As stated earlier, this product has the same significance as the input data, assuming that the coefficient is interpreted as fractional.

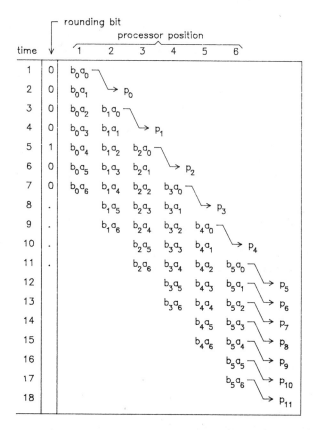

Fig. A.4 Hodograph showing product formation in a linear processor array, with processor place (horizontally) against time step (vertically). The product bits P_0, P_1, P_2, P_3, P_4, appear internally (at the outputs of processors 1, 2, 3, 4, 5) at times 2, 4, 6 ,8, 10 and the remaining product bits $P_5 - P_{11}$ apear at the output of processor 6 at times 12–18.

A rounded n-bit product may be formed by adding a rounding bit as input to the first processor, at the correct time step. Alternatively a double precision product may be formed by extracting the internal product bits. For the purpose of this study, we focus on the truncating/rounding multiplier form.

A hardware mapping follows directly from the hodograph, as shown in Figure A.5. The principal computational unit in this linear cellular array is a serial adder (subtracter in the case of the last cell) with a latency of one bit. The carry is recirculated, whilst the sum is passed forward to the next stage. The coefficient bits are propagated through a one-bit-per-stage delay line and are latched into their appropriate positions by the delayed LSB control signal $c1$. Like $c1$, the data is propagated through the array by a two-bit-per-stage delay line; $c1$ is also used within each cell to clear the internal carry and to sign-bit extend in all but the final cell.

In continuous operation, the data and the coefficient words are supplied serially without interruption. The hardware can be most efficiently used by allowing the earlier processors in the array to commence the formation of one product whilst the later processors are completing the previous product. This pipelining of product formation makes 100% use of the processors, as shown schematically in Figure A.3 and implied by the control conventions used in Figure A.5.

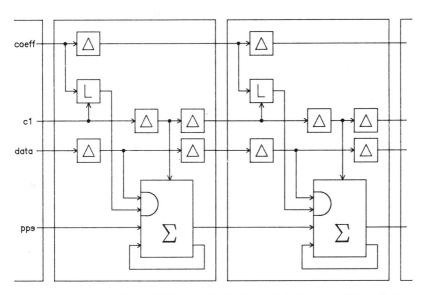

Fig. A.5   Hardware map of the multiplier array derived from the hodograph of Figure A.4.

A.4   The modified Booth multiplier

A principal constraint on bit-serial systems is the latency of the primitives. It is possible to reduce the latency of the multiplier by using the modified Booth algorithm. This recodes the coefficient in such a way as to halve the number of computational steps involved, and so halve the length of the processor array.

The modified Booth algorithm recodes each pair of coefficient bits as a five level digit, in the range $-2,-1,0,+1,+2$. The attraction of this recoding scheme is that the products of these digits with the data word are simply implemented by optional shifts. In this way only one partial product word is formed for every two coefficient bits, and the number of partial product sums is reduced accordingly. The new partial products and partial product sums become one bit longer, so we require a further sign extension of one bit in the data word. Also the relative weighting from one partial product sum to the next is increased to 2^2.

The recoding algorithm relies upon examination of triples of coefficient bits comprising the bit pair under consideration along with the next least significant bit. The initial least significant bit is an inserted trailing zero. The recode operation is defined in Table A.1 (cf. Rubenfield, 1975).

Table A.1   Modified Booth Recoding

Coefficient bits	Operation
$b_{i+1}\ b_i\ b_{i-1}$	
0 0 0	$PP \leftarrow (1/4)PP$
0 0 1	$PP \leftarrow (1/4)PP + a$
0 1 0	$PP \leftarrow (1/4)PP + a$
0 1 1	$PP \leftarrow (1/4)PP + 2a$
1 0 0	$PP \leftarrow (1/4)PP - 2a$
1 0 1	$PP \leftarrow (1/4)PP - a$
1 1 0	$PP \leftarrow (1/4)PP - a$
1 1 1	$PP \leftarrow (1/4)PP$

The new multiplier array cell embodying this algorithm is shown in Figure A.6. The principal computational element is now a programmable serial add/subtract with the carry fed back internally, as before. The coefficient is propagated on a one-bit-per-stage tapped delay line, modified to enable the three relevant bits to be latched and recoded under control of the 'latch' signal. This is related to but separate from c1 to enable a single coefficient to be permanently latched, if required. By connecting 'latch' to c1 at the multiplier input, continuous operation with varying coefficients can be effected.

The data is propagated via a three-bit-per-stage delay line (to accommodate the additional one bit delay between partial product sums) and this is tapped accordingly, to effect the 1x, 2x partial product formation.

The add/subtract cell is initialised from c1, as before, but sign extension is separately controlled to effect a 2-bit extension of the partial product sums. The sign extension feature is omitted from the last cell, which is now identical to the other cells with respect to arithmetic operation.

The first cell of the array differs from the remainder in respect of the least significant input to the recoder, which is set to zero. The final cell of the array differs from the others in that correct interpretational scaling requires only a single bit extension and shift.

A.5   Floor planning

As with any FIRST primitive, the instantiation of the multiplier must respect the geometrical and electrical conventions set out in Chapters 1 and 2. These define the availability of power and clock services and constrain all input/output ports to lie along the waterfront.

Intrinsically the multiplier is a modular, linear array, but the input/output port constraints require linear arrays to be folded. A plan for multiplier construction is shown in Figure A.7. This includes the folded array, with services distributed through a central umbilical supply. Provision must also be made for direct inter-cell connection instead of a multiplier cell, for cases where only an odd number of multiplier cells is needed. This is indicated in Figure A.7.

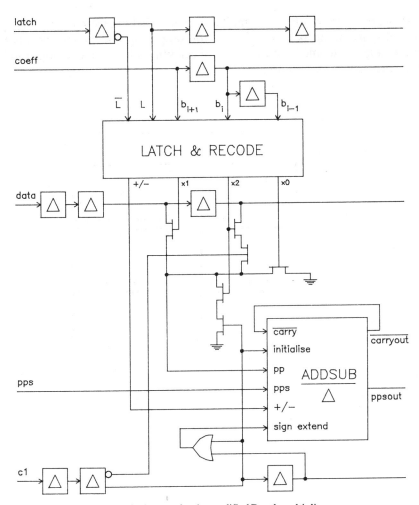

Fig. A.6 Block diagram of a single stage for the modified Booth multiplier.

A.6 Leaf-cell logic and layout

We now expand the 'black-box' functions of Figure A.6. The technology of implementation is silicon-gate, single-metal nMOS, using two-phase non-overlapping synchronous clocking. Figures A.8, A.9 and A.10 show respectively a one-bit delay circuit, the coefficient latch and recode circuit and the programmable add/subtract element. Both the recode and add/subtract functions use pass-transistor logic techniques where appropriate.

Plate 8 shows full layout of one internal multiplier stage, including examples of the bit-delay, recode and add-subtract cells. This stage measures $258\lambda \times 193\lambda$. The first and last stages include minor modifications, as indicated previously.

Altogether the multiplier primitive contains 17 different custom designed leaf cells, including pieces of layout for supply routing, input and output buffers, etc. A detailed outline of a leaf cell library in this technology can be found in Newkirk and Matthews, 1983.

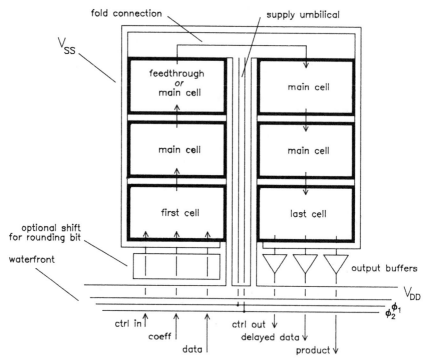

Fig. A.7   Floorplan template for the multiplier layout.

A.7   Incorporating a primitive into FIRST

The physical design subsystem of FIRST comprises a set of software routines which generate chip mask geometries. The programming basis for the physical design subsytem is an embedded language (cf. Locanthi, 1978; Gray *et al.*, 1983). This allows parameterised procedural definition of symbols (which represent groups of geometric shapes) within a high level programming language.

We now consider the assembly of the bit-serial multiplier as a primitive composition routine. We commence with the collection of leaf cells, held as layout in files of CIF code.

Given that the sizes of the leaf cells are known (from layout), the following outline for the composition routine, when expanded, may be used to assemble the multiplier as a function of one parameter – the coefficient wordlength.

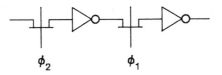

Fig. A.8   Logic detail for stage functions: one bit delay

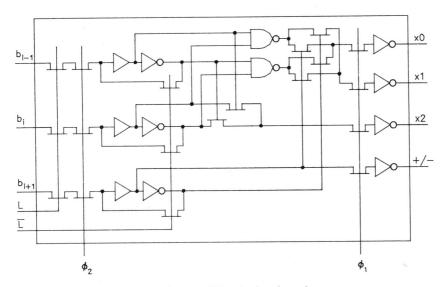

Fig. A.9   Logic detail for stage functions: coefficient latch and recode

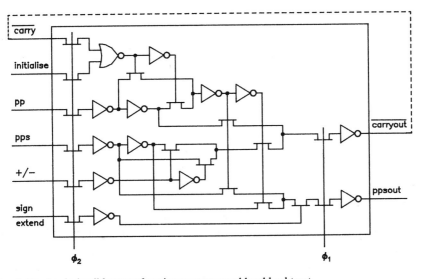

Fig. A.10   Logic detail for stage functions: programmable add-subtract

```
multiply()
{
        declarations
        retrieve parameter values for this instance
        calculate internal constants
        check parameter values
        compose symbol identifier (name)

        if(!symbol__exists(name)) {
                symbol(ttname)
                draw("MULTAT")
                draw I/O buffers
                draw("MULTB")
                draw("MULTC")
                draw("MULTE")
                for(k = 1;k <= limitb;++k)
                        draw("MULTB")
                for(k = 1;k <= limitdt;++k)
                        draw("MULTD")
                if((coeffbits–4) % 4 != 0)
                        draw("MULTG")
                else if(coeffbits > 4)
                        draw("MULTD")
                draw("MULTH") for(k = limitdb;k >= 1;--k)
                        draw("MULTD")
                endsymbol()
        }
        evaluate and return height and width
        evaluate and return I/O port relative positions
}
```

Where the following routines are examples of calls to the embedded language and have the function described. The routine draw() outputs the CIF shapes of the symbol named as its argument; this is done so as to achieve the correct position and orientation. Note that suitable values for position and orientation must be passed to the draw() function, and must subsequently be updated for the next call. At this level the details are suppressed for clarity. The function symbol() is a routine to generate a CIF definition start and endsymbol() to generate a CIF definition end. The function symbol_ exists() interrogates the data structure generated so far to see whether the symbol has already been defined or not; it returns TRUE or FALSE. The pseudo-code given above can be expanded directly into an appropriate high level language function or routine to define the multiply primitive. An example of full layout generated by the multiply composition routine is shown in Figure A.11.

This block of layout, representing the full primitive module, is then available to subsequent routines of the Physical Design Subsystem for placement and

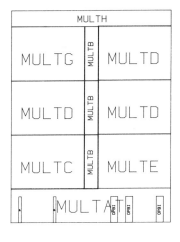
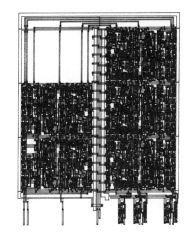

(a)   (b)

Fig. A.11   A compiled multiplier:
(a) leaf cell composition
(b) fully instantiated layout

routing. There is no restriction to the use of a single parameter, many of the primitives have two or three parameters.

Plate 2 shows detail of an assembled, placed, routed and fabricated multiplier from one of the FIRST case studies.

References

Gray, J.P., Buchanan, I. and Robertson, P.S., 'Controlling VLSI Complexity Using a High-Level Language for Design Description', *Proc. International Conference on Computer Design*, 1983.

Locanthi, B., 'LAP: A Simula Package for IC Layout', Caltech SSP Report 1862, California Institute of Technology, 1978.

Mead, C. and Conway, L., *Introduction to VLSI Systems*, Addison-Wesley, 1980.

Newkirk, J. and Matthews, R., *The VLSI Designer's Library*, Addison-Wesley, 1983.

Rubenfield, L.P., 'A Proof of the Modified Booth's Algorithm for Multiplication', *IEEE Trans. Comput.* **C-24**, 1975.

Index